my
head
was
a
sledgehammer

my head was a sledgehammer

RICHARD FOREMAN

six plays

THE OVERLOOK PRESS
WOODSTOCK • NEW YORK

First published in 1995 by
The Overlook Press
Lewis Hollow Road
Woodstock, New York 12498

Library of Congress Cataloging-in-Publication Data

Foreman, Richard

My head was a sledgehammer : six plays / Richard Foreman.
p.   cm.
I. Title.
PS3556.07225M9   1995   812′.54—dc20
94-37369   CIP

Manufactured in the United States of America
Book design by Bernard Schleifer

ISBN: 0-87951-575-9 (HC)
ISBN: 0-87951-622-4 (PB)

First Edition

contents

Introduction

Marc Robinson

"If this were a play . . ." With these words, the opening of *Eddie Goes to Poetry City,* Richard Foreman sets the tone for a wistful and introspective new collection. How often his audiences must have said the same words to themselves: If this were a play . . . then we would know how to watch it—and how to respond. It would have a clear narrative propelling us forward. It would be filled with well-rounded characters baring their souls. Its beginning would be explanatory, and its ending would seem inevitable. It would conjure a time and place in which we could lose ourselves for an evening.

But *Eddie Goes to Poetry City* is not that kind of play, nor are the other works in this collection. Like all of Foreman's theater, these plays celebrate flux. The characters are incurably disoriented, unsure of where the stage begins and ends, always tripping over the decor. They are caught up in inscrutable plots, and speak as though they have only just begun to learn the language. Nothing ever coalesces in their world. Just as they settle, grow familiar with one another, and understand what is at stake, the action stops short—only to start over in a different place. These chronic disruptions make it difficult even to recognize Foreman's characters *as* characters. They reinvent themselves with every sentence, acquiring new virtues and vices, discarding their original beliefs before they (or we) have examined them adequately. They sever relationships with one another and welcome distraction. Sometimes, they even change their names. The entire play seems to shed a skin—and then another skin, and still one more.

The process makes most audiences dizzy. But in exchange for comfort, spectators can experience a rare degree of engagement with the stage. At other theaters, Foreman believes, the audience lapses into passivity early in the evening, once it discovers the play's architecture and can predict the direction of the play's action. The audience stops watching, perking up only when an event onstage confirms expectations. At Foreman's theater, in contrast, we learn to be on guard throughout the performance, ready to refocus our attention and revise our interpretations with each disruption. Foreman prevents us from reaching premature conclusions about even the most basic aspects of stage action—much less about a play's meaning. But while he never reveals a play's pattern, he counts on us to want a glimpse of it. Our desperation, he believes, will make us watch and listen more intensely.

Foreman discovered how this principle works in his own experience as a spectator. He once described how much he loves watching the first ten minutes of a film—any film, regardless of its quality. During those minutes, nothing is clear. He doesn't know who's who, where the characters are, or how they are tangled up in each other's lives. The characters don't have a visible past, and their future is as yet unknown. He can't decide who will be a major character and who, after this scene, will end up a mere bystander. As the actors speak in fragments, he can't always tell what they are referring to, or evaluate the importance of the information. Faced with so many unsolved mysteries, he hangs on every word and scrutinizes every frame, piecing elements together, hoping for a story to take shape. In his own theater, Foreman tries to stretch the charged atmosphere of these ten minutes over an entire evening. He wants to keep his audience asking questions and looking for clues through the final scene.

Foreman also learned how to honor the here-and-now of theater from Gertrude Stein. In her many plays, Stein tried to achieve a "continuous present"—her term for a style in which each moment of performance stands alone, announcing the play's substance anew. Like Foreman at the movies, Stein formed her style while watching other people's art. She never enjoyed going to the theater, she wrote in her famous essay "Plays," because she was always either "ahead of" or "behind" the action onstage. Either she could predict what was going to happen in a story, or she dwelled on a moment of performance long after it had passed. She never found herself watching a production at its own pace. Moreover, she had grown frustrated by actors who seemed so busy sorting through a character's biography that they never adequately explored something as simple, and as crucial, as presence. Most playwrights, she had come to believe, were equally distracted: They were spelling out messages when they could have been exploiting the musical possibilities of speech. And most directors, Stein felt, were so preoccupied with such matters as arcs, transitions, and denouements that they never perceived the grace of a gesture or utterance at the moment it took shape. Stein took it upon herself to restore these neglected beauties of stagecraft, and thereby reforge the link between performer and spectator. In her own plays, she scorned cause-and-effect plotting, dialogue in which some lines are subordinate to others, and the linear evolution of characters—thereby freeing herself to concentrate on the essence of theater: being.

Reading Stein, Foreman recognized his own discomfort with theatrical convention—and his own ambition. In 1968, he began to adapt Stein's approach and formed the Ontological-Hysteric Theater in New York City to direct his own plays on his own terms. Those early works were so sprawling and overpopulated that a spectator had to watch them one minute at a time: They couldn't be summarized. The action traveled around the world—conjuring up Africa (*Egyptology* and *Africanus Instructus*), the Far East (*Hotel China*), Europe (*Blvd de Paris*), and places as yet uncharted (*Rhoda in Potatoland*). Eventually, however, Foreman put down roots. *The Cure* (1986) and *What Did He See?* (1988) introduced a new, hushed tone to his theater. The present volume is the logical development of those plays: It is a collection of chamber theater, contemplative and private. In this volume, Eddie does go to Poetry City, or at least tries to, but few other characters venture further than the confines of their maze-like and often tormented imaginations. Their imaginations reflect Foreman's own: In these pages, he steadily turns inward, mapping a spiritual geography and touring invisible sites.

In retrospect, Foreman's evolution in this direction was inevitable. After so many Ontological-Hysteric plays in which he reckoned with the pleasures of the material world—plays in which hysteria took precedence over ontology—Foreman was bound to grow curious about everything he hadn't yet represented: spiritual dimensions, invisible regions of silence and stillness. The shift in interest coincides with a shift in artistic allegiances. Having made good use of Stein's inheritance, he now claims the legacy of the turn-of-the-century symbolists—Stéphane Mallarmé, Hugo von Hofmannsthal, William Butler Yeats, and Aleksandr Blok, among others—and echoes their enthusiasm for the secret world that lies behind appearances. (Alas, Foreman continues to be isolated from most contemporary American playwrights. He suggests that to place him in context, we turn to poets, painters, and philosophers, instead.) The European symbolists hoped to create an art in which the sensual and material aspects of their craft— the verse, the setting, the sounds of voices—would serve primarily as gateways to the spirit. Once the artist reaches this arcadia, they believed, the chaos of competing images and sensations will subside. Crowded stages will clear. Words themselves will shed their ordinary meanings to reveal their true radiance. Here, the symbolists promised, it will be possible to "listen to incense," as Yeats put it, and to experience what Mallarmé called an art of "perpetual allusion without breaking the ice or the mirror." In fact, artists of this realm will no longer simply create, and spectators will no longer observe. Both will experience revelation, and will be transfigured by what they discover.

Readers who have seen the plays in this volume performed may wonder how successfully Foreman has achieved symbolist tranquillity. After all, despite the text's meditative content, the productions are among his most scenically cluttered. Each play unfolds on a small stage amid ornate furniture, brightly colored paintings, carpets with clashing patterns, books, newspapers, plastic flowers, tiny flags, candy wrappers, and mechanical devices of uncertain function. The remnants of a just-finished party are visible in many productions—balloons, streamers, confetti, funny paper hats. Music plays continuously. As the actors stagger through the mess, one senses that the party had lasted too long, or shouldn't have occurred at all. How is one to escape daily life and be contemplative in such a place?

Foreman hopes that we will ask just such a question. In earlier Ontological-Hysteric productions, the characters delighted in debris. Each object invited them into a world of fantasy and prompted them to poetic reverie. The setting became a playroom. Now, however, the characters seem suffocated by the setting and frightened by the many objects. In many of these plays, one character longs for escape, and squares off against adversaries who constantly put temptation in his way. The protagonists, and sometimes even the other characters, wish they could clear away the junk, especially the artistic junk. Eddie wants to burn a painting. The Angel in *The Mind King* erases blackboards and yearns for sleep. In *My Head Was a Sledgehammer*, gnomes tear the pages out of books. In *I've Got the Shakes*, everyone rips up blank sheets of paper. Before long, Foreman's characters feel the need to tear up more blank paper, and erase an already clean board again. This nervousness pervades the production: The dances that were so delightful in earlier Foreman productions are still here, and still entertaining, but now they also seem darker—as though the characters had been shoved by an invisible hand into a dance that embarrasses them. Wide-eyed and frozen-faced, they wish they could sit still and be quietly attentive, but can't stop themselves from running headlong into another routine.

Foreman shares his characters' inability to resist distraction. All of Foreman's plays, starting in 1968, track the route of his obsessive mind—so much so that the true subject of each play, regardless of its apparent story, is Foreman himself. Foreman's early manifestos describe how much he enjoyed letting his subconscious lead the way, but these new plays suggest a change in that attitude. As the characters talk of silence and stillness, one hears Foreman himself asking for an end to his usual intellectual wanderlust. He seems to want to erase himself—or at least his old artistic identity—along with the play. "All manifestation takes a powder," says one of his surrogates, hopefully, in *Eddie Goes to Poetry City*. But the harder Foreman works to fulfill this and other symbolist ideals, the deeper he sinks into the material world. He is wedged there against his will. New inspiration, new ideas, new images—they are always demanding his attention, and he is powerless to keep them at bay. This collection, then, is a record of yearning and frustration, each play marking another attempt to bridge the gulf between his surroundings and his vision of equilibrium.

In dramatizing that process, Foreman explores what few symbolists ever admit: difficulty. With the seriousness of a believer, he reminds himself that spiritually charged art is never simply a matter of translating dreams to the stage, or pursuing an interest in the occult, or detecting the "magical" properties of ordinary phenomena. Just when Foreman's characters are on the edge of revelation, they bump into a pillar, or someone hits them with a hammer, and they fall back into the real world of things and the pain they cause. Those actors dressed as rabbis or scholars (as several are) seem especially vulnerable: Their vocational interest in hidden knowledge makes them suffer disillusionment more often. Even the God who appears from time to time in these plays looks earthbound—a construction of cardboard wings, stilts, and a phony beard. He should never have shown Himself, for now He can't be believable. As such disappointments accumulate, the entire play indicates only what cannot be shown. But the plays are not failures. Far from it: By constantly sabotaging his symbolist efforts, Foreman creates some of his most personal and revealing theater.

Few critics have been comfortable discussing Foreman in psychological terms, and few spectators have felt moved to sympathize with his characters. But with this collection, Foreman encourages us to discover his work's emotional depth. He is preoccupied with mortality in these plays, as his characters balance on the edge of nervous collapse. In their anxiety, they try to outrun a world where death is inevitable. Behind the dialogue, and especially in the voice-overs (performed by Foreman himself), we can hear Foreman hoping to erase the boundaries between life and death, so that no experience, and no person, will be lost to him. Yet, as with everything else in the material world, death is stronger than art's power to transcend it. Foreman's scenic design continues to taunt him: Skulls fill the stage in one play: A coffin appears in another. Doctors (of a kind) preside over numerous crises. Throughout these plays, the dialogue wends it way through various topics but always returns to death. Foreman doesn't wallow—these aren't manipulative tearjerkers—but neither can he deny death's presence in even the most remote philosophical dimension of his theater. These plays, in other words, address more than formal issues— one "ism" versus another. The vulnerable body, with its fears and afflictions, is always on view—as the titles of three plays remind us: *My Head Was a Sledgehammer, I've Got the Shakes, Samuel's Major Problems.*

The mere presence of death doesn't account for the poignancy here. Foreman's struggle with this theme offers a more complex object for our sympathies. If a reader moves through the plays in sequence, he or she follows the ordeal of a writer who becomes more and more consumed by his topic, as if against his will. In the opening pages, Foreman's characters discuss his familiar concerns—the place of art in life, the power of the imagination, the need for surprise. They are cool and detached. But soon they are revealing their inner sterility, and expressing feelings of depletion and aimlessness. They are humiliated by their physical weaknesses and urges. Before long, their anguish has spread throughout the play. Foreman has often referred to the Ontological-Hysteric Theater as his "paradise"—a place in which, during the run of a production, he can hide from and control life at the same time. But in these plays, as for his characters, no evasion is possible. Each performance brings him face to face, night after night, with what he most fears and hopes to flee.

Lest Foreman buckle under such an obsession (and lest readers despair), he discovers relief in the last play collected here. *I've Got the Shakes* is no less feverish than Foreman's other plays, but in its final moments Madeline X, its heroine, reassesses her situation. Like her cousins before her, she searches for a pure space free from contingency. Like her cousins, she never finds it, and learns how bound she is to cycles of life and death. Other Foreman plays end here, accepting this knowledge. Madeline X, however, lingers in her defeat until she decides to "stretch out a moment, any moment, until it lasts a whole lifetime." She could "try to say what's hidden," as other Foreman characters have done, but, she explains, if she did so her words wouldn't "be like the thing that's hidden." Its mystery is essential to its meaning. Better to concentrate on what is visible, she implies. If she looks at the tangible world with sufficient intensity, without blinking, perhaps she can master it: It won't overwhelm her, and it won't cause her pain. She ends the play asking the others to "hold it right there."

Foreman's new collection ends where his writing life began—on the brink of perception, entranced by mere presence. But nearly thirty years later, he demands more from what he sees. When he first experienced the theater of Gertrude Stein, and those first ten minutes of a movie, his interest was purely formal. He learned to watch (and to make) art one moment at a time; a story's ending, then, was never as important, or as fascinating, as what was happening in the present. Now, Foreman has acknowledged the reality of endings in his life, and Stein's thinking influences him for different reasons. Perhaps now, Foreman suggests, her lessons can address his needs outside the theater. If Madeline believes she can "stretch out a moment until it lasts a whole lifetime," perhaps he shouldn't flee the material world. In a place shaped only by the present-tense, where its inhabitants never stop perceiving their surroundings, it seems possible to transcend death—or at least to meet its gaze. Can the continuous present—a structural device—become his route to continuous life? Can close observation of that life (as Madeline teaches) foster the spiritual clarity he always seeks? Foreman leaves the questions unanswered. But he knows that if he continues to engage the questions by making one play each year, as he does now, and continues to delay answering them, his art can hold his own experience "right there," where everything is still possible— and theater will indeed become his paradise.

Marc Robinson
New Haven 1995

Eddie Goes to Poetry City: Part One. Produced by The New City Theater, Seattle, Washington. September-October 1990. John Kazanjian, Artistic Director. Written, directed, and designed by Richard Foreman.

MARIE:	Mary Ewald
EDDIE:	Brian Faker
ESTELLE:	Amy Perry
DOCTOR:	Ben Prager
WOMAN IN BLACK:	Jennifer Steil

A dim stage, full of strange objects. A tilted table with a low built back that contains small arches. Two padded walls against which the actors occasionally bounce with great force. Many chairs of different, nondescript style. Far rear, a circular wooden revolvable merry-go-round frame, a couch and a piano, tables loaded with objects. To one side is an antique wind machine—a revolving drum covered with a piece of canvas. Scattered about are microphones, which the actors speak into on many occasions. The actors always speak quietly, and there is often soft music behind the action, continually changing, and sometimes building to deafening climax. A sign on the rear wall says "Poetry City." A light bulb in its center goes on at selected moments during the play.

As the audience assembles, the actors are visible, relaxing at the rear of the set. At a certain point, they begin whispering, then tickle each other and try to suppress fits of giggling, as the sound of a drum roll rises. A WOMAN who sits alone at the rear of the stage on a high stool for the whole play, wearing a black dunce cap, shouts out aggressively, "Excuse me!"—and the actors stop tussling with each other and race forward. MARIE and ESTELLE, the two women, quickly pull a black curtain which rides on a wire eight feet above the floor. After a while, EDDIE appears in a slit in the curtain, coming just halfway out. There is another pause, and then the voice of the DOCTOR, the other male actor in the play, is heard, speaking softly over a loudspeaker.

VOICE OF THE DOCTOR: If this were a play, a curtain would be drawn. And the audience would be in darkness.

VOICE OF MARIE: *(After a pause)* If this were a play, a room would be visible . . . *(Curtain is quickly reopened. A giant abstract head is seen on the DOCTOR's body as he stands in the shadows, rear)* Into which one would project one's imagination.

ESTELLE *(Into a microphone. Everyone speaks softly, as if in a dream)* If this were a play, a line of dialogue would suddenly emerge from the silence of dimly illuminated space.

EDDIE: If this were a play . . . *(He takes a step back into the playing space)*—the room would be crowded with men and women in evening dress. Cigar smoke would hover in the air. And a chosen someone would lean forward as if his face were exploding. He wouldn't speak, because he wouldn't have to. But . . . he would speak.

MARIE: *(Sings softly to herself)*
Secret door
Secret door
Can I find
The secret door.

DEEP VOICE OVER LOUDSPEAKER: *(The stage tableau is frozen)*
The center was nothing
The edge was nothing
The bottom was nothing
The root was nothing
The depth was nothing
The extension was nothing
The kernel was nothing.

WOMAN ON STOOL: Excuse me!

EDDIE: Let me introduce you to a man who tried to turn himself into a work of art.

MARIE: A work of art must push open a door to another world—isn't that right?

EDDIE: I'm trying to find a secret door.

MARIE: Is it a door to another world?

EDDIE: Well . . . yes.

MARIE: Then don't move.

EDDIE: *(Pause)* Why?

MARIE: *(After a pause)* I wanted to see how long it would be before you moved.

> *(EDDIE races to one of the padded walls and bounces off, as MARIE runs to sit, putting on a bonnet, and EDDIE, fallen to the ground, crawls across the floor, then rises and goes to the tilted table to become fascinated by the built up rear side with holes, which looks a bit like a tiny Roman arena in which demonstrations might be imagined. As this is happening, the deep VOICE begins speaking over the loudspeakers)*

DEEP VOICE OVER LOUDSPEAKERS: Eddie went to Poetry City.

The soft air, gray and granulated, offered itself to his sniff. Somebody must be burning logs, said Eddie. But in fact, he was wrong.

Global forces were at work, but Eddie was localized.

He opened a local window, and before he could open a local window, something came whirling into his mind's eye like a photograph of the whole planet from a place far in space. *(EDDIE has knelt at the table, and MARIE also kneels, and the sawing stops)* Look, there's Poetry City under a cloud of fog—

Oh, Eddie, from where you sit, it's so atmospheric to be looking at the sun bursting into the city through clouds of soft fog.

Eddie realized that by midday the air would be clear, and Poetry City would be like any place else.

Would it still be Poetry City? Of course, offered Marie. Maps don't change. (*The DOCTOR and ESTELLE run to separate sawhorses with logs strapped on top, and begin furiously sawing at the logs, and EDDIE rises and runs to crash into the padded wall. He recovers and staggers to a chair, where he sits, holding his head and clutching a briefcase. The others quiet down*)

Maps don't change.

Maps don't change. (*ESTELLE comes behind EDDIE, and as the voice continues, she leans over him from behind and puts her arms around his neck, which makes him uncomfortable*) Is this the city where

looking out the window

in late afternoon,

a beautiful vista seems dominated by the faint tracer-bullet patterns of many automobiles in motion, evoking,

as they cross the visible-from-a-distance multitude of bridges spanning the magic river that gives mythic dimension to this city nestled in its curve

—automobiles evoking that specific seen-from-far-away energy that paints precise,

punctuated,

energy strips in the imagination of someone

who perhaps relies too much upon that same imagination? (*EDDIE rises unsteadily to come forward to the audience*) There he goes, encasing himself in a work of art— (*The noise of a small collision bounces EDDIE back into his chair*)—in a prototype, at least (*ESTELLE swings a movable railing in a semicircle, which, as it happens, passes over EDDIE's chair and knocks him off. He struggles back onto the chair*)

So.

He made plans.

But here's the important part.

He didn't try to define them.

Plans?

Plans. (*EDDIE reaches into his briefcase and takes out a map, which he slowly smooths out over his lap*) It all adds up to the same thing, no? He made a work of art for himself, into which he might hopefully disappear. Then, seeing corners at the corners, and in response pulling the entire edifice of his sometimes comfortable enough life,

over his body like a blanket,

could he be in fact so blanketed?

Time to escape, the new woman said. (*MARIE has posed her body on the tilted table, spreading her legs, slowly unwrapping a bandaged leg to reveal a red wound on her inner thigh, and holding out an apple in one hand to tempt Eddie, who slowly crosses to her*)

But.

Escape what, escape to what?

The new woman did not say escape to what

and we all knew to escape,

but we did not know to escape to what.

So what made her new, this new woman?

She was always new because she was so . . . ethereal.

MARIE: I take no responsibility for my own etherealness, that's what she should have truly said.

DEEP VOICE OVER LOUDSPEAKERS: That was not new. (*EDDIE is creeping up onto the table toward MARIE's apple, but in reaching for it he somehow stumbles and falls on his back, between MARIE's now uplifted legs, and her apple drops and bounces off his head*) What was new was that he began to perceive, under this blanking artifact, artifactually enough,

that what was new and strange was his own relationship to whatever spewed forth, because now, believe it or not,

he did not have the feeling it was necessary for him to be mountainous in his efforts of will,

all directed to making his life cohere into one of the twenty-seven life models ordered specifically into HIS consciousness on pain of death, which certainly could not be avoided

down the road someplace. *(The DOCTOR is at the rear, cleaning a large shovel and crying softly to himself, as EDDIE and MARIE remain frozen on the table)*

Road, road, road, he said to himself in the hopes it might indicate a direction.

Also realizing it could be more than one.

And again automobiles started jumping a little bit like pretend molecules of a very bright light—

and he decided to spend a lot of time and effort creating what was more than a simple lament, because it was never simple.

There was a lot of debate later—which route did he take to success and glory that was—

Oops, I almost said "unprincipled" when I mean to say "unparalleled."

And with the parallel—though words are not things that can ever be parallel to each other like worlds can—

he nevertheless fell quite off the track. *(The DOCTOR and ESTELLE have gathered around the table where EDDIE and MARIE lie frozen and entangled, and all now start shading their eyes against what might be a terrible vision, or a very bright light)*

Into the car?

But do cars ride on steel tracks, or on asphalt pavement sometimes?

Put them together this way—

Have you ever imagined one of those incredibility ravishing contests between automobile and passenger train?

Somebody thought you'd have to go back to the turn of the century for that,

but what they were really imagining, his friends volunteered, was the nineteen-thirties.

But the confusion was understandable, because the turn of the century was the epic,

par excellence,

of that powerful iron-horse metaphor-as-drug,

and if there's one thing that did need to be drugged,

it was this sensibility in question that above all
was scheming to GET OUT OF HERE any way possible.

(*MARIE* gives *EDDIE* a shove off the table, and he falls and
grabs onto a cardboard industrial drum that stands at the
foot of the table. Then he feels his way over the top of the
drum and goes to the ground head first, but as his feet
follow, his legs grasp the barrel and he begins crossing the
room in a crawl on the floor, legs locked around the barrel,
which follows him upstage, and *ESTELLE* runs and puts a
little mechanical toy on its top. It waddles around in a circle
on the barrel top, as *EDDIE* drags everything upstage. *MARIE*
and *ESTELLE* then run to saw on the logs, and the *DOCTOR*
makes the wind machine turn at a great rate. Finally things
quiet down, and *MARIE* and *ESTELLE* race to one of the side
walls and begin feeling along the wall for a secret door)

MARIE: (Singing to herself as she feels the wall)
    Secret door,
    secret door . . .

DEEP VOICE OVER LOUDSPEAKERS: Here's the main thing. You're
    looking for an escape route—

EDDIE: (Who has arrived at one of the padded walls, also feeling
    along it for an opening) Am I?

DEEP VOICE: It could manifest itself in different ways. A route, a
    method of locomotion. A secret door.
        You can't find the secret door, because it isn't in this
    world, but in the other. The one you want to escape to.
        So use it. Use the secret door. Remember—
        It isn't in this world, it's located in the world you want to
    escape to.
        Use it.

MARIE: (Comes away from her wall, a few steps toward Eddie,
    and speaks in a nearby microphone) Confused?

I'll change the subject a little. *(She holds out a strange painting of a head with a halo that she has been hiding behind her back)* What do you think of this painting?

(The DOCTOR, at a microphone in the rear, whispers echoes of all the lines that follow)

EDDIE: I like it.

MARIE: You do?

EDDIE: Yes. I like it.

MARIE: *(Smirking, as ESTELLE giggles)* Then there's no more to be said, is there?

EDDIE: *(After a pause, very quietly)* Burn it.

MARIE: What?

EDDIE: Burn it.

MARIE: Ah, because you like it so much?

EDDIE: Exactly.

MARIE: What a spiritual trip. *(She starts to go, then turns back to the mike)* You really want it burned?

EDDIE: Yes.

MARIE: Then I'll take it into the next room, where we always perform such rites of sacrifice. *(She goes upstage, and ESTELLE comes to EDDIE and acts as if she were pulling back the front curtain, so EDDIE could watch)*

ESTELLE: *(Very quietly, with a smirk)* Maybe you want to watch?

EDDIE: No. I trust you.

ESTELLE: *(Pause)* No. I trust . . . *(She lifts a finger and points to his head)* You. *(She turns away, as MARIE returns without the painting and walks straight up to EDDIE)* It's done. *(She slaps him sharply on the cheek and he steps back, holding his face)*

EDDIE: That was quick.

MARIE: Yes. *(Pause)* You should have opened the door.

EDDIE: Did you really burn it?

MARIE: *(Into a microphone)* Yes.

EDDIE: *(Under his breath, as he sits)* Bastard.

MARIE: Why do you say that?

EDDIE: I have my reasons.

MARIE: You must be of two minds.

EDDIE: Not at all.

MARIE: Am I a bastard a hundred percent of the time?

EDDIE: No. You have me there.

MARIE: Have you?

EDDIE: You're not a bastard a hundred percent of the time. Therefore I have to try to be in sync with you, but I know I'm relatively fallible and can't pull it off all the time.

(There is a pause. MARIE has forgotten her next line, and the WOMAN in black shouts out, "Now that you burned the

painting which you say you liked so very much!" *MARIE
turns and gives her a dirty look, and then goes to another
mike and speaks her line)*

MARIE: *(Very softly)* Now that I burned the painting which you
say you liked so very much—

EDDIE: Oh, I did.

MARIE: Do you want to see another?

EDDIE: You have lots of them stored away.

MARIE: Yes. I only exhibit one at a time.

EDDIE: *(Staring into space)* It's snowing.

MARIE: So it is. *(Pause)* Anyway, do you want to look at another
painting?

EDDIE: No.

MARIE: Suppose I told you I didn't really burn the painting.

EDDIE: Did you?

MARIE: *(Crossing)* Yes. Come take a look for it in the next room,
Eddie. *(She is wiping her hands, as the DOCTOR comes forward to join them. The DOCTOR is now dressed strangely. He
is wearing a pig's nose, with tubes from the nose circling his
body. He also wears an apron and a stocking cap, which
gives him the semblance of a bald skull. He carries a briefcase)* All you'll find is ashes. And by the way, the reason it
was able to burn so quickly is that I use a blowtorch.
Ashes were prefigured in our train references.

DOCTOR: *(Smiles threateningly)* That's one way of looking at it.

MARIE: *(Pause)* The race between the automobile and the passenger train could also be thought of as our symbolic confrontation.

DOCTOR: *(To EDDIE, tossing him the briefcase)* Which is which?

MARIE: *(Smiles)* I take it back.

DOCTOR: *(Turns to her)* You can't, you've committed yourself. *(The DOCTOR and ESTELLE run to the merry-go-round, rear, and run it in a full circle—and it makes a loud rattling noise as it is revolved, and Eddie hurries to a corner and extracts another small painting from the briefcase—very similar to the other, a head with a halo)*

WOMAN IN BLACK: *(Over the noise)* Excuse me! *(Everything stops)*

EDDIE: *(Staring forward into the light, wearing dark glasses now)* . . . The automobile is racing to be able to cross at the railroad crossing before it gets smacked by the locomotive of the passenger train carrying, as fate would have it, the unbeknownst beloved. *(Pause, he looks at MARIE, who steps toward him)* So you must be the passenger train. And I'm the one about to get smacked by the loco.

MARIE: *(Into a mike)* I'd say the one who wants to burn a painting he likes very much, and you really did—that's the loco I'd think.

DOCTOR: *(Coming close to EDDIE, thrusting his chin almost onto EDDIE's shoulder)* The one who carried out the wishes of the loco with such dispatch is also a kind of loco.

MARIE: *(Under her breath)* Bastard.

ESTELLE: *(At a mike upstage, carrying another painting, which is hidden under a cloth)* I couldn't help overhearing your conversation and realizing that you want someone to disagree, but that's impossible. (*MARIE starts toward ESTELLE, who steps forward a bit to stop her, also thrusting her covered painting out in front of her*) I mean, you WERE speaking in what seemed an unnaturally loud tone of voice, so you obviously did want to be overheard and judged, but unfortunately I judge you in a way that's not to your liking.

MARIE: Unless?

ESTELLE: Unless what? (*Pause*) Oh, I get it. Unless your liking is to be not to my liking. (*She whips the cloth away, revealing another similar painting of a head with a halo. There's a pause. The light changes*)

EDDIE: Didn't you notice the sun came out? (*The light softens*) One minute it's snowing, the next minute the sun's out. The only implication is you get melted snow. Unless, of course, the snow was a mistake.

DOCTOR: How can snow be a mistake?

EDDIE: Well, somebody could torch it. Isn't that what they say people do to houses? Gangsters—they torch a house. (*Turns to MARIE*) Just like we—you—torched a painting. (*MARIE throws her arms around EDDIE and kisses him on the mouth, and he struggles and frees himself with a lurch, and he gasps for breath and equilibrium*) You know, I can no longer remember even who's responsible. The one who physically executes, or the one who provides the inspiration.

MARIE: Could I invite you back to my apartment for a look at a very unique art collection?

EDDIE: What's unique about your art collection?

ESTELLE: (*Smirking*) She'll make you burn all your most beautiful pictures.

MARIE: There are other ways paintings can be sacrificed to the gods.

EDDIE: The who? *(They are both downstage, talking into a mike)*

MARIE: The gods. I see you don't believe what I'm talking about.

EDDIE: You think you mean gods that I don't believe in, but I do— my own.

MARIE: Here's one. *(She turns upstage, looking to where the DOCTOR, in the shadows, has been winding white surgical gauze over his head so he looks like a mummy. He also takes a small painting, which he carries under his arm, but EDDIE has seen none of this)*

EDDIE: You anticipate that long before it happens. *(He turns and is shocked to see the mummy)*

MARIE: I told you it would happen. What I didn't tell you was that he would come through HIS door into OUR world. But from our perspective, that's not the important thing. Poor us. Look what he's got under his arm, by the way.

ESTELLE: Your favorite painting, Eddie.

MARIE: *(Running against the wall in mock surprise—or is it horror?)* Oh, YOU'RE Eddie!

ESTELLE: What does that explain?

EDDIE: Isn't anybody else surprised to see a godlike mani- festation?

MARIE: We're not sure what it is.

DOCTOR: *(From under his bandages, intoning like a mummy)* I am . . . ! *(He begins shuffling across the stage)*

EDDIE: Sure?

DOCTOR: Yes, VERY sure . . . !

EDDIE: *(Turning away to speak to himself through a microphone)*
A painting that returns from the dead either wasn't dead, or
else has regenerative powers related to a god's interest in
such a potent image.

MARIE: It's wonderful that you and your god have the same taste
in paintings. *(The DOCTOR bangs into the wall and drops the
painting)*

EDDIE: *(Worried)* I don't know that we do.

MARIE: But he's the sacred messenger! *(The DOCTOR has bent
down to laboriously retrieve the painting)*

DOCTOR: May I speak?

EDDIE: Does a god have to ask permission?

ESTELLE: Weren't you shocked at the timbre of his voice? It wasn't
expectedly godlike, was it? Which implies, on my part, how
much happier we'd all be if he or it didn't speak. *(There is a
pause. At first it seems that everyone has been stunned into
silence at the god's surprise appearance. Then it's made
clear that EDDIE has simply forgotten his next line, since the
WOMAN IN BLACK shouts out his line: "May I look at the
picture?")*

EDDIE: *(After giving her a dirty look, mumbles his line into a mike)*
May I look at the picture?

MARIE: Is it exactly the same?

EDDIE: It looks the same.

MARIE: Should we reburn it?

EDDIE: I don't think so, since it was remanifest in such a miraculous way.

(The DOCTOR (Mummy) has made his way center stage, lifting the painting in the air doing a slow ritual dance as the music rises to a deafening level. ESTELLE has distributed snow shovels, and EDDIE follows the women's lead as they begin pantomiming the shoveling of dirt onto the god and his painting as the god begins howling rhythmically over the music. Then they throw away their shovels and run away to watch from a distance, as EDDIE shouts over the decreasing music)

EDDIE: Sometimes it's definitely chaotic!

MARIE: I wouldn't use that word for a miracle.

EDDIE: You think it's a real miracle?

MARIE: Well, let's say yes.

ESTELLE: Hey, you must love pictures more than you love anything, Eddie!

(The DOCTOR has wandered to the side, and again bounces against a wall)

EDDIE: I don't think miracles are handed out right and left. Therefore if one occurs, it must be linked to a pivot point inside your private value system.

DOCTOR (MUMMY): *(Recovering from his bang against the wall, looking about dazed)* Hey! What time is it?

EDDIE: I'm sorry. You can go on theorizing if you like—*(The DOCTOR starts unwrapping himself)*

MARIE: You think it's so banal?

EDDIE: I'd rather clear the airwaves of all possible interference.

MARIE: That's not possible, Eddie.

EDDIE: It's possible. I'm encasing myself in a work of art. You know what that means? My life, really. (Pause, advancing forward) That's why I wanted to burn a painting I liked very much. A distraction, right? It had to be cleared out of my life totally. I think you get the point even though I've been careful to circle rather than zeroing in. (During this speech, ESTELLE has taken a pose on the tilted table. She holds a big red-and-white beach ball over her head, as if posing for a cheesecake photo)

MARIE: (Leaning into a mike, as the lights brighten on ESTELLE) Now, let's pretend we've finally made it to the beach—

EDDIE: (Turning) What?

MARIE: It's a warm, sunny day. We doff our workaday apparel. We strip down to bathing suits or perhaps no clothing at all,
    and slowly march into the shining ocean.
    From which, within the briefest possible period of time, one or two of us start to rise, as if we weighed now,
    no more than air, into the sun.

EDDIE: Why talk about a beach, we could do that right here.

MARIE: I don't see it happening.

EDDIE: I was allowing myself a moment of reverie.

ESTELLE: (Still in her pose) What's the question, Eddie?

EDDIE: Question?

MARIE: Perhaps it's a question that's supposed to provoke other questions.

ESTELLE: It's too bad our picture can't speak to us, Eddie.

EDDIE: *(To himself, testing out his own name)* Eddie . . . ?

DOCTOR: *(Leans in threateningly, but still in his ridiculous nose with tubes, bald pate, and apron, all of which he wears for the rest of the show)* Should we BURN it, Eddie?

EDDIE: *(Very quietly)* My name is Eddie and I plan to escape to Poetry City.

DOCTOR: Escape?

EDDIE: Don't be upset if I tell you, you participate in a life I find oppressive.

MARIE: Why, Eddie?

EDDIE: I find oppressive, life that is not centered, continually, on concern for the human spirit. That has to be the center.

DOCTOR: But Eddie, you've described life as it is here, where you are this very minute. *(The WOMAN IN BLACK shouts out a repeat of the DOCTOR's line: "But Eddie! You've described life as it is here, where you are this very minute." Then with much giggling, the DOCTOR, MARIE, and ESTELLE run to spin the merry-go-round once, then they grab wineglasses, and taking a drink, come forward tempting Eddie to join their party)*

EDDIE: In a hidden sense, maybe.

DOCTOR: Not hidden, Eddie. It wobbles, perhaps, because that's the human condition.

EDDIE: Wobbles?

DOCTOR: Yes. You know—wobbles. *(They giggle)*

EDDIE: It's true, I wobble when I walk.

DOCTOR: Be careful, Eddie, you're going in circles.

EDDIE: What?

DOCTOR: *(A pretend smile)* I didn't say anything.

EDDIE: I thought you did. *(Turns away)* I was talking to myself.

DOCTOR: *(With a little wave)* Goodbye. *(But instead of leaving, the DOCTOR, MARIE, and ESTELLE all sit to sip at their wine-glasses. Eddie then sits also, tentatively, as if afraid to do the wrong thing. He is facing them, his back to the audience. Then he turns in his chair to face out)*

EDDIE: *(After a pause, quietly, as if convincing himself)* Here I am. Totally okay.

MARIE: Totally happy?

EDDIE: Yes.

(A loud noise knocks the others off their chairs onto the floor. They reseat themselves, and try to recover their composure)

ESTELLE: Totally at peace?

EDDIE: Yes.

(A noise again knocks the others to the floor. This time it continues, and they twitch on the floor for a few seconds,

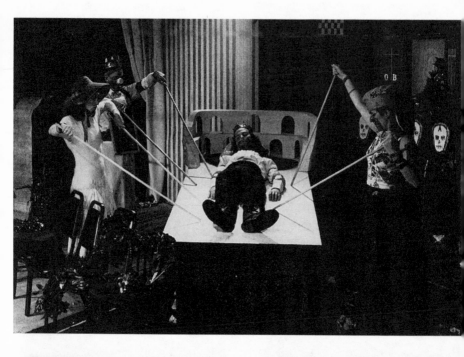

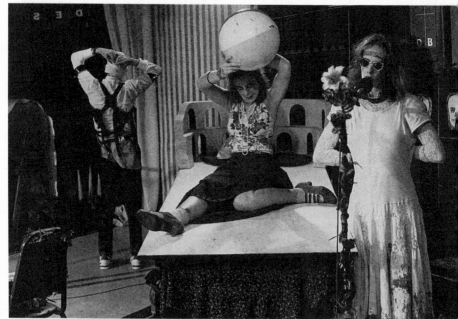

like fish out of water. Then it stops, and they recompose themselves, but remain on the floor)

MARIE: What city is this?

EDDIE: Poetry City.

MARIE: Are you sure?

DOCTOR: Harmony comes from opposites, Eddie. Everything originates in strife.

ESTELLE: Guess who said that?

EDDIE: *(Pause)* Where's a map?

ESTELLE: *(A gentle threat)* Look on the table.

(EDDIE goes to a table rear, where props are piled. He pushes a few to the floor in his search and comes back with a map, which he unfolds and holds in front of him, trying to read it)

MARIE: *(Very slowly, deliberately)* It was the wrong . . . table.

EDDIE: Oh? . . . This is the wrong map?

MARIE: It was the wrong . . . table.

EDDIE: *(Pause, he presses the open map to his chest)* So, this is where we are now. Could I put this map of Poetry City on the wall?

MARIE: How?

EDDIE: *(Pause)* Do you have any . . . thumbtacks?

MARIE: Wouldn't that . . . hurt the wall?

EDDIE: *(Pause, considering this carefully)* Well, it would put very small holes in the wall. *(Pause)* It's okay, then?

MARIE: Best not.

EDDIE: Okay. I'll just fold it up and put it in my pocket. *(He starts to do so, when ESTELLE comes up behind him and shoves him into the padded wall. He bounces off and falls to the floor and starts crawling to a chair on the other side of the room)*

DEEP VOICE OVER LOUDSPEAKERS: Eddie knew the streets of Poetry City by heart, so when a map appeared in his pocket, he wasn't confused.

He flipped through the streets in his mind, and a door opened across the street.

That's a good fifty yards from me, thought Eddie, but still he jumped out of the way.

But Eddie, he realized, that jump was unnecessary, he realized.

And he noticed his map, on fire.

(By now, MARIE has run to another table and taken a stack of books (poetry books?). She has started throwing them, one by one, at the crawling EDDIE. At the same time, as the music rises and falls several times, the DOCTOR and ESTELLE run rear, grab snow shovels, load them with trays of food, and run and bounce the shovels on the backs of chairs till the food bounces off (amid much noise, of course) and scatters on the floor. MARIE and ESTELLE finally sit together, entwined, staring at EDDIE, who has by now found a seat, as the DOCTOR races rear, seizes a bowling ball, and bowls it from the rear into the middle of the assembled group, knocking over a few chairs)

ESTELLE: *(As EDDIE sits panting and disheveled across from her)* 'Fess up, Eddie—

WOMAN IN BLACK: *(Shouts)* Oh, Eddie! 'Fess up!

ESTELLE: Is this really your kind of town?

EDDIE: I haven't been here very long.

ESTELLE: But you get the feel of things kinda fast, Eddie—

WOMAN IN BLACK: EDDIE!

ESTELLE: —or I miss my guess.

WOMAN IN BLACK: EDDIE!

> *(The DOCTOR bowls another ball through the center, and EDDIE gets out of the way, but tries to act as if he isn't upset)*

EDDIE: I'm the kind of person—

ESTELLE: Nothing satisfies you, yes?

EDDIE: You're right.

ESTELLE: *(She is speaking into a mike on a cable, which she manipulates seductively, still entwined with MARIE, who is trying to read one of the books she was recently hurling at EDDIE)* So this isn't really your kind of town, Eddie.

WOMAN IN BLACK: EDDIE!

ESTELLE: I mean, for the first day or two, Eddie says to himself—

WOMAN IN BLACK: EDDIE!

ESTELLE: —"Hey, maybe this is okay." You managed to squeeze out a little poetic frisson from a turn around the corner into this vista, then that vista, but then with a little more time, it didn't really seem to hold up for Eddie, did it?

WOMAN IN BLACK: EDDIE!

EDDIE: *(After an uncomfortable pause)* You're right.

MARIE: *(Smiles)* No, YOU'RE right. *(She and ESTELLE look at each other and share a laugh)*

ESTELLE: Of course I'm right. This town is a shit town. Take it from me, Eddie. I had deep experience of this shit town, and a shit town is what it is.

EDDIE: That doesn't leave much doubt.

ESTELLE: On the other hand, a lot of opportunity is here, for somebody looking for a certain kind of something.

EDDIE: Oh? What kind of something?

ESTELLE: You don't expect me to make myself overly clear, I think.

EDDIE: Well, I don't know if that's your habit or not.

MARIE: *(Moving toward EDDIE, who has risen, ready to run)* What about your habits, Eddie? Don't YOUR habits have something to do with the overall situation?

EDDIE: I get myself into certain situations where I don't know quite . . . how to respond. *(Pause; he looks about nervously)* Like now?

MARIE: Yes. Why the hell don't you know how to respond?

WOMAN IN BLACK: Do you want: absolute clarity, Eddie!?!

MARIE: You want absolute clarity? Or are you aware of the disadvantages built into absolute clarity. That seems to be the question I'm putting to you, and you seem to me perfectly capable of coming up with some kind of response.

EDDIE: Yes. I should be. Certainly . . .

DOCTOR: So? Do you want absolute clarity? (*He is now sitting with ESTELLE, his hands exploring her body as she sedately rubs her body against him*)

WOMAN IN BLACK: Do you want: absolute clarity, Eddie!?!

(*EDDIE turns to run, hits the padded wall, bounces off, and staggers a few feet*)

EDDIE: (Recovering) Let me ask, if I can—can we define again the area under discussion?

MARIE: (*Suddenly more aggressive, as the DOCTOR and ESTELLE get even more deeply involved with each other*) Suddenly things get clarified. You're interested in entertainment. (*ESTELLE giggles, then she and the DOCTOR run to the merry-go-round and spin it once, after which they freeze, waiting for the next activity with which to befuddle EDDIE*) You're one of those people who can't be alone with his life! This perpetual drift from city to city, a diversion. That's all!

EDDIE: Go on—

MARIE: Go on to what?

EDDIE: Go on with what you were saying.

MARIE: (*Shouting into a mike*) What do you want from me, anyhow? That's not what you're gonna get, buster! You're gonna get a truckload of shit, that's what you're gonna get, and don't tell me you don't like it, because by the time I'm finished with you, you're gonna LOVE it.

(*MARIE*, *ESTELLE*, and the *DOCTOR* run to get three cardboard industrial drums from the rear. They set them center stage and pose over them, watching *EDDIE*. He gets the idea, runs to get one of his own, brings it center and waits)

EDDIE: (After a pause, for lack of anything else to say) Okay.

MARIE: Okay!

DOCTOR AND ESTELLE: Okay!

(The *DOCTOR*, *ESTELLE*, and *MARIE* bend down, and the top halves of their bodies disappear into the drums. After looking about for a beat, *EDDIE* decides to join them, and he too disappears. Terrible groaning music builds, as all slowly emerge from the drums, their faces smeared around the mouth with a thick, sticky brown substance. As the music gets louder, the *DOCTOR*, *ESTELLE*, and *MARIE* lift their barrels and hold them, horizontal—and *EDDIE* tentatively follows. Then he crosses and places his barrel against one of the padded walls, the top open part flat on the wall. The others line their barrels up behind him, so the held barrels form a kind of segmented snake, head against the wall. The music is deafening now. They all retract the barrels a few inches so a slight gap opens up between each barrel, and then suddenly all barrels are smashed together and against the wall. This is repeated. The music is deafening. After several of these, all retreat, worn out, and lay their barrels carefully on the floor. Slowly, they first sit on the barrels, then immediately crawl forward and twist and crawl halfway inside the barrels, their legs sticking out. The music finally fades. As *EDDIE* emerges slowly and collapses into a chair)

EDDIE: At a certain point in my life, I realized that my mind had been incorrectly focused. (The others are out, sitting exhausted also) It would be, I realized, a terribly difficult task to reorient the focus mechanism. I doubted that I had the energy and determination. Therefore, I tried to imagine other, less demanding procedures whereby I might achieve that identical goal. That is, the effect of refocusing, without refocusing.

MARIE: *(Calls out softly, as if from far away)* E . . . ddie . . .

(After a pause, the DOCTOR, ESTELLE and MARIE rise and start rearranging the furniture. They are fashioning a sort of restaurant setting, with the barrels, turned upside down, serving as tables. As this is done, the deep VOICE is heard over the loudspeakers)

DEEP VOICE OVER LOUDSPEAKERS: In Poetry City,
I bet I stay
a real long time, in fact,
because more poetry means more fun. *(A loud crack, and all freeze for one sentence, then continue)*
What was that noise,
That metallic crack, in fact?
Something in my heart?
Not at all;
a vehicle exploded,
or rather began to and stopped,
because nothing in Poetry City fulfills itself.
Which is why it's Poetry City,
get it?

I bet you didn't
but it happened like that
and whatever it is that happens
gets into you, somehow
in Poetry City.

I've had fine, fine meals here.

The philosopher turned over his plate
In Poetry City.

In the restaurant called JOY
He finished his lunch from
a series of uncomfortable positions.

JOY, JOY, the passerby was corrected
as he almost thought of asking
old-timers
for the most dependable restaurant
in Poetry City.

The gray clouds hung over something
beyond street corners
that evoked
what should have been docks
but no river flowed or ever,
cut wet
in between the semi-tall buildings.

What's the best way in and out
Of Poetry City?

Not by water of course,
there is none.
And the philosopher dried his throat.
Not by air
which compacts over the city whole
like a blanket of foam,
and the philosopher swallowed hard.
Not by rail,
for once,
where streetcars cut electric slap paths
into the interior
now rest assured with lying wherever you find yourself.
And the philosopher turned to dessert
which had been served first anyway—
and made a smile out of his mental muscles.

You look happy,

claimed his companion and vanished.

Which one of them?
An answer was
Shhh, forever.

(ESTELLE has pulled the black curtain, so the reset room is hidden. As she does so, we hear one more roll of a bowling ball across the floor, and the crash as it hits a wall. Sickly sweet music is playing, as the DOCTOR appears through the curtain. He has been transformed into a waiter. He carries a tray, and a rose, and smiles dopily at the audience, as if he has taken some kind of pacifying drug. From behind the curtain we hear EDDIE calling in irritation—)

EDDIE: *(Behind the curtain)* Waiter!?!

DOCTOR: *(Smiling at the audience)* Helloooo!

DEEP VOICE OVER LOUDSPEAKERS: *(As the DOCTOR smells his rose)* Oh, Eddie. Sweeten the self, and do not act, which will sweeten the self through not acting, not projecting the self into gross matter through the act, which falls into the real world that is not sweet.

EDDIE: *(Appearing through the curtain)* Why not employ a more efficient waiter?

MARIE: *(From behind the curtain, into a microphone)* Oh, Eddie, what's the name of this town of famous restaurants?

EDDIE: Why employ a waiter that does not act?

MARIE: *(Still hidden)* Guess again. *(The curtain has opened, and the DOCTOR takes up an ecstatic pose in the center of the room, smelling his rose and ignoring the restaurant's one customer—Eddie)*

EDDIE: *(Seating himself at a table)* Waiter?

DOCTOR: *(Dopily ecstatic, waves at Eddie)* Hello.

EDDIE: I'd like some fish. *(Pause. Nobody moves)* Is that possible?

MARIE: *(She sits at a table, laying out cards like a fortuneteller. A mike has been positioned so she can speak into it)* It is possible.

EDDIE: Will you bring me some fish?

DOCTOR: *(Shakes head, sadly)* Ahhhhh . . . No . . .

EDDIE: Why employ a waiter who does not act?

MARIE: He sweetens himself, and my restaurant burns, lightens.

EDDIE: I don't understand "lightens."

MARIE: I can't explain "lightens". *(A noise, and she throws her cards in the air as ESTELLE grabs EDDIE and pushes him to the center of the room. He composes himself, and begins to recite, as if in school, a memorized text. He is perhaps this evening's entertainment in the restaurant?)*

EDDIE:
The night was outside the window,
as well as inside where Eddie was.
Nothing . . . turned into a poem.
And a great weight lifted from Eddie's chest, from his shoulders and forehead.
Poems exited from all parts of his body.
And in leaving
they turned to nothing.
That nothing was Eddie's medium.
He drank deep, and picked up the telephone.

Hello? Who is nobody;
On the other end of the line.
Many faces flashed from Eddie's mind
onto the wallpaper
that curled up like burnt leaves. (*His recitation finished, he finds his way back to his seat. There is another pause. He decides to try again*) Waiter, I'd like some fish.

WOMAN IN BLACK: Excuse me!

EDDIE: (*Pause*) Would I really?

DOCTOR: (*Smiles, staring into space*) Please, don't pay me for fish.

EDDIE: (*Confused and irritated*) Normally, I don't pay for fish until I've received it.

DOCTOR: (*Sitting beside EDDIE, puts an arm around him, which makes EDDIE very uncomfortable*) Would you like to look at it, sir?

EDDIE: I try to imagine it.

DOCTOR: Try . . . (*ESTELLE has one of the snow shovels, loaded with fish, which she smacks against a wall behind EDDIE. Then she immediately holds it over his head*) . . . to imagine it.

EDDIE: (*Under his breath*) Look at this river . . .
    No fiery angels on this river.

MARIE: This river?
    Is that a river?

EDDIE: (*To himself*) I can imagine a river. I can imagine fiery angels on the river, and fish leaping into the sky in happiness.

MARIE: We let them leap, I believe.

DOCTOR: I'm a waiter who does nothing, and in the end, it makes
   you happy, also.

EDDIE: I'd like to eat. Why? Because dinnertime has come, you
   see? (Shows his watch)

MARIE: I see. (She jumps up to go rear to sit at the piano)

EDDIE: (Calling after her, in irritation) Would your restaurant be
   more successful—(He jumps up, hits his head on the fish
   shovel, the others shout "Owww!" but EDDIE speedily recovers, and takes a few steps to call after MARIE)—as a
   restaurant, if you employed a waiter who did not—NOT
   act?

   (MARIE starts playing the piano, as the DOCTOR is next to
   EDDIE and slumps against his body as if his passive and
   ecstatic state would make him collapse, so EDDIE grabs him
   to keep him from falling, and starts trying to hold him up,
   which turns into an awkward dance of embrace)

DEEP VOICE OVER LOUDSPEAKERS: (As MARIE plays, and EDDIE and
   the DOCTOR dance)
   Heart carved
   he opened his palm
   A light spread
   left to right;
   insignia of flash,
   idea imprint
   over vista-weight.
   Rapid into
   a clutch
   that spasmed
   itself.
   A mix
   total.

EDDIE: *(Still holding the DOCTOR up, trying to talk past his body to the audience)* This waiter does not act. He does not descend into the real world, where he takes my desire for fish and gratifies it. *(The DOCTOR is standing on his own now, and EDDIE takes a step away)* I taste the imaginary fish in my mouth. I feel what it does to my throat, as the taste seems to spread in multiple directions inside me. By what pathways I do not know.

DOCTOR: How did I become a waiter? *(He starts to fall, EDDIE again catches him)* How did I come to dress, and be here? Now I remember. *(He regains his balance and frees himself)*

MARIE: *(Moving downstage)* It was as if you were doing a walk that was a kind of revolving perpetual, and that spin, that wobble, as it were, spun you into my restaurant. *(A loud noise, and MARIE is isolated in a spotlight, pointing aggressively at the DOCTOR)* I HAVE ANOTHER IDEA!

Which I admit is inspired by viewing this waiter that I employ, or seem to. Do I employ?

He WOBBLES into my employ! He is, wobbling, sustained within my employ. This waiter does not fall into concrete being with acts, but hovers—always on the verge of delivering the meal that will satisfy. *(EDDIE turns to go and runs into the padded wall and bounces back, almost colliding with ESTELLE, who stands there holding a large pot filled with water)*

ESTELLE: I decided to help out and bring you your fish.

MARIE: *(Turns away and sings softly)*
Secret door
Secret door . . .

EDDIE: *(As ESTELLE lifts a fish from the pot)* But it hasn't been cooked.

MARIE: Ah, then it would be far past living— *(EDDIE turns and bangs into the wall)*

ESTELLE: *(Whispers)* A fish!

MARIE: *(Continues)*—while here in a previous state, there is still the chance, returned not too far off into a water environment, it may be able to function as a live, fulfilled being which it is or at least was, but we can hope still is.

ESTELLE: *(Whispers to Eddie)* That's your generic fish.

MARIE: Shall we try?

ESTELLE: Oh, yeah!

DEEP VOICE OVER LOUDSPEAKERS: Shall we succeed? I think we succeeded. *(As the VOICE continues, all but the DOCTOR are given a fish and go to separate corners of the stage, holding a fish above their open mouths as if ready to drop it down their respective throats)* The man in the bar said, "Careful Eddie, Poetry City is on the verge of destruction." He put his finger to his lips, and Eddie fought the impulse to seize the man's hand and return it forcibly to the side of his body.

The man seemed not to notice what was going on inside Eddie, which made Eddie very suspicious.

So he pretended he was looking for something inside his pocket. "Here it is," cried Estelle, who had just returned from the country several days earlier, and she handed Eddie a bunch of keys.

Eddie, momentarily baffled, realized the best thing to do was accept the keys and act as if he knew what they were intended for.

DOCTOR: *(Coming forward excitedly, as if he's solved a mystery and he wants to tell the world)* The taste is where? In my mouth. In the sensation which is registered in the brain or elsewhere?

In the tasted item, of course—? But of course not! It
seems to CIRCULATE!

EDDIE: *(Taking a step forward)* My mind wandered. Was I
speaking?

DOCTOR: It was a taste.

EDDIE: What?

DOCTOR: For speaking.

EDDIE: *(Holding up his fish and looking at it)* My fish? *(EDDIE,
MARIE, and ESTELLE go, "Meow!" and throw their fish to the
center of the room)* I dare not ask.

DOCTOR: *(Radiant, starting a goofy dance)* Ask me, your waiter!

MARIE: I'm surprised the customer hasn't exploded.

EDDIE: I've exploded? *(Coming forward to watch the DOCTOR's
dance, he slips on a fish and takes a pratfall)* I have! But it
seems to distribute itself over such a wide landscape, that
the explosion itself is no explosion . . . but more a gentle
wave.

MARIE: Oh, Eddie, wait; patient; while the large silver tray from
the kitchen arrives—

ESTELLE: Shhhh.

DOCTOR: Poetry City, kid.

MARIE: Bottomless! Which means what?
    "Meaning" arrives, and the entire fabric so self-grown
in radiant, fiery . . . "AM-IS!" *(Music starts to build, and
a "fish dance" is commenced, with swimming motions,
and with breathing like fish, and also yelping like puppy*

dogs, and the line of dancers circles amidst the objects of the cluttered stage) "Am-IS!" *(The dance starts to end as EDDIE and the DOCTOR and ESTELLE collapse on the couch at the back of the room and wave their legs in the air, and MARIE runs downstage and declaims for the audience as the music is fading)* A kind of flap—"am-is!" he flapped himself in the flapping—"am-is! am-is!"

WOMAN IN BLACK: EXCUSE ME!
EXCUSE ME!

MARIE: *(The music continues lower, as she sweeps across the stage still declaiming)* A waiter? Irrelevant. Because the fish arrive— *(The three on the couch, still waving their legs in the air, pipe out a falsetto "Wheee . . . !")* and flap upon the strand!
Grand and wonderful indeed.
Heed them with care!
He is not there, in the morning air!
Sliced by sunlight
that blinds, not at all;
that dazzles, not at all. *(Her energy running down now, as the music disappears completely)*
Too bad.
Too sad. *(Pause. EDDIE comes forward. Silence. Dejectedly, he goes and sits in a corner)*

MARIE: *(At a mike)*
Oh, Eddie.
Why retro-relax
when you can dazzle me effectively.

WOMAN IN BLACK:
RETRO-RELAX!
RETRO-RELAX!
RETRO-RELAX!

MARIE: *(Softly)*
> You have no story to tell.
> So. You're a winner.
> You want a story so you can believe in the world.
> My message is quite the opposite.
> Believe no longer.
> You made it happen—okay, but the happening got stopped. *(EDDIE has come slowly downstage to face her)* That is to say, the world goes on, but you see what's going on right through the middle of it going on?

DOCTOR: *(Singing softly, mockingly, in the rear shadows)*
> "Get your coat
> and grab your hat.
> Leave your worries
> On the doorstep . . ."

MARIE: A new plan for life surfaces, Eddie.

ESTELLE: *(Calling in a whisper)* Eddddd . . . ie?

MARIE:
> Everything that took you back
> now takes you forward.
> So you say.
> "Am I confused?"

> But whether it's a statement or a question of fact
> is equally so.

ESTELLE: *(Coming forward with the DOCTOR)* Bundles of being. *(The DOCTOR gestures shooting a pistol at EDDIE, and there is a loud BANG)* He was that kind of hero. *(Another gesture with a BANG. And EDDIE slowly and gently holds his head, as ESTELLE comes and gently embraces him)*

DOCTOR: *(Whispering into a mike)*
> The darkness falls.

Fish drop gently through the suburban landscape.
Floral displays were considered.
Feet bringing one to the edge.
Upside-down . . .
A dilemma noncontradictory.

ESTELLE: *(Still holding EDDIE)* We lose our way—*(Does a slow dance step out from his body, holding his hand)* and benefit.

DOCTOR: All manifestation takes a powder.

ESTELLE: *(To EDDIE, whose hand she still holds)* Lift off.

MARIE: Caress

ESTELLE: Lift off

MARIE: Oh, Eddie, everything comes to he who waits.

EDDIE: This: waiting for language to turn on by itself.

MARIE:
This . . . waiting for language to turn on by itself;
like waiting for rain
when the day has rained itself out.
Conditioned as you are to expect more—
but there is no more.
That kind of waiting.

DOCTOR: That kind of waiting

MARIE: That kind of waiting.

DEEP VOICE OVER LOUDSPEAKERS: The city existed in silence.
    (EDDIE is crossing slowly center)
    And as Eddie approached, it was as if a temperature were palatable, rather than the usual buzz of conversation.

The passing time itself, implied silence.

The feeling of "could" . . . that seemed to hover over the streets did whisper the same message. But Eddie had prepared himself.

So there was no problem.

There was nothing to talk about . . . because there was no talking.

EDDIE: *(Standing alone in dim light, the others scattered at the sides of the room)* If I told the truth *(The others all give a loud, artificial sigh)* If I told the truth about all things, guess what?

It wouldn't be MY city you'd be visiting.

Follow this? All things have their own—shall we call it, a sense of direction? I wanted to participate in a real world but then it just got so painful.

Here's what I did. *(He slowly crosses to a small table, with a single rose in a bud vase sitting on it)* I went to lunch.

MARIE: *(Very softly)* We know where you went to lunch.

EDDIE:

And the tablecloth was white, and sparkling, and the napkins were,

and even a flower was on my table in a little glass jar.

And I picked it up. —I mean my fork,

and imagined what lunch was going to be like.

Waiters were looking at me.

Many waiters.

As I was there in purposeful, frozen, I mean—

that was the state I was in.

A very frozen state.

(The black curtain closes very quickly, hiding the restaurant. Then EDDIE appears, stepping through the curtain. To the side is an illuminated painting on an easel, with a painting of fruit and flowers displayed on it. Covered with real flowers. We realize it has been at the side since the

beginning. *ESTELLE is looking at it. Now we remember that during the course of the play, it has occasionally been illuminated, for no reason that was evident at the time)*

EDDIE: That's what made it a different kind of city. It wasn't necessary to move, in the sense of moving on, see what I mean? *(ESTELLE and MARIE run forward and kiss EDDIE on the cheek, then they immediately turn and reopen the curtain)* You interrupted my train of thought. Should we call that polite, or think about it? *(In the dimly illuminated main stage, we see that the DOCTOR again wears the giant head, and he stands behind the wind machine. EDDIE takes a step toward the audience. He has been holding a microphone on a cord, and now he lifts it and speaks softly into it)* These are attributes of YOUR city, not my own.

See: the web I spin out of suddenly—okay. Say "suddenly" . . . just lifted me into a sphere of being that nobody else recognized but you, me, and a hundred million Chinese. *(MARIE and ESTELLE sigh audibly, and the giant head on the DOCTOR tilts to the side)* Why do I say Chinese? Because when I'm crying sometimes, I accidently pull the sides of my eyes up, and I've seen other people in tears also, where I've come from, and so now, to make everything really different, let me say, this bite is for you. *(Another sigh from MARIE and ESTELLE, and the head on the DOCTOR tilts slightly to the opposite side)* Then, an amazing thing happens. He lifts his fork—I've already done that. . . . *(He lifts his fork)* And here, spread on the end of it, a whole, roast, morsel of some sort.

No psychology anywhere here. No veined tracing of deliberate logical types.

A morsel.

This bite is for you

DEEP VOICE OVER LOUDSPEAKER: *(As the VOICE speaks, EDDIE slowly moves to look at the illuminated painting. ESTELLE goes to the pot in which she had brought the fish. She extracts a gold ball and holds it up so that it shines in the light)* Eddie knew that something was missing from his life, and suspected that he would never find it. (*EDDIE is moving to look at the gold ball*) Eddie went to Poetry City to find it, but he didn't necessarily believe he would find it, but he believed and discovered he was right to believe that something was missing from his life, and his experiences in Poetry City intensified that belief, which was good, said Eddie, because it changed his relationship to the world he lived in, because he knew there was something missing that he couldn't find in the world, but because it was missing didn't mean it wasn't valuable. So Eddie knew he longed for and was devoted to something valuable, even if he couldn't find it or imagine it or therefore put his finger on it.

That was Eddie's problem. (*ESTELLE is moving the ball onto the tilted table. She has a thin stick she uses as a billiard cue, and she sets in a position to make a shot, using the gold ball*) That was also Eddie's solution to his problem . . . which was . . . to HAVE the problem. (*ESTELLE slowly changes her position and hands the ball to EDDIE. He takes it, and immediately cries out in pain, dropping the ball, which was burning hot, and runs to put his burnt hand into the pot filled with water. He then moves quickly onto the table and lies on his back on the table, as the others take a stick in each hand, and all scattered about the table point the sticks to EDDIE as if they were pinning a rare butterfly to the tilted table. After two seconds, they all let their sticks fall, making a terrible clatter as EDDIE leaps up and runs center, and THE DOCTOR and ESTELLE are busy setting small golden road pylons in a circle and MARIE, carrying a small suitcase and wearing her bonnet, comes slowly into the circle as the deep VOICE speaks*)

DEEP VOICE OVER LOUDSPEAKERS: Eddie went to Poetry City, and there, on one of the major boulevards, he met Marie.

"Marie! Marie!" he cried. "I didn't expect to find you in Poetry City."

"Don't be a fool." Marie frowned. "I only come here to get gas."

She opened her small suitcase. . . . *(Her suitcase opens, many small containers tumble out and roll across the floor)* . . . and some small metal bottles rolled out onto the sidewalk. *(EDDIE bends down and starts gathering them)* Eddie hurriedly bent down and gathered them in his arms. "Here. Here's your gas, Marie."

She kissed him on the cheek, to say thank you. *(He offers his armful of bottles to MARIE. She looks at him. There is a pause. Then she slowly turns and walks rear into the darkness)*

"Ah . . . this could only happen in Poetry City," said Eddie. *(Now MARIE is sitting at the piano. EDDIE is standing center, alone and dejected)* Oh, Eddie, Eddie—you broke my heart, with your stories about a brilliant childhood. I also, wanted to track down those elusive vapors. But when the duck pond froze, opened, and then recoagulated, where could the ducks go? *(MARIE has opened music on the piano, and at the same time, four small white duck cutouts appear on the piano top)*

How could they climb mountains, any of them, without my help? But I'm so weak, Eddie, compared to you. The pencil falls from my hand. *(The DOCTOR has positioned himself downstage, and pantomimes shooting a pistol, as if in a shooting gallery. The noise of a shot accompanies his gesture, and one of the ducks falls)*

I drift slowly *(Another duck is shot)* and by the time the telephone rings *(Another shot, another duck falls)* I've lost all cause and effect as a way to realize what I signed up for in the name of responsibility. *(EDDIE starts to a rear prop table upon which three of the industrial drums are piled one on top of the other, and he carefully lifts them all, keeping them balanced one on the other)* All of a sudden, slumped over my table, I regained my balance and attributed it to the natural magnetism of whatever I'm really leaning on.

Because you're still here, Eddie . . . *(EDDIE approaches a railing which stands between him and the main part of* the room, balancing his barrels) . . . and I resolve to make myself invulnerable . . . just like you.

(The music builds, and another voice is heard intoning "X MARKS THE SPOT . . . !" and EDDIE carefully lets his barrels drop over the railing and come crashing down into the set. At the same time, MARIE has picked up a bowling ball at the rear, and standing in front of the piano, she bowls down toward the footlights, where the ball crashes into a low guard rail and bounces back into the set. The music is loud, and she bowls another ball. And EDDIE leans exhausted on the railing, and the sweet music is loud so that it no longer seems sweet, but frightening now, and the lights fade and the play is over)

THE END

eddie goes to
poetry city

(part two: new york version)

Eddie Goes to Poetry City: Part Two. Produced by the Ontological-Hysteric Theater at La MaMa E.T.C., N.Y.C. April 1991. Written, directed, and designed by Richard Foreman.

ESTELLE:	Rebeca Ellens
EDDIE:	Henry Stram
DOCTOR:	Brian Delate
MARIE:	Kyle deCamp
FIGURE:	Colin Hodgson

The actors are *EDDIE*, a young man in a business suit; the *DOCTOR*, also in suit and tie, and two women who might be secretaries, but who in fact are something else—*ESTELLE* and *MARIE*. They all slowly enter a large room that seems to be a kind of office. And yet there is something artificial about it. Flags hang from a high ceiling. Many clocks on the wall, many tables and chairs, and on either side padded sections of wall, against which the actors occasionally bounce. A few microphones stand about. This is an office, but also a studio of some kind where art is made, practiced, and produced.

The stage is strewn with crumpled-up newspaper. When the actors walk through it, we can hear the noise it makes.

The actors are all wearing body mikes (headset style, so they can speak very quietly), so when the Soft Voice of the narrator comes over the loudspeaker, its quality is not unlike the quality of the actors miked voices. Sometimes the actors will also cross and speak into the visible microphones, which have a somewhat different quality from the sound of the body mikes that will normally transmit their quiet voices to the spectators. Different loops of soft music play now and throughout most of the play.

After a pause, all the actors but *ESTELLE* run from the room. Then, after another pause, *EDDIE* reenters slowly, and faces *ESTELLE* tentatively.

ESTELLE: *(Into a microphone)* Oh, Eddie, you're less conventional than you believe. *(Pause)* Do something, Eddie. Do something to surprise us. *(ESTELLE strides out of the room. Eddie moves, then hesitates)*

SOFT VOICE OVER LOUDSPEAKER: Oh, Eddie, make a surprising
move, right in front of our very eyes.

(The others return quickly, and cover their eyes)

EDDIE: My speaking alone pleases me.

DOCTOR: You're big on speaking, but not on communication.

EDDIE: That's because happiness floats into my language.
Like a dream. Probably you're quite blind to that fact,
but okay, I smile so much it hurts.

DOCTOR: What city is this?

*(EDDIE exits, the others run about, one holding a small
curtain on a stick, like a tiny theater curtain, and EDDIE
pushes through that curtain in order to exit, and another
strides across a tabletop, as the VOICE speaks over this flurry
of activity, and someone tries to pose in a suddenly visible
spotlight beam and is quickly pulled away)*

SOFT VOICE: The theater, the perverse theater, the joyous theater,
the noble theater, abandoned finally. And something else
takes its place. Talking in the dark. Inhabiting rooms with
no access, in this location a god will manifest himself. His
presence already intimated in this vibrating light and temperature. But the time, far off of course, of his true manifestation. An unplaceable time.

(EDDIE reenters)

EDDIE: I want something . . . out of the ordinary to happen.

DOCTOR: Be patient, Eddie. A god will manifest in this very
room.

EDDIE: Will I recognize him?

MARIE: You're a mirror, Eddie.

EDDIE: A mirror?

ESTELLE: So is the world, Eddie.
  Bounce back and forth. (*EDDIE turns away from ESTELLE, and somehow hits the padded wall he hadn't expected to run into, and bounces back into the room as the VOICE speaks*)

SOFT VOICE: He looks into a mirror, tries to comb his hair, but it isn't there. So much for the surface of things, he says, but I don't cry, I just try to balance good on my own side of a spinning what-d-ya-call-it? And nobody could tell if I fell off the bed because it happened so fast I came in a seeming wink of the eye but who winked? Nobody I know. But then, I don't know everybody. I'm too much into milk, chocolate, and sometimes, maybe, a slice of apple pie. Who'll join me?

ESTELLE: (*She has mounted a table, and holds an apple to EDDIE, as in the rear MARIE and DOCTOR seem to be engaging in some kind of perverse practice that involves MARIE striking poses on what seems to be a wooden rack*) This perfect apple is not edible, Eddie.

SOFT VOICE: What's really happening?

ESTELLE: You're anticipating.

EDDIE: What?

ESTELLE: The arrival of somebody invisible. He or she will walk onto the stage—

EDDIE: What stage?

ESTELLE: —but you won't know it happened. Don't cry, Eddie. (*She jumps down from the table and runs off, as do the*

DOCTOR and MARIE. EDDIE starts to follow, then stops and crosses to a microphone. He bends down to speak quietly into the mike)

EDDIE: I arrived at the theater for a performance: I opened my eyes, I took my fists, which had been jammed into my two ears, away from my ears.

I was ready to be . . . filled with images and words that would have upon me, great purgative emotional effect.

And then, the theater was taken away. Wiped out. Totally.

And I was left with nothing into which I could plunge . . . with my emotional identification.

I was left with nothing to think about.

DOCTOR: *(Who has tiptoed in carrying a box he quietly places on a table across from EDDIE)* What are you frightened of, Eddie?

EDDIE: Nothing I can put my finger on. What's in that box?

DOCTOR: Something to eat. Take a look. *(EDDIE tentatively peeks, and the DOCTOR whispers)* Dig in, Eddie. It's lunch.

EDDIE: *(Ecstatically, sitting)* It looks . . . wonderful.

DOCTOR: Do you really think so?

EDDIE: But is it lunchtime already?

DOCTOR: Haven't you noticed? It's much later than that. *(He goes; EDDIE as if "wakes" from his ecstasy)*

EDDIE: What did you say?

SOFT VOICE: The next thing I knew, I was flooded with richness, that had no content. Blank fullness.

And in that blankness, because it was full, there was a

continual, yet totally evasive, multitude of things that left me as quietly as they arose.

EDDIE: *(He's been smiling as if the soft VOICE was speaking for him. Then he makes a hand gesture)* Zip: except it was faster than that.

And I was perfectly, fulfilled. *(ESTELLE and MARIE have placed themselves on the rack, which is in shadows)*

ESTELLE: Oh, Eddie, turning yourself into a work of art?

EDDIE: Well, if I looked out the window—

ESTELLE: I don't see a window.

MARIE: *(Smiles to herself)* Zip.

DOCTOR: *(Sticking his head back into the room)* Poetry City?

ESTELLE: Convince me.

DOCTOR: *(Entering)* Let me introduce you to a man who tried to encase himself in a work of art. Oh, said the Doctor. I can help this man escape from a work of art, but only if he genuinely wishes to do that.

ESTELLE: Office party! *(She hits a table bell, and she and MARIE run from the room, giggling)*

DOCTOR: Understand, Eddie. I'm not a real doctor. Exercises into something quite unobtainable, that's what I'm into. So here you are in Poetry City, but under false premises.

EDDIE: I don't think so.

DOCTOR: Please don't be angry when your anticipations are frustrated. Anger reaps no permanent rewards.

EDDIE: I know that.

DOCTOR: Dare I ask what the goal is, Eddie?

EDDIE: I'll never tell. *(Pause)* I want to take over the world.

> *(A strident female voice is heard over the loudspeakers: "Excuse me!" Eddie looks about, startled)*

DOCTOR: *(After EDDIE is quiet)* I'll never tell.

EDDIE: I want to take over the world by getting control of myself.

DOCTOR: What should I teach, Eddie—free-floating attention?

EDDIE: What does that mean?

DOCTOR: It means—what hurts doesn't, even though it hurts.

EDDIE: Sounds good.

DOCTOR: You don't know what you're talking about, Eddie.

EDDIE: You have other patients?

DOCTOR: Didn't I tell you? I'm not a doctor. *(He opens a filing cabinet drawer to take out a blindfold, and he puts it over EDDIE'S eyes)*

EDDIE: Maybe I should tell you I spend my days worshiping my approaching blindness.

DOCTOR: Why worship that, Eddie?

EDDIE: It seems perverse.

DOCTOR: Something I said?

EDDIE: I think blindness will send me deeper into myself. Make me stronger than I am.

DOCTOR: It might hurt.

EDDIE: I suppose it might hurt. *(Holds a beat, then suddenly covers his ears)*

DOCTOR: Hear something unusual? *(He slams shut a filing cabinet drawer)*

EDDIE: *(Uncovers ears and takes off blindfold)* What was that?

DOCTOR: Time for explosions, Eddie.

EDDIE: Metaphorically, of course?

DOCTOR: If you say so.

EDDIE: Internally explosive.

DOCTOR: If you say so.

EDDIE: Nobody but me would notice.

DOCTOR: I wouldn't notice?

EDDIE: *(Pause)* Does the devil withstand evil?

DOCTOR: The devil's supposed to be evil personified.

EDDIE: But can he withstand evil?

DOCTOR: That remains to be seen.

EDDIE: Can you tell whether or not I exploded?

DOCTOR: An educated guess?

EDDIE: Guess.

DOCTOR: Guess my guess.

EDDIE: I'm not up to that.

DOCTOR: Then don't expect that for no reason at all, I'll start giving away my secrets, Eddie. Especially since you wouldn't benefit in the least. *(Pause)* By the way, I'm not the devil.

EDDIE: You just gave away a secret.

DOCTOR: Ah. Then maybe I'll give away one more.
    I can withstand evil, when I want to.

EDDIE: Maybe my question . . . was, Can it be resisted?

DOCTOR: Ah. Not the same thing, is it? But I don't have to tell that to Eddie.

EDDIE: Tell me everything.

DOCTOR: Careful, Eddie. "Bravado" is a word nobody should memorize.

(An explosion. EDDIE goes to door)

DOCTOR: Did you do that, Eddie?

(ESTELLE and MARIE run on, each spins one of two strange wheels attached to logs strapped to sawhorses)

ESTELLE: Office party!

SOFT VOICE: *(As the VOICE speaks, EDDIE tries to compose himself at one of the tables, and MARIE and ESTELLE run to the rack that houses a small curtained box perched on top. They lift an edge of the curtain as if to invite EDDIE to peek, but as he advances, they run back to sit at the table, and* EDDIE *loses courage and finds his way back to the table, to sit and try and compose himself across from their provocative presences)* Eddie went to Poetry City.

The soft air, gray and granulated, offered itself to his sniff.

Somebody must be burning logs, said Eddie. But in fact, he was wrong.

Global forces were at work, but Eddie was localized.

He opened a local window, and before he could open a local window, something came whirling into his mind's eye like a photograph of the whole planet from a place far in space.

Look, there's Poetry City under a cloud of fog—

Oh Eddie, from where you sit, it's so atmospheric to be looking at the sun bursting into the city through clouds of soft fog.

Eddie realized that by midday the air would be clear, and Poetry City would be like any place else.

Would it still be Poetry City?

Of course, offered Marie. Maps don't change. *(*MARIE *and* ESTELLE *again spin the wheels and then run from the room)*

Maps don't change.

Maps don't change. *(*EDDIE *runs to hide his head behind the curtain that hangs down from the box over the rack)*

DOCTOR: Use your head better than that, Eddie.

EDDIE: *(He reappears, tentatively)* How could I?

DOCTOR: Cover more territory, then
　　　　you wouldn't suffer your normal anguish.

EDDIE: Oh?

DOCTOR: That sounds tentative, Eddie.

EDDIE: I've been promised similar things, on other occasions.

DOCTOR: Disappointed?

EDDIE: Other times.

DOCTOR: But Eddie keeps trying.

EDDIE: Didn't you recommend certain exercises?

DOCTOR: Not me.

EDDIE: You said that if I—

DOCTOR: I know perfectly well what I said, Eddie.
    Cover more territory.
    Try using your head like a bicycle *(He spins his fists, as if they were pedaling)*

EDDIE: *(Frowns)* That could be interpreted in different ways.

DOCTOR: I hope so.

    (Door opens; MARIE is there)

MARIE: Eddie?

DOCTOR: Don't think Marie can help.

EDDIE: You have a self-satisfied smirk.

MARIE: *(Hurt)* Eddie. That's not polite.

EDDIE: It's true, Marie. Look at the smirk on his face.

DOCTOR: *(Making the cycling motion with his fists)* Like a bicycle, Eddie. No big mystery. *(He exits and immediately re-enters, pushing a bicycle)*

MARIE: He's been helping you like a friend, Eddie.

EDDIE: Reviewing the history of our relationship—

MARIE: I'm the only one in this office who can't ride. Please? Help me?

EDDIE: *(Considers, then tentatively)* Sure.

DOCTOR: Mistake number one, Eddie. But okay, let's find out what it leads to.

(EDDIE helps MARIE onto the bicycle)

MARIE: Promise me you won't let go until I say it's okay.

EDDIE: Marie, I promise. *(EDDIE pushes the bicycle offstage with MARIE on it. A crash is heard, then she screams. After another pause, EDDIE enters)*

DOCTOR: What happened, Eddie?

EDDIE: Well, I thought Marie was giving me the "let go" sign, so I did. But we had our signals mixed, and she wasn't ready for me to let go, and when I let go, she crashed into the wall. *(Pause)* She wasn't hurt badly. Just a scrape on her left knee.

(MARIE appears, pouting)

DOCTOR: A scrape?

EDDIE: I suppose so.

MARIE: You can do one thing to make up for this scrape on my knee, Eddie. Kiss it to make it better.

EDDIE: Okay. *(He does)*

DOCTOR: What's that on your lip, Eddie?

EDDIE: Huh?

MARIE: I think it's a little bit of blood from my scraped knee.

EDDIE: I guess so. *(Takes out handkerchief and wipes lips)*

MARIE: Oh, Eddie, I'd imagined you licking it from your lips with your tongue, not wiping it with a dirty handkerchief.

EDDIE: My handkerchief is clean, except for the blood.

DOCTOR: She's flirting with you, Eddie. She knows it was clean.

EDDIE: How would she know?

DOCTOR: It's in your character, Eddie.

MARIE: Oh, Eddie, there seems to be a little blood still on my knee.

EDDIE: Are you flirting with me, Marie?

MARIE: Probably, Eddie.

EDDIE: *(Pause)* Guess what. I think I'll have to kiss that knee again to make it better. That's the least I can do, under the circumstances, I think.

MARIE: *(As he awkwardly kisses her knee)* Oh, Eddie—you have no idea how it makes me feel.

EDDIE: Ready for another try?

MARIE: *(Pause)* On the bicycle?

EDDIE: Well, yes. Is that what I mean?

DOCTOR: Picture it in your head, Eddie. Is there a relationship between Marie and the bicycle?

EDDIE: Well, I visualize Marie . . . and then she's falling off. . . .

DOCTOR: Deeper, Eddie.

MARIE: *(Quiet)* Don't let him trick you.

EDDIE: You said he was my friend.

DOCTOR: Deeper, Eddie.

EDDIE: Give me a minute to collect myself, please.

DOCTOR: Deeper, Eddie. What's happening?

EDDIE: My head is . . . spinning, that's all.

DOCTOR: How come?

EDDIE: Well—my head must be spinning.

MARIE: I hope so.

DOCTOR: Deeper, Eddie. *(Eddie faints)* Eddie? Look what's happened, thanks to Marie.

MARIE: *(Offended)* Hey—!

DOCTOR: Don't worry. It's all for the best.

MARIE: I never worry.

DOCTOR: *(Suddenly vicious, points to MARIE)* Ah! That made the lights go out!

(*They both exit, and at the same moment a strange* FIGURE *in black with a black mask and pointed hat, holding a black megaphone to his mouth enters the rear of the room and poses as still as a statue.* EDDIE *lies unconscious on the floor. There is a pause, and then we hear* ESTELLE *calling from outside the room*)

ESTELLE: (*Off*) Eddie? Eddie? Are you in there? (*Pause*) Eddie? This is Estelle.

MAN IN BLACK THROUGH MEGAPHONE: Oh! Eddie! This! Is! Estelle! (*He turns and strides out mechanically as* ESTELLE *enters from the other side, not seeing him*)

ESTELLE: (*Bending over* EDDIE) What took you so long to open the door, Eddie?

EDDIE: (*Rising*) I was unconscious.

ESTELLE: Eddie! How come?

EDDIE: Well, it started, I think, when I was trying to help Marie learn how to ride a bicycle.

ESTELLE: I should have known she'd be involved.

EDDIE: Why are you so down on Marie?

ESTELLE: Because I think she's a no-good tramp, Eddie. Plus I'm jealous of the time you spend together.

EDDIE: Really?

ESTELLE: Yes.

EDDIE: I'm flattered.

ESTELLE: And a little flustered?

EDDIE: *(Laughs shyly)* Well . . .

DOCTOR: *(Entering)* Vanity, Eddie.

EDDIE: What?

DOCTOR: Don't let Estelle fluster you, Eddie. Keep your equilibrium.

ESTELLE: Right, Eddie. . . .

LOUD VOICE OVER SPEAKERS: Right!

ESTELLE: *(Overlapping)* He's right of course.

EDDIE: He is?

ESTELLE: I think so, but I bet Marie wouldn't think so.

EDDIE: Oh no, she's his defender also.

ESTELLE: No kidding?

EDDIE: I detect a note of sarcasm.

DOCTOR: Learning about life, Eddie? *(Offers EDDIE an apple)*

EDDIE: *(Looks from one to the other)* I'm not sure. . . . I think I'm making progress.

DOCTOR: This perfect apple . . . is not edible, Eddie. *(He tosses it away, and EDDIE runs to exit at the back but is immediately thrown back into the room with such force that he falls to the floor. The soft VOICE has already begun speaking)*

SOFT VOICE: Eddie went to Poetry City.
  He cracked his head on the sidewalk, trying to express something by taking a sudden, demonstrative plunge.

A stranger stopped and bent over the bleeding Eddie and said, "Can I help?"

It wasn't like that, said Eddie, trying to smile, hoping the stranger would understand how appropriate a smile truly was under the circumstances. *(As the VOICE continues, EDDIE, the DOCTOR, ESTELLE, and MARIE have moved to arrange themselves in a stretched-out line, holding hands, staring at the deep end of the room with their backs to the audience, as if in listening to the story the VOICE tells they expect it to be manifest somehow against the back wall)* You're a lucky guy, Eddie—and the stranger helped him to his feet, glancing at his watch almost coincidentally.

Be on your way sir, said Eddie. The blood was a miscalculation— *(MARIE utters a piercing scream, and the line breaks, and they slowly find their way to seats, as the VOICE continues its story)*—but it can be rectified by this handkerchief.

What a beautiful handkerchief, offered the stranger, but it's true I'm behind schedule.

You did all you could, said Eddie, and I'm in good shape—which allowed the stranger to be on his way, and Eddie to make a second try.

This time it was well done

and Eddie felt good in the sunlight.

EDDIE: *(After a pause, quiet and ecstatic)* Here I am. Totally okay.

MARIE: *(Soft, as if not to frighten him awake)* Totally happy?

EDDIE: Yes. *(A loud noise knocks the three others off their seats to the floor)*

ESTELLE: *(After recovering, holding her irritation in)* Totally at peace?

EDDIE: Yes. *(Another noise, they are again thrown to the floor)*

MARIE: *(Recovering, trying to act calm and controlled and sweet)* What city is this?

ESTELLE: *(As EDDIE doesn't respond—he's too spaced out. In fact they all seem a little spaced out)* Remember?

EDDIE: *(Pause)* Where's a map?

MARIE: *(A gentle threat)* Look in the drawer.

> *(EDDIE goes and opens a drawer in the filing cabinet. He takes out a map and slowly starts unfolding it)*

ESTELLE: *(Very slowly, deliberately)* It was the wrong . . . drawer.

EDDIE: Oh? . . . This is the wrong map?

ESTELLE: It was the wrong . . . drawer.

EDDIE: *(Pause; he presses the open map to his chest)* So this is where we are now. Could I put this map of Poetry City on the wall?

MARIE: How?

EDDIE: *(Pause)* Do you have any . . . thumbtacks?

MARIE: Wouldn't that . . . hurt the wall?

EDDIE: *(Pause; considering this carefully)* Well, it would put very small holes in the wall. *(Pause)* It's okay, then?

MARIE: Best not.

EDDIE: Okay. I'll just fold it up and put it in my pocket. *(ESTELLE has snuck up behind EDDIE. She pushes him violently into the wall; he bounces off, dropping a briefcase he's been clutching for security. He recovers and runs to the rear wall*

to escape, but miscalculates and bounces off that also,
falling to the floor, and as he rises *MARIE* and *ESTELLE* are
holding a metal bar above his head, so he lifts to his feet but
clunks his head on the bar and reels dizzily to a chair,
where he collapses)

SOFT VOICE: (*As* *EDDIE* *tries to collect himself, slumped in the
chair. And* *MARIE* *begins crossing the rear of the room,
wearing high spiked heels, arriving at the rack, upon which
she poses as the* *DOCTOR* *starts stroking her body with a
towel as if erotically washing her arms and legs*)
Is this the city where
looking out the window
in late afternoon,
a beautiful vista seems dominated by the faint tracer-bullet
patterns of many automobiles in motion, evoking,
as they cross the visible-from-a-distance multitude of
bridges
spanning the magic river that gives mythic dimension to
this city
nestled in its curve
—automobiles evoking that specific seen-from-far-away
energy that
paints precise,
punctuated,
energy strips in the imagination of someone
who perhaps relies too much upon that same imagination?
(*EDDIE* *rises unsteadily to come forward to the audience*)
There he goes, encasing himself in a work of art— (*The
noise of a small collision bounces Eddie back into his
chair*)—in a prototype, at least.

EDDIE: (*ESTELLE* *is blindfolding him as he speaks*)
The darkness falls
I come hurtling toward you
In my language. (*He drops his briefcase, slides off his chair
as if it were slippery, and as he continues talking, climbs
onto the large table behind his chair*)

Feet, head
arms and lungs
all exchange superior position
in rapid succession.

ESTELLE: *(Softly mocking)* Office Party . . .

SOFT VOICE: *(As it speaks, a still blindfolded EDDIE reaches out to two table flaps and begins slapping them up and down a few times, like the wings of a giant bird)*
Outsiders howl
Insiders lift their skirts.
While everything on the opposite side of expectation,
plunges
into the landscape of
Oh—this remark, that remark.
Quick!
What I said was etched
In some kind of nonrefundable gold.

EDDIE: *(Removing his blindfold)* If one anticipates the good moments too enthusiastically, it lowers one's resistance for being able to deal with the bad moments that come later, I suppose.

DOCTOR: What's that red blotch on your face, Eddie?

EDDIE: *(Worried, feels his face)* What?

DOCTOR: I had you worried, I guess.

EDDIE: Yes—

DOCTOR: Be reassured, for the moment. You're okay.

EDDIE: But it certainly reminds me—something COULD go wrong, even with my own body, which up to now has been in pretty good health. *(He suddenly doubles over in pain)*

Oww! *(But he fights back the pain and gingerly feels his way against one of the padded walls against which he places his body as if to calm it down. The others tiptoe close, to study him)*

SOFT VOICE: Oh, Eddie, Eddie—you broke my heart with your stories about a brilliant childhood.

I also, wanted to track down those elusive vapors.

But when the duck pond froze, opened, and then re-coagulated, where could the ducks go? *(EDDIE moves away from them, uneasy at their proximity)* How could they climb mountains, any of them, without my help? But I'm so weak, Eddie, compared to you. The pencil falls from my hand. I drift, slowly. And by the time the telephone rings, I've lost all cause and effect as a way to realize what I signed up for in the name of responsibility. *(By now, EDDIE is leaning on one of the tables. Is he feeling pain again? We can't be sure)*

DOCTOR: What name did you use, Eddie? Right . . . "Poetry City."

SOFT VOICE: *(As all but Eddie rearrange the furniture, making a veritable "Poetry City" of chairs and tables)* All of a sudden, slumped over my table, I regained my balance and attributed it to the natural magnetism of whatever it is I'm really leaning on.

Because, you're still here, Eddie, and I resolve to make myself invulnerable . . . just like you.

DOCTOR: What's up, Eddie?

EDDIE: Well, a sort of . . . sharp, shooting pain.

DOCTOR: Where, Eddie?

EDDIE: I'm a little ashamed to say.

DOCTOR: Nonsense, Eddie. The human body is a wonderful machine. No part of it should cause shame or embarrassment.

EDDIE: Theoretically, I know that's right. But I can't help— OWW! *(He holds his groin)*

DOCTOR: Apparently the pain is in your groin, Eddie.

EDDIE: Yes—

DOCTOR: Let's have a look.

EDDIE: Oh, no—

DOCTOR: You mean you don't want the pain dealt with? I might be able to help—

EDDIE: It's not that—

DOCTOR: Yes, Eddie?

EDDIE: I don't like to uncover that part of my body.

DOCTOR: Eddie, what have we just been saying?

EDDIE: I know, but—

DOCTOR: *(Calls off)* Estelle, come in here, please?

EDDIE: I'd rather not have Estelle involved in this.

DOCTOR: Why not, Eddie?

EDDIE: Things about her.

DOCTOR: What?

EDDIE: Private things.

DOCTOR: What effect does she have on you, Eddie?

EDDIE: She smells . . . funny.

DOCTOR: Funny?

EDDIE: Funny.

DOCTOR: Funny?

EDDIE: *(Soft)* Like raw apples.

ESTELLE: What do I smell like?

EDDIE: Jesus, she heard.

ESTELLE: Of course I heard you.

EDDIE: *(To Estelle)* I was only looking for an excuse to keep you out of this situation. Because, pain—
    Well, it was suggested that you try and help somehow, but I don't think that's a good idea.

ESTELLE: Where's the pain?

DOCTOR: Tell her, Eddie.

EDDIE: Well, in the groin area.

ESTELLE: Is it in your penis, Eddie?

EDDIE: Well . . .

ESTELLE: Or maybe it's in your scrotum.

EDDIE: I think . . .

ESTELLE: Which?

EDDIE: Well, both maybe. It's hard to tell.

ESTELLE: That's because you haven't had much experience distinguishing between them, am I right?

EDDIE: Well, it IS the first time I noticed a pain in that area.

ESTELLE: I think you should let me look.

EDDIE: Okay. *(He sees the white medical screen that has been placed behind them)* Suppose I just get behind this screen for a minute.

ESTELLE: Oh, Eddie.

(He goes behind a screen that leaves his head and chest still visible. We can tell he's undoing his pants)

EDDIE: My pants are down, if you want to see.

DOCTOR: Go ahead, Estelle. Eddie's a little shy.

(She goes behind, her head disappears as she looks)

ESTELLE: Gee, Eddie, everything looks okay. Let's see if you can get an erection.

EDDIE: Well, I think so.

ESTELLE: Thinking isn't doing, Eddie. *(Pause, Eddie makes an effort, strains)* Yeah, that seems in order.

EDDIE: Yes.

ESTELLE: Nothing wrong with that erection, Eddie.

DOCTOR: May I look?

ESTELLE: Sure.

DOCTOR: Estelle's right, Eddie. That's a perfectly good erection.

EDDIE: I never thought I'd be showing such recent acquaintances my . . . ostensible tumescence—

DOCTOR: Oh, Eddie, sad to think you consider us strangers.

ESTELLE: As long as you have that good erection, Eddie, would you mind putting it into my vagina for a few minutes?

EDDIE: Well, okay.

DOCTOR: *(Looking down behind the screen)* Thank goodness those attacks of pain seem to have subsided, though I probably shouldn't tempt fate.

EDDIE: *(To the DOCTOR)* I wish you wouldn't watch this.

DOCTOR: *(Turns back; pause)* I have to admit, it's a kind of test.

EDDIE: *(Half orgasm)* Oh.

> *(The DOCTOR watches. ESTELLE withdraws and whispers, "Thanks." Goes and sits elsewhere)*

DOCTOR: *(Taking down the screen, and EDDIE has to hurriedly hitch up his pants)* How about it, Eddie? Ready for a little psychoanalytic adventure?

EDDIE: Now?

DOCTOR: You know how it operates?

ESTELLE: Hi. *(She waves)*

EDDIE: As I understand it—

DOCTOR: Shhh.
     Why don't we have a moment of silence?

MARIE: *(Racing into the room, carrying a notepad)* Why don't I
take notes?

> *(ESTELLE groans at MARIE'S pushing herself into the situa-
> tion, and the DOCTOR and MARIE and ESTELLE go to a corner
> and gently move to the center of the room three big indus-
> trial drums made of cardboard. They look at EDDIE expec-
> tantly. He finally gets the idea and finds the fourth drum,
> which he moves forward to join the three others. Then the
> DOCTOR, MARIE, and ESTELLE put on party hats they find
> inside the drums. And EDDIE copies them and does like-
> wise. Then the DOCTOR, ESTELLE, and MARIE reach into the
> drums and pull out wads of crumpled newspaper, which
> they throw up into the air so they fall to the floor, joining
> the papers that have been littering the stage from the
> beginning.
>   The strident FEMALE VOICE over the loudspeaker shouts,
> "Excuse me!" and the paper throwing stops and they all
> look at EDDIE. He looks at them, and then . . . copies them
> and reaches in for paper, which he throws about the room.
> He stops to see what happens next. The DOCTOR smiles,
> starts to exit, and stops)*

DOCTOR: *(To the audience, gesturing with his thumb to EDDIE and
the women)* Office party. *(He exits; there is a pause)*

ESTELLE: *(Advancing on EDDIE)* Question for Eddie. Do you like a
girl to be very verbal about her inner feelings? *(She has
backed him up against one of the industrial drums, and he
bumps into it, and to recover his "cool" bounces up to sit on
top of it, only he falls halfway in and ends up with his
behind deep into the drum)* Or more reticent?

EDDIE: *(Considers)* It all depends.

ESTELLE: Depends?

EDDIE: Gee, Estelle. I think you're pulling me into very deep waters.

ESTELLE: Swim, Eddie.

EDDIE: *(Pause)* Look, aren't you really asking—which of you two do I feel more attracted by?

ESTELLE: Yeah. We're asking. *(Pause. EDDIE points to MARIE, then embarrassed at having made a commitment, hides his hand)*

ESTELLE: Never point, Eddie. Can't you say it?

EDDIE: Maybe I made a mistake.

ESTELLE: In not speaking? Or in the one you chose to point to?

EDDIE: *(Laughs)* Suppose I did it through saying . . . Estelle. *(As he says "Estelle," however, he rapidly points to MARIE)*

ESTELLE: Why are you pointing to Marie if you're saying Estelle?

EDDIE: Come on, you understand why. *(ESTELLE goes and pulls MARIE's hair)*

MARIE: Oww! Aren't you going to defend me, Eddie? *(She pulls free)*

ESTELLE: I think he didn't want to tip his hand.

MARIE: Oh. He's saying, in effect, it's okay for YOU to physically attack ME. *(Pause)* I wonder if the opposite is true—

ESTELLE: Don't try it, Marie.

(MARIE looks at EDDIE, then tries to slap ESTELLE, who catches her hand, twisting her arm as EDDIE looks about nervously)

MARIE: *(Writhing under ESTELLE'S grip)* So. You're obviously stronger than me. I wonder how Eddie feels about that.

EDDIE: *(Running out of the room, embarrassed)* I'll see you later.

ESTELLE: *(Dropping MARIE'S wrist and moving away)* I guess you'd call me impetuous maybe.

MARIE: *(Rubbing her wrist)* Men like that.

ESTELLE: Sometimes. *(ESTELLE turns to go, but MARIE suddenly reaches out and pulls her hair)* Ow! Stop that! *(Breaks away)*

MARIE: *(They face each other a moment, then MARIE turns to call to the next room)* You missed something, Eddie! Estelle grabbed my hair and gave a good strong pull, which hurt like the devil! *(ESTELLE looks outraged at the lie, but MARIE ignores her and goes to the door to look for EDDIE)*

ESTELLE: What do you see?

MARIE: He's sitting in the next room, reading something. *(ESTELLE comes to see. The DOCTOR enters and watches from the rear)*

ESTELLE: I don't believe you.

MARIE: Look for yourself.

ESTELLE: What on earth could he be READING?

DOCTOR: *(From the rear)* Well, ladies? *(They are startled by him and whirl to look)* Interpersonal relations are structured like a circle. *(He revolves his fists like a bicycle again)* So I assume you're ready for a hundred-and-eight-degree reversal.

ESTELLE: Like what?

DOCTOR: Are you thinking about it?

MARIE: Not very effectively.

ESTELLE: Speak for yourself, Marie, darling.

DOCTOR: Oh? Estelle has a new idea?

ESTELLE: I think I might throw myself at Eddie.

DOCTOR: I thought that's what happened.

ESTELLE: Oh, no, I can be much more aggressive. Sometimes I do it to amuse myself—*(The DOCTOR is whispering to MARIE)* Hey, are you two trying to provoke me?

DOCTOR: Doesn't it say something, that you're so easily provoked?

ESTELLE: Wrong.

DOCTOR: Think about it.

ESTELLE: I don't consider that a viable option.

DOCTOR: Good. *(ESTELLE sits)* Try seriously NOT thinking— learn from Marie.

MARIE: *(Offended)* I beg your pardon?

DOCTOR: *(Turns to her)* A compliment, sweetie.

ESTELLE: Because we're women?

DOCTOR: *(As he picks up another one of the strange curtain-on-a-stick structures, hanging the little curtain in front of MARIE's face)* Oh, being ladies has nothing to do with it, because after all, Eddie makes the same mistake—if you see what I mean. *(MARIE immediately pushes through the curtain as EDDIE enters from the rear with his pants carried over his arm. He is in his underwear)*

DOCTOR: Don't get too big for your britches, Eddie. Careful, Eddie. Don't fall.

EDDIE: *(Circling the room)* Where could I fall? I'm not near anything dangerous.

ESTELLE: *(To herself)* Can you believe it? Eddie says "I'm not near anything dangerous." As a matter of fact, he's right. But nobody can take that for reality.

DOCTOR: *(Holding out a box of matches)* Marie, would you light this match, please? *(EDDIE has stopped center stage, amid the industrial drums. He is staring forward, and somehow he doesn't register MARIE, crouched down at his feet, partially obscured by the drums, as she lights a match and seems to apply it to his shoe)*

MARIE: *(Standing up in front of him)* Did you feel anything, Eddie?

EDDIE: No. When did Marie put in an appearance?

MARIE: I gave you a hot foot.

EDDIE: What's that?

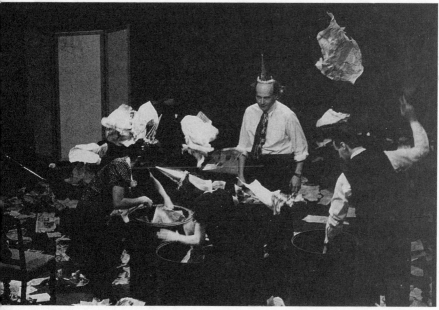

MARIE: Oh, Eddie!

ESTELLE: *(Whispers)* A hot . . . foot!

MARIE: You put a match in someone's shoe. Between the sole and the other part. Then you light it—with a second match.

EDDIE: Was that your idea? *(He holds up his foot to look at the damage, balancing precariously on the other foot)*

MARIE: No.

EDDIE: Then why did you go along with it?

DOCTOR: Don't judge other people's motives, Eddie.

EDDIE: But I seem to be in a very vulnerable position. *(He is hopping about on one foot)*

MARIE: More than me?

ESTELLE: More than me?

MARIE: More than ME?

ESTELLE: More than ME?

EDDIE: *(He has lost his balance and fallen amid the drums. There is a silence. Then he slowly surfaces from behind one of them and speaks in almost a whisper)* Something's missing.

DOCTOR: What's wrong, Eddie?

EDDIE: Something's being left out.

DOCTOR: What could that be, Eddie?

ESTELLE: Is that why you have your pants off?

EDDIE: It expresses something.

ESTELLE: What's that?

EDDIE: *(Thinks)* I have my pants off. . . .

ESTELLE: What's being left out, Eddie?

EDDIE: I came into the room, half undressed like this, in order to speak to you. . . .

DOCTOR: Yes, Eddie?

EDDIE: Well . . . about God.

DOCTOR: Ah, is that why Eddie made a sudden appearance in—

EDDIE: Don't say it!

ESTELLE: Is that why Eddie took his pants off?

EDDIE: *(Red in the face now)* This expressed my stupidity, my crudeness and obviousness—all of which are NECESSARY!

DOCTOR: A preamble, as it were.

MARIE: *(She has a glass of water which she presents on a tray)* Refresh yourself, Eddie—*(The tray bangs into EDDIE's chest as he reaches for the glass, which falls, and MARIE mutters, "Asshole," under her breath)*

DOCTOR: Careful Eddie, that was the ceremony of the spilled glass of water.

ESTELLE: *(As EDDIE starts racing about the room)* This is the ceremony of the severed head.

EDDIE: I'm rendered irrelevant!

ESTELLE: *(As the DOCTOR repositions the little red curtain on a stick so EDDIE is behind it)* What do you see, Eddie?

EDDIE: *(Behind)* Red, mostly! *(He pushes through)*

ESTELLE: The most attractive color, isn't it?

EDDIE: Red?

ESTELLE: Kiss me, Eddie.

EDDIE: *(Still racing about)* I'm busy!

> *(A funny taped voice is heard speaking rapidly in crescendo—"Busy, busy BUSY, BUSY!"—and the man in black with the megaphone repositions himself in the shadows rear)*

EDDIE: *(Coming to a screeching halt. Making a decision)* Take off your clothes, Estelle!

ESTELLE: No go.

EDDIE: *(Red in the face with embarrassment)* I want to understand my motives.

ESTELLE: No go, Eddie.

MAN IN BLACK WITH MEGAPHONE: *(Preceded by a loud noise)* I! WANT! YOU! TO! UNDERSTAND! MY! MOTIVES!

> *(MARIE has somehow reappeared in the room, wearing a number of colored panels strapped to her body. Everybody is frozen in shock for a few seconds)*

ESTELLE: Is she supposed to be imitating the good fairy?

EDDIE: Seriously, Marie, why are you dressed like that?

MARIE: Believe it or not, it gives me a feeling of power.

EDDIE: Oh? *(Pause; frowns)* You'd better go into detail.

MARIE: Whatever's passing through your head right now, Eddie, that's the power I'm talking about.

ESTELLE: *(Sarcastically)* Is that supposed to be armor?

MARIE: Oh, no.

ESTELLE: Full speed ahead!

MARIE: I'd expect you to pick up on the silly aspect, Estelle—but there's more to it. It's magic, actually.

ESTELLE: We don't believe in magic

MARIE: *(Turns to EDDIE, as the DOCTOR and ESTELLE start making a repetitive series of gesture, as if magically invoking something in the room)* What's going through your head right now, Eddie?

EDDIE: Oh . . . random. As usual. *(Sees the DOCTOR, gets an idea)* You're asking me to free-associate?

MARIE: Yes.

EDDIE: *(Thinks, then begins)*
   Estelle, ding-dong dell
   Red white and blue, pell mell,
   Skin, nose, shit
      Hey, this is getting a little embarrassing. *(Pause; he takes a deep breath to make another effort)* Estelle—
      I don't know WHY I keep saying Estelle—it's Marie I'm associating on really, but it comes out Estelle.
      Fuck-fuck-fuck! Hey, maybe I can't pierce Marie with my libido, because she's wearing a libido protector!

ESTELLE: Uh-oh, she's got you going through the back door, Eddie.

EDDIE: You mean Estell— MARIE'S! Private asshole? *(They all feign mock shock)* See? I started to say Estelle even THEN, and corrected myself. *(Points to MARIE)* Those could be reflectors she's wearing, so a thought goes to her, and bounces off and lands on you—Estelle.

ESTELLE: What I was trying to make you understand is there's a trick in it, because I know that actually, Marie has the hots for YOU, Eddie.

EDDIE: *(Quiet, close to Estelle)* Do you believe in magic?

ESTELLE: Yes.

EDDIE: In that costume, I see Marie as a psychic tank.
I'm waiting for her to come and roll over me. *(EDDIE hesitates, then goes up close to MARIE. She circles around him and presses him up against one of the padded walls. He doesn't move. Nobody moves. Then there is a loud noise)*

MAN IN BLACK WITH MEGAPHONE: OKAY! WE! COULD! STAY! LIKE! THIS! FOR! A! LONG! TIME!

EDDIE: *(After a pause, repeating the line under his breath, pissed off)* Okay. We could stay like this for a long time.

MARIE: *(Moving away a step)* Get undressed Eddie.

EDDIE: *(Showing her his pants, which he still carries)* Now? More than this? *(Pause; she doesn't give an inch)* Aren't you going to meet me halfway?

MARIE: No.

MAN IN BLACK WITH MEGAPHONE: RIIIIGHT!

MARIE: I just wanted to get you in my power. I'm going. But I'll be back. *(She exits, as does the man with the megaphone)*

EDDIE: *(Calling after her)* Marie? Is it perfectly okay with you that I'm undressed, alone in a room with Estelle?

ESTELLE: You're a free agent, Eddie.

EDDIE: *(Thinks for a bit)* Well, to make this a little more comfortable, one of two things has to happen. Either you get undressed too, or I get redressed.

ESTELLE: Guess which.

EDDIE: No. On second thought, I think I'll DEAL with that lack of comfort. *(ESTELLE has turned her back on him and is polishing her nails on her blouse)* Maybe it can be a mental resonator. *(ESTELLE turns, blows on her nails, which is in EDDIE'S direction, and as a mysterious tone is heard it's as if her breath blows him back into the padded wall, much to his surprise)*

ESTELLE: *(Smiling at her demonstrated power)* "Marie?" Knows her stuff? Is that it?

EDDIE: *(Worried)* Yes and no.
        Maybe. *(He takes a step toward ESTELLE)*

ESTELLE: *(Holding up a hand like a stop sign)* No. You're not going to kiss ME!

EDDIE: Frankly, I thought you were attracted to me.

ESTELLE: Frankly, I am. But there ARE other things in life, aren't there? *(She puts her hands on her hips and breathes in and out rapidly three times, a kind of yoga)* Poor Eddie. I do think your relationship with Marie has deteriorated considerably over the last two hours.

EDDIE: Why were you breathing funny?

ESTELLE: Guess.

EDDIE: Were you imitating . . . a locomotive?

ESTELLE: You give yourself away, Eddie.

EDDIE: How do I give myself away?

ESTELLE: Try striking a pose like a certain famous statue.

EDDIE: What statue?

ESTELLE: Obviously, Eddie, "The Thinker."

EDDIE: I think too much.

ESTELLE: Just the pose, Eddie.

EDDIE: *(Sitting, chin in hand—not quite correct)* Is this the pose?

ESTELLE: I think not.

EDDIE: This is how I remember it. Auguste Rodin's "The Thinker."

ESTELLE: It's wrong, Eddie.
        But it serves a purpose.

(The lights are dim. EDDIE sits dejectedly on his chair, ESTELLE is standing on a table with her hands on her hips, and the DOCTOR, in the rear, leans into a microphone and speaks quietly)

DOCTOR: Eddie was on the train to Poetry City. (*ESTELLE again breathes three times in a sharp, puffing rhythm. Then she kneels, offering EDDIE an apple*) Then he took a particular drug that altered his consciousness, but Estelle said, "Look Eddie, it's a perfect apple." Why did Eddie want to alter his consciousness?

EDDIE: I had remembered to ask myself, Why did I want to alter my consciousness at a time when altering my consciousness seemed self-evidently a desirable thing to do? I was not interested in thrilling experiences, believe me, I was interested in self-development, I told myself. Potential development of my potential, that was the way I circled my subject. (*He has walked slowly toward the audience. The three others are holding three small paintings that represent red theater curtains in line behind his head*) I was on this . . . train. And I took this . . . drug. It was not that I expected experience to come rushing toward me. I did expect experience, but experience was not the aspect toward which I traveled, with pleasure. (*The paintings are manipulated, and the other side shown—three still-lifes with a skull prominently featured*)

SOFT VOICE: I was on a train to Poetry City, and an image came into my mind.
   I saw visionary fields.
   I was on a train to a dead city.
   From the window of that train, I saw amazing transformations of the landscape.

SOFT VOICE AND EDDIE:
   Because whatever was dead
   was dead, and when I saw that
   I was able to function
   as I hadn't been able to function. . . .

EDDIE: (*Alone in the room now*) . . . when I didn't know the dead, was the dead.

ESTELLE: *(Reenters with* MARIE*)* Whatever is dead, Eddie, is dead. It's useful to be able to make such distinctions.

MARIE: Eddie agrees, or Eddie wouldn't be visiting.

ESTELLE: I think he's looking for an escape route—

EDDIE: Am I?

ESTELLE: You tell me.

EDDIE: Poetry City. Please.

ESTELLE: Of course, Eddie. But I don't know if you like living in paradise. Feel the ground shifting under your feet?

EDDIE: *(Sits)* That's not desirable.

ESTELLE: Feel it?

EDDIE: No.

MARIE: He must have a problem. *(She exits)*

EDDIE: *(As* ESTELLE *reshows her skull painting)* Maybe it isn't paradise after all.

ESTELLE: Don't count on it.

EDDIE: You convinced me.

ESTELLE: Not quite. I cut through the whole question with a single flash of my double-edged blade saying, "Happy to have you on board, Mr. Sliced-in-Two!"

EDDIE: Funny, it didn't hurt.

ESTELLE: That's a provocation, but I won't bite.

EDDIE: Thank goodness.

ESTELLE: From your point of view or from mine?

MARIE: *(Reentering with a new painting)* Let's change the subject a little—*(She holds up the painting, which is a face, very white, with strange decorations)* Is Eddie frightened by THIS wonderful painting?

EDDIE: I don't recognize it.

MARIE: How come?

ESTELLE: It looks a little like Eddie. Before and after.

EDDIE: Before and after what?

ESTELLE: Notice?

EDDIE: I like it.

MARIE: You do? *(Pause)* Tell me again—you really like it?

DOCTOR: *(In the rear, in the shadows, he echoes what's being said in whispers into the microphone, overlapping before they've finished)* You really like it?

EDDIE: *(Coming downstage to push through an imaginary curtain)* Yes.

DOCTOR: Yes

ESTELLE: Then there's nothing more to be said, is there?

EDDIE: *(A pause, very quietly)* Burn it.

DOCTOR: Burn it.

MARIE: Ah. Because you like it so much?

DOCTOR: Because you like it so much.

EDDIE: Exactly.

ESTELLE: What a spiritual trip.

MARIE: You really want it burned?

DOCTOR: You really want it burned?

EDDIE: Yes.

MARIE: Then I'll take it into the next room, where we always perform such rites of sacrifice.

DOCTOR: I'll take it into the next room.

ESTELLE: *(As MARIE goes upstage)* Maybe you want to watch?

EDDIE: No. I trust you.

ESTELLE: *(Smiles, whispers)* No. *(Points to EDDIE'S head)* I trust . . . YOU.

VOICE OVER THE LOUDSPEAKER: Riiiiiight!

SOFT VOICE: *(As the DOCTOR, MARIE, and ESTELLE move, rearrange the furniture, and put up streamers as decoration for an anticipated "Office Party")* Here's the main thing. You're looking for an escape route, a method of locomotion, a secret door. You can't find the secret door, because it isn't in this world, but in the other: the one you want to escape to. It isn't in this world— *(EDDIE is feeling the wall, looking for the door as the others watch)*—it's located in the world you want to escape to. So use it.

MARIE: Use the secret door.

EDDIE: Everything looks different.

ESTELLE: Wrong.

EDDIE: But it looks different!

ESTELLE: *(Smiles, standing by the rack, where the small red curtain has been removed and a tiny dollhouse room is revealed perched on top of the rack—a room that is a close model to the one in which they are in fact located)* This is it.

EDDIE: What?

ESTELLE: This is it.

EDDIE: What?

ESTELLE: The room . . . in which God speaks to us, Eddie.

EDDIE: I don't believe you.

ESTELLE: How come?

EDDIE: I don't believe you.

ESTELLE: How come you don't believe me?

EDDIE: It doesn't look like the right kind of room.

MARIE: Suppose I told you I didn't really burn that valuable painting?

EDDIE: Did you?

ESTELLE: *(Behind him)* It sneaks up on you.

EDDIE: *(Whirls)* What does?

ESTELLE: What did you say, Eddie?

EDDIE: I said, "What sneaks up on you?"

ESTELLE: *(Getting irritated)* Well . . . maybe a phone rings. Maybe somebody knocks and you think lunch is being delivered—

EDDIE: It's too late.

ESTELLE: What time is it, Eddie?

EDDIE: I lost my watch.

ESTELLE: *(Crossing to the filing cabinet, flipping out loose pages so they add to the mess on the floor)* Then we'll just have to find it for Eddie, since Eddie can't pull it off for himself, and in MAKING an extensive and deliberate search— guess what! We don't seem to come up with anything VALUABLE and all of a sudden the phone rings—

EDDIE: *(Reaching for a ringing phone)* I didn't know you had a telephone.

ESTELLE: *(As the phone is grabbed away from him)* You MUST have known because you TELEPHONED!

EDDIE: *(Grabbing back at the phone)* Excuse me while I make a telephone call! *(In a fast whirling struggle, they get the phone back, and the activity leaves EDDIE stymied and out of breath. He takes a moment to recover, and his expression darkens)*

EDDIE: What happened to seeing God?

ESTELLE: It's taken care of.

EDDIE: I didn't hear the phone.

ESTELLE: It's taken care of, Eddie.

(There is a pause; the room is dim. EDDIE goes and looks at the dollhouse room on top of the rack. Then turns back and speaks quietly)

EDDIE: It's snowing.

ESTELLE: *(Whispers to herself)* Forever.

EDDIE: *(Sits)* Don't try to turn me into a little boy.

ESTELLE: Why not, Eddie. It's a bedtime story.

EDDIE: Time for bed?

ESTELLE: No.

EDDIE: Yes.

ESTELLE: It's not a sexual overture, Eddie.

EDDIE: It's getting personal.

ESTELLE: In what sense?

EDDIE: Okay. Tell me about what really manifests in this room.

ESTELLE: Either . . . or.

EDDIE: Yes. Tell me.

ESTELLE: No. Be . . . REALLY interested.

EDDIE: I am.

ESTELLE: *(After a pause)* Okay. I'm not who you think I am.

EDDIE: Who are you?

ESTELLE: *(Very softly)* I'm Eddie.

EDDIE: Prove it.

ESTELLE: I just did.

EDDIE: How?

ESTELLE: *(Turns away)* Ah, too dumb to figure THAT one out!

MARIE: *(Entering)* Let's take a vote.

EDDIE: *(Whirling)* On what?

ESTELLE: Oh, Eddie, you know on what.

EDDIE: No. Really I don't!

MARIE: All in favor?

ESTELLE: Me.

MARIE: Opposed? *(A pause)* You're not opposed, Eddie?

EDDIE: I don't know what's up for consideration.

ESTELLE: Mystery, Eddie.

EDDIE: I'm not opposed. I'll take the risk—anyway, no matter how I voted I'm outnumbered, aren't I? *(They turn their backs and walk out on him and he calls after)* Hello? Am I locked in here? *(He sits quickly and talks to himself)* Why do I assume that? But I think I'll stay anyway. *(He looks *about the room, and whispers)* Gods? Here I am. . . . *(A pause)* What a disappointment that nothing happened.

(ESTELLE and MARIE reenter and begin talking as if they never left—but in the rear, in the shadows, unseen by either EDDIE or the two women, a Godlike figure with a halo and long white beard slowly edges into the room, holding a painting under his arm)

ESTELLE: In your element, Eddie?

EDDIE: You're trying to be mysterious.

ESTELLE: *(Mocking him)* It's "snowing."

EDDIE: I don't think so.

MARIE: Eddie doesn't believe in what he believes in.

EDDIE: You think you mean gods that I don't believe in, but I do—my own.

MARIE: *(At a mike now, she whirls and shouts into the mike, while pointing at the God figure in the shadows)* Here's one!

EDDIE: *(Still not seeing him)* You anticipate that long before it happens. *(As he speaks, he turns, and steps back, shocked to see the figure)*

MARIE: I told you it would happen.

ESTELLE: What she didn't tell you was that it would come into our world through YOUR door.

MARIE: But maybe that's just our own perspective on things.

ESTELLE: Did Eddie remember to burn a particularly wonderful painting?

MARIE: Look at that painting he's carrying!

ESTELLE: *(As the GOD lifts his painting, which is the same white Eddie-like face that MARIE had ostensibly taken out to burn)* But Eddie! It's your favorite painting!

MARIE: *(Whirls to face EDDIE, running backwards to crash against one of the padded walls)* You mean HE'S Eddie?!

ESTELLE: What does that explain?

EDDIE: Isn't anybody else surprised to see a godlike manifestation?

ESTELLE: We're not sure what it is.

GOD: *(Thundering yet childlike voice—in fact, the DOCTOR, muffled under a God mask)* I . . . AM!

MARIE: *(Acting frightened)* Sure?

GOD: Yesss, very sure. *(He bangs the painting down on the table)*

EDDIE: A painting that returns from the dead either wasn't dead, or else has regenerative powers related to a god's interest in such a potent image.

MARIE: *(Hurrying to Eddie)* It's wonderful that you and your god have the same taste in paintings.

EDDIE: I'm not sure about that anymore.

MARIE: Careful, Eddie, he's the sacred messenger.

GOD: May I speak?

EDDIE: Does a god have to ask permission?

ESTELLE: Weren't you shocked at the timbre of his voice? It wasn't expectedly godlike, was it? Which implies, on my part, how much happier we'd all be if he, or it, DIDN'T speak.

(*Unnoticed by everyone, the man with the megaphone has managed to reappear at the rear, in the shadows behind the* GOD. *There is a pause, and as if* EDDIE *has forgotten his next line, the man with the megaphone suddenly bellows out through his megaphone, "MAY! I! LOOK! AT THE! PAINT-ING!"* EDDIE *looks irritated, as if worried the audience will realize he's forgotten a line. He bites his lip, and then speaks in a kind of mumble of embarrassment*)

EDDIE: Right. May I look at the painting. (*But he doesn't move to go to it*)

MARIE: Do you really like it?

EDDIE: I think so.

MARIE: (*As* ESTELLE *runs out and returns with three snow shovels*) Should we reburn it?

EDDIE: I don't think so, since it was remanifest in such a miraculous way.

VOICE ON TAPE: RIIIGHT!!

(*As* EDDIE *speaks, music is building, and* ESTELLE *distributes the shovels, and then as the* GOD *lifts and lowers his painting in a ritualistic pattern,* EDDIE *follows the lead of* ESTELLE *and* MARIE, *and all three circle the awesome* GOD, *and to deafening organ music, start shoveling as if they were heaving dirt over the image of the* GOD *and his painting—as if they were burying him.*)

Each time they throw imaginary dirt, some flies back into their eyes and painfully blinds them, from which they quickly recover and regroup and reshovel—after three shovels and three blindings, they throw down their shovels and are so full of crazy energy that they lift a heavy table and march around the room carrying it high in the air, finally collapsing in exhaustion as the music fades)

EDDIE: *(Out of breath)* Sometimes it's definitely chaotic.

MARIE: I wouldn't use that word for a miracle.

EDDIE: You think it's a real miracle?

MARIE: Well, let's say yes.

ESTELLE: *(Having grabbed the picture from the GOD, she shoves it in EDDIE'S face)* Hey, you must love pictures more than you love anything, Eddie.

EDDIE: *(Pushing the picture away)* That's not completely true.

(Behind their backs, the DOCTOR has been removing his mask and halo, and now he leans forward aggressively)

DOCTOR: Shall we BURN it, Eddie?

EDDIE: *(Sees him. Turns away. Talks to himself in their presence)* I'm encasing myself in a work of art. You know what that means?

DOCTOR: Yes indeed.

EDDIE: My life really. *(He is at one of the microphones)* That's why I wanted to burn a painting I liked so very much. A distraction, right?

VOICE OVER LOUDSPEAKER: RIIIIIGHT!

EDDIE: *(Very quietly)* My name is Eddie and I plan to escape to Poetry City.

DOCTOR: Escape?

EDDIE: Don't be upset if I tell you, you participate in a life I find oppressive.

MARIE: Why, Eddie?

EDDIE: I find oppressive, life that is not centered, continually, on concern for the human spirit. That has to be the center.

DOCTOR: But Eddie, you've described life as it is here, where you are this very minute.

EDDIE: In a hidden sense, maybe.

DOCTOR: *(As he and the women start to wiggle in a kind of dance)* Not hidden, Eddie. It wobbles perhaps, because that's the human condition.

EDDIE: Wobbles?

DOCTOR: Yes. You know—wobbles. *(They demonstrate for EDDIE, wobble-dancing across the room)*

MARIE: Wobbles, Eddie!

ESTELLE: WOB-BLES!

EDDIE: It's true, I wobble when I walk

DOCTOR: *(Shouting over the dance and music)* Be careful Eddie— you're going in circles—

EDDIE: What? *(Music abruptly cuts)*

DOCTOR: (*Freezing*) I didn't say anything.

EDDIE: I thought you did. (*A frozen silence*) I was talking to myself.

DOCTOR: Talking to yourself!?!

ESTELLE: Oh, Eddie!

(*EDDIE is, as if magically, thrown by their disapproval against one and then another of the padded walls, being bounced around the room as the DOCTOR and MARIE and ESTELLE all shout one additional disapproving "EDDIE!" and the loud VOICE booms out over the loudspeaker*)

LOUD VOICE: (*Deafeningly*) You're disturbing the other guests!

EDDIE: (*Shouting as he careens out of control about the room*) What guests?

LOUD VOICE: You're time is up! You're being evicted for disturbing the neighbors!

EDDIE: What neighbors!?

LOUD VOICE: You won't get away with this outrageous behavior! I swear you won't goddammit! (*EDDIE has collapsed in a corner*) I swear you won't get away with this!

If it's the last thing I do. I won't let you get away with this outrageous behavior!

(*Very slowly, EDDIE picks himself up and sees the others, seated, staring at him*)

EDDIE: (*Quietly, nervously*) Why is everybody looking at me?

DOCTOR: You're in a play, Eddie.

EDDIE: I'm not in a play!

DOCTOR: You're in a play, Eddie.

EDDIE: No. *(He comes slowly forward toward the audience)* I'm not standing in bright light. I'm not in front of hundreds of people. I'm talking . . . language. But I'm in the middle of my own life. *(They each suddenly grab a flag—one of several that have been standing about the room in floor stands, and point the flag poles directly into EDDIE's body, flags trailing on the floor, focusing on EDDIE—and he contracts in fear)* Hey!

ESTELLE: Remember, Eddie, poetry melts language.

EDDIE: Debatable pleasure, maybe. Hacked off parts of the body.

DOCTOR: Offered by the mouth, Eddie.

EDDIE: *(Quiet)* Okay. If this were a play—

DOCTOR: Tell us about it, Eddie.

EDDIE: If this were a play, a curtain would be drawn. *(He steps forward, through an imaginary curtain, as the others drop their flags and run to different corners of the room and bend over to whisper in microphones)* And the audience would be in darkness.

DOCTOR: *(Far upstage)* No. If this were a play, a room would be visible into which one would project one's imagination. *(As he speaks, a giant head floats in behind him, and seems to stare downstage at EDDIE)*

ESTELLE: Would a line of dialogue suddenly emerge from the silence of dimly illuminated space?

EDDIE: (*Pause*) No. If this were a play . . . the room would be crowded with men and women in evening dress. Cigar smoke would hover in the air . . . and a chosen someone would lean forward as if his face were exploding. (*He puts gentle fingers up to his face*) He wouldn't speak, because he wouldn't have to. But he would speak. (*All break from their positions as the lights brighten*)

DOCTOR: (*Speaking with a rhetorical flourish as a thin white cord is stretched with MARIE'S help from his hand to EDDIE'S chest*)
  Oh Eddie,
  why retro-relax—

MARIE: (*Whispers an echo*) Retro-relax

DOCTOR: When you can dazzle me effectively?
  You have NO story to tell,
  so—
  you're a WINNER! (*EDDIE turns away from the string that pins him*) You WANT a story to tell
  so you can believe in the world?
  My message is quite the opposite.
  Believe no longer
  You made it happen,
  but the happening got stopped.
  That is to say—
  The WORLD GOES ON!

(*EDDIE has turned from the string, and retrieves the box from the beginning of the play that was described as holding his lunch. MARIE and ESTELLE have repositioned the string so that it cuts across EDDIE'S path, like a finish line through which he must push himself, but he hesitates*)

MARIE: Lunch, Eddie.

EDDIE: That's all?

DOCTOR: Isn't that enough?

EDDIE: Is that enough?

MARIE: Take what's yours, Eddie. It's wonderful.

EDDIE: *(Hesitates)* I don't think I'll look inside.

ESTELLE: Don't you remember? You already peeked.

EDDIE: Did I? I don't remember.

ESTELLE: *(As she collapses the string and MARIE retrieves it)* Matched? Outwitted?

MARIE: Eddie's experiences were profound.
   For that reason, he triumphs.

   (MARIE, ESTELLE, and the DOCTOR are picking up three-foot wands from various hiding places in the room, and they circle EDDIE and apply their wands to his body so he is pinned in space between them, at the center of a radiant circle)

DOCTOR: It was not his own doing, of course.
   He seized the "seize-me."

EDDIE: Seize me. *(Pause. He remains at the center of the network of wands)* If I told the truth *(ESTELLE and MARIE sigh audibly, and the circle revolves slightly)*
   If I told the truth about all things, guess what?
   It wouldn't be MY city you'd be visiting.
   Follow this? *(They all allow their wands to drop with a clatter, and all three go off in different directions leaving alone at the center of the room. EDDIE crosses to a table to deposit the box with his lunch)* All things have their own— shall we call it a sense of direction?
   I wanted to participate in a real world

but then it just got so painful.
Here's what happened.

I ordered lunch, but to my amazement,
I arrived in a city so confusing, it was homogeneous in that,
at least.
Which was comforting, to some.

ESTELLE: What city, Eddie?

EDDIE: That's what made it a different kind of city. It wasn't necessary to move, in the sense of moving on, see what I mean? (*ESTELLE runs to EDDIE, kisses him on the cheek, and then goes quickly to the back of the room*) You interrupted my train of thought! Should we call that polite, or think about it?

DOCTOR: (*Coming forward as EDDIE goes rear, when MARIE recovers his face with one of the small red curtains on a stick*) Eddie thought ideas got pressed between the pages of a book like fruit, so the sweet flow of ideas could run down over his fingers like rose water.
  That made him think of his own potential beauty, interior and exterior, and so he combed his hair.

EDDIE: (*Pushing through the red curtain to speak, brushing away imaginary cobwebs as he does so*) Eddie looks out over the city and it speaks to him. But how does an entire city form words? Phrases arise in Eddie's head, no question about it. He turns to Marie as if to speak, then hesitates.

MARIE: Marie senses his hesitation and says, "Eddie, are you trying to put feelings into words?"

EDDIE: And Eddie turns the pressure in his throat into a smile, and directs his gaze toward the window, that isn't there.

SOFT VOICE: "Look at me" is what Marie feels an urge to shout, but that doesn't mean she is in any way arguing with Eddie.

They go for a drive. (In the shadows rear, the God figure reappears, walking very slowly, a giant now on tall shoes, carrying a white box—the very image of the box resting on the table with EDDIE's wonderful lunch. As the VOICE continues, EDDIE and ESTELLE and the DOCTOR move and gesture during its speaking) Where did the automobile come from? Eddie was about to say—I borrowed it from a relative named . . . Father, but he was long since dead so that couldn't be possible. (Eddie sees the God figure—his father? And moves toward him, then hesitates, and slowly retreats, covering his eyes) Was Eddie dead? No, just because there was a certain problem with certain words coming or not coming out of his mouth, even after they had well started inside his throat, where did they disappear? Maybe Eddie was dead, and his father was alive in him or not in him and look—speeding around a corner a man in a checkered jacket—go slow, said Marie under her breath, and where did those words come from, thought Eddie? (The God figure has slowly brought his box to rest on top of the box EDDIE had placed on the table. The God figure slowly turns and begins to drift out the other side of the room, in a shaft of dim light) But the man who was not Eddie's father cast his eyes down the street toward the car, which he definitely heard make a noise. And something in that maneuver vanished, or wasn't there to begin with. Certainly it wasn't Eddie, or Marie either, but a part of the city that decided to appear through Eddie, and he tried not to be too preoccupied, but still it vanished as he noticed the man looking in their direction.

I almost, exclaimed Eddie, decided to stop the car and run over to the man to tell him how much he looked like my father. This was later at a cocktail party. (EDDIE and MARIE and ESTELLE quickly change positions, exchange glances, then look away from each other) Eddie was drinking soda water. He spilled some of it on his jacket, but it was soda water. *(Eddie wipes at it)* Eddie wiped at it, rather more "blotted" it with a napkin. That was that. He closed his eyes—just for a second—and listened to the hum of conversation that was going on around him rather than to here or there a specific word or phrase. *(EDDIE has covered his eyes. And ESTELLE is watching him. He uncovers his eyes, looks to ESTELLE, and she—unable to receive his gaze—covers her own eyes quickly and turns away)* By the time he had opened his eyes, only about three seconds had elapsed and whoever it was he was talking to hadn't moved. It wasn't Marie—she wasn't even at the cocktail party. And Eddie smiled and looked across the room and waved at someone almost imperceptibly, and he wondered if anybody noticed, and then he thought—of course, whatever I do, people notice. *(The God figure, about to vanish from the room, has slowly turned back toward EDDIE and lifted his hand, slowly, in greeting)* And to verify that for all time, as it were, he heard a voice saying "You waved, Eddie." And he tried to imagine somebody in the room waving back. The effort made the room shimmer, slightly, under his eyes. *(The God figure is gone, and they all stumble slightly)* Was it a shimmer? Something sped around his head in a circular motion. And Eddie forgot where he was, but a voice brought him back to reality, saying, "Eddie, are you paying attention?"

ESTELLE: *(After a long pause, tears in her eyes)* Eddie, have you really seen God?

EDDIE: Of course not.

ESTELLE: Marie says you have.

EDDIE: *(Pause)* But there's no way of knowing, is there?

ESTELLE: One can have one's opinions.

EDDIE: *(Sadly)* That's all they are, really.

ESTELLE: Opinions.

EDDIE: Right.

ESTELLE: *(Sadly)* Right.

DOCTOR: *(Aggressively)* Right!

VOICE OVER THE LOUDSPEAKER: RIGHT!

ALL: *(Leaping into the air in place, and shouting in desperate defiance)* RIGHT! *(They fall back from their leap and stumble a bit, then recover and rush from the room in opposite directions—but at their respective exits, each bounces back as if from an invisible wall and turns and exits running in the opposite direction, as the voice on the loudspeaker continues barking out words)*

VOICE ON SPEAKER: Right! Right again! Right! Right still! Right completely! Totally . . . RIGHT!

(The music builds, the lights fade, then the music cuts. The play ends)

THE END

the mind king

The Mind King. Produced by the Ontological-Hysteric Theater at the Ontological at St. Mark's Theater, N.Y.C. January–March 1992. Written, directed, and designed by Richard Foreman.

THE ANGEL:	David Patrick Kelly
PAUL:	Henry Stram
LADY (ANNA MARIE):	Colleen Werthman

Organ music, in the style of the popular Sunday religious radio hour, is heard playing softly. The setting is a dimly illuminated room, walls painted gray, and with a gray carpet covering the floor completely. A narrow table, perhaps sixteen feet in length, lines up along the wall to the audience's right. On the other side of the stage, a table not quite as long sits parallel to the audience. Both are covered with gray cloth that hangs to the floor.

At the rear of the room, a large cabinet. A few large checkered geometric objects hang above the room, looking like giant children's toys. Several posts with light bulbs are scattered about the room, and many chairs. To the audience's right, a low, sculpted cabinet in a shape that evokes a primitive head. Fixed to its top is a tray on which stand a dozen of so empty crystal champagne glasses. To the left, high on the wall, is a white screen with delicate propeller-like apparatuses protruding. Around the room, resting on the floor and leaning against the walls, are two small blackboards, also several panels, on each of which has been painted a faded, life-size image of an antique chair.

Scattered on the walls are images of a hand, and assorted letters from the Hebrew alphabet, some arranged in magic squares.

The light is so dim that we hardly notice PAUL entering the room. He wears traditional Jewish teffilin strapped to his forehead and his left arm. A brocaded prayer shawl is wrapped over his shoulders, and his bald head has a mystical letter painted on one naked temple. On his hands he wears leather gloves that leave the fingers uncovered.

Suddenly, THE ANGEL enters vigorously and races to a central position in the room. He wears a black suit, with lace cuffs and collar, and wears two ties at once. He also wears what looks like an oversized, brocaded nightcap.

Both PAUL and THE ANGEL wear radio mikes, which enable them to speak very softly throughout the play.

As THE ANGEL races to his position, crackling sounds drown out the soft organ music. A variety of softly played repetitive tape loop musics alternate with faint electronic tones throughout 90 percent of the performance. They rise and fade, following the course and intensity of the action onstage.

A photo flash illuminates the stage, then within five or ten seconds the lights have faded back to their normal dimness. This same flash of light, which then fades, recurs many times during the course of the play.

PAUL slides into a chair at the main table and dares not look at THE ANGEL, whom he senses standing behind him. The noise fades.

Throughout the entire play, both characters speak very quietly, and very slowly—except when specifically indicated otherwise.)

PAUL: (In a low whisper) An angel appeared, and I lifted my hat, because above all else I wanted to be polite to angels.

THE ANGEL: (He has slowly pointed to his own head. Then the lights flash and fade. THE ANGEL slaps his head and then points to it with his finger) Angels know not from politeness.

PAUL: Now I know. Before I didn't.

THE ANGEL: (Advancing on PAUL, resting his palm on his head) So your hat is not in evidence.

PAUL: Correct. (A low tone is heard)

THE ANGEL: Did the angel stay?

PAUL: Yes. *(Slowly rising)* It integrated itself inside me. It's here. *(He is standing with his back to the audience, facing the large cabinet. THE ANGEL comes beside him and blows once into his ear)*

THE ANGEL: It's inside you.

PAUL: Yes.

THE ANGEL: Is it speaking?

PAUL: Yes. *(THE ANGEL touches PAUL gently on the shoulder, and PAUL is magically thrown to the side of the room)*

THE ANGEL: I believe you should cast it out, Paul.

PAUL: *(Slowly stretching out his arms)* An angel is a higher being. *(Lights flash and fade)*

THE ANGEL: But it isn't you, Paul. Being a human being, I would assume your destiny is to realize yourself rather than to escape yourself.

PAUL: To have an angel inside me is my ideal. Because where I am, or was, is a void.

THE ANGEL: Grow into it.

PAUL: I am trying. With an angel.

THE ANGEL: That's from the outside. *(He rises, looks toward a door, then back to PAUL, and the lights flash and fade, as THE ANGEL goes into the next room, glancing back at PAUL as he does so)*

PAUL: *(He races after the disappearing ANGEL, then stops at the door as if a force field had intervened. Then he slowly crosses to the other side of the room and picks up a pair of wooden wings)* My belief system is attacked. Who would have thought I was so dedicated to beauty?

THE ANGEL: *(Reappearing in the doorway)*
My belief system is under attack.
My personal habits are criticized.

PAUL: *(Having strapped on the wings)* My taste is questioned

THE ANGEL: Tell the real story.

PAUL: Tell the real story, which is of course very hard, because in the real story nothing happens.

THE ANGEL: I don't think you can tell the real story, Paul. *(PAUL takes off his wings, tucks them under his arm, and exits quickly into the next room. There is a pause, as THE ANGEL now sits in a downstage chair with his back to the audience and yawns and stretches. Then PAUL reenters)*

PAUL: Once upon a time . . .

THE ANGEL: Are you blocked? *(He laughs to himself)* That's understandable.

PAUL: *(Coming quickly toward THE ANGEL, who suddenly holds up a hand to freeze him in his advance, as the lights again flash and fade. PAUL stops, then decides to persevere)* Now look, if somebody wanted to escape normal language, normal meaning, everything normal, where would they go?

THE ANGEL: To me. I'd help.

PAUL: How?

THE ANGEL: That's the wrong question

PAUL: I'm one of those people. I want to escape everything normal.

THE ANGEL: Rationality?

PAUL: Yes.

THE ANGEL: Feelings?

PAUL: Yes.

THE ANGEL: The ability to utter coherent sentences? (*Sad, wistful music*)

PAUL: (*Hanging his head in shame*) Yes.

THE ANGEL: Why?

PAUL: (*Growling an answer*) That's the wrong question.

(*THE ANGEL runs to pull PAUL to the upstage cabinet, as the lights again flash and fade and the music gets louder and the crackling noise begins. A giant-sized light bulb on top of the cabinet lights to a soft glow, and with repeated coaxing THE ANGEL gets PAUL to the cabinet. The music softens. THE ANGEL opens a lower drawer, inserts his two hands, and twists to look up at PAUL, who stands beside him nervously*)

THE ANGEL: This machine helps.

PAUL: What is it? (*THE ANGEL doesn't answer*) Please!

THE ANGEL: I shrug. (*He lifts his shoulders in a giant shrug. PAUL goes and puts his own hands in the open drawer*)

PAUL: I don't feel different.

THE ANGEL: Not yet. *(The lights flash and fade. THE ANGEL hits his head and then points to his forehead with an extended finger)* It takes time.

PAUL: How long?

THE ANGEL: Years. *(THE ANGEL is taking an envelope out of another drawer)*

PAUL: How many?

THE ANGEL: Different in different cases. You? I'd guess thirty—forty—

PAUL: How do I speed it up?

THE ANGEL: You don't. *(He laughs, as the lights flash and fade, and he lightly taps PAUL on the head with the envelope, and does a little jig to the wistful music, which gets louder. He puts the envelope back in the cabinet and exits. As he gets to the door, the music cuts and PAUL reopens the drawer and looks at the envelope. Seeing nothing but a blank sheet of paper inside, he quickly returns the envelope, while THE ANGEL has returned almost immediately, standing in the doorway unseen by PAUL, wiping his hands on a white towel. PAUL turns away from the cabinet, sees THE ANGEL watching him, and quickly turns back to the cabinet and takes out six plates, which he clumsily places on a ledge on the front of the cabinet. Then he takes his own towel from the cabinet and maniacally rubs at a plate as he mutters under his breath—)*

PAUL: Here's a slice from MY plate of experience—I don't even talk about it. It simply floats in front of my eyes.

THE ANGEL: *(In a grotesque voice that makes PAUL whirl to see him)* I'm with you in the watering mouth you thrust in my direction. *(His voice slows and softens again)* But just one thing—

PAUL: Twisting my body slightly, to deflect a blow.

THE ANGEL: *(Holding plates that he polishes with his towel)* I wasn't going to hit anything.

PAUL: Too true.

THE ANGEL: Only too true. *(He purposely drops two plates to the floor, to startle PAUL)* Don't flinch.

PAUL: I thought I was "quenching my thirst." *(He runs to get a glass from the cabinet)*

THE ANGEL: Drinks from the same source aren't equally tasty. *(There is an unnaturally loud noise as PAUL drops ice cubes into his glass, and THE ANGEL performs a sudden ritual-like series of gestures)* Guess why.

PAUL: *(Freezes, then looks around the room in awe)* Everything is different

THE ANGEL: Not specific enough, Paul. Don't you know they call me Mr. Specific? I could lose lots of things under my own name, but your name interests me.

PAUL: You don't know my name.

THE ANGEL: I can choose.

PAUL: It won't be right.

THE ANGEL: Oh yes it will. Language goes slithering through its own underpass: and when names get named—?

PAUL: They stick.

THE ANGEL: What's mine?

PAUL: I'm drinking your image right now. *(He puts a finger under THE ANGEL's chin)* I wait before I spit it back. *(He flicks THE ANGEL's chin, and THE ANGEL staggers, then recovers)*

THE ANGEL: That gives me an out. *(He takes off his hat, only to reveal a gray skullcap underneath. He drops his brocade hat on the table, and continues out of the room, as the lights flash and fade, but as he reaches the door, he begins retracing his last few steps and seems unable to pass through the door)*

PAUL: Well. Here I am. Alone with my memories.

THE ANGEL: *(Continuing his efforts at the door)* Could be I tripped over another one of my connectives. I'm just a tissue of connectives.
   There's power in this kind of indecision.

PAUL: You read my mind.

THE ANGEL: Sweetness.

PAUL: . . . delicacy.

THE ANGEL: Ah, that's my MIND talking.

(A flash of light, which this time doesn't fade but slowly gets blindingly brighter. The tone and music get louder. THE ANGEL races to one of the chair paintings. PAUL sees this and hurries around the table to get a closer look. Then THE ANGEL takes a crown from the cabinet and puts it on his head, as PAUL turns his back and, folding his arms, tries to sit on the painted chair. A little nursery rhyme tune is heard on a child's piano, as PAUL falls to the floor in slow motion, and THE ANGEL starts frantically erasing the already smudged blackboard. As PAUL hits the ground, he

startles *THE ANGEL* away from the blackboard. *THE ANGEL* looks about, sees the second blackboard, goes to it, folds his arms as he turns his back, and succeeds in slowly sitting on the painted image. Unrecognizable words are heard being whispered over the music, as *PAUL*, seeing *THE ANGEL* sitting successfully, rises and takes a birthday cake with one large candle from the table and runs out of the room. From the flickering of a tiny light outside the door, we can see what he is doing, and he immediately returns with the lit cake, now wearing a crown of his own, to place the cake on the table right by the spot where *THE ANGEL* sits poised in space against the painted chair. Then he hurriedly circles the room and tries to sit again on his original painted chair, but again slowly falls to the floor. As he does so, *THE ANGEL* comes and blows out the candle and hurries with the cake to the other table. Then, as *PAUL* hits the floor, and quickly rises, to run from the room humiliated, *THE ANGEL* gets a small one-foot-high folding white screen from the side and sets it up as a low barrier in front of the sculpted face table. He then races to the cabinet, and making a great clattering noise, he rapidly opens and closes drawers, as *PAUL* races back into the room—the whispering is now very loud over the loudspeakers—circles the tables, and tries to sit once more, falling to the floor with a thud as the noise stops, and *THE ANGEL* stops his search through the drawers and bends suddenly over *PAUL*, who sits on the floor and plucks *PAUL'S* crown from his head, tossing it to the side)

THE ANGEL: Now. Are you thoroughly humiliated? Your thinking is fuzzy. Are you humiliated?

PAUL: No. I'm quite happy.

THE ANGEL: Your fuzziness is like a warm blanket.

PAUL: Yes.

THE ANGEL: It's not right, Paul.

It's a waste.

You make me so angry—I just want to . . . tear out my hair! Yes! I feel like I could tear myself to pieces. *(He throws his arms around his own body, and trying to tear himself to pieces, crashes to the floor, thrashing about. PAUL rises to watch, and THE ANGEL stops just as suddenly, smiles up at PAUL, as the lights flash and fade, and he then rises and runs out of the room. PAUL runs after, and just as he's about to pass through the door, THE ANGEL reappears to block his exit)*

PAUL: *(As the tone rises and then cuts off)* I displaced myself. It hurt.

THE ANGEL: I rewarded myself. It came loose.

PAUL: That happened before I said— Shut up about it! *(THE ANGEL lifts a fist and PAUL cowers and holds his mouth)* I said I lost a tooth.

THE ANGEL: Was it magic?

PAUL: No. It was backwards. *(Lights flash and fade, as THE ANGEL is thrown back to hit the wall, and PAUL is whirled into space, and starts to prance about the room as jiglike music is heard)*

THE ANGEL: *(Very soft, in a squeaky voice, as he makes ritual-like passes with his hands)* Help me. Help me!

PAUL: *(Ending downstage, thrown off balance as the music cuts and THE ANGEL claps his hands. Then PAUL recovers and speaks to himself)* Time covered my bets, so I was allowed to carry on.

THE ANGEL: Under a different name.

PAUL: Beginnings were not my strong point.

THE ANGEL: Name it! Name it!

PAUL: Taking this life for granted.

THE ANGEL: Name it.

PAUL: *(Slowly spreading his arms)* . . . The Mind King! . . . let tiredness enter his body, entering at last, or was it retiring into a real distance? No one knew him from a distance.

THE ANGEL: Then, a man taking a walk on a normal afternoon, sees a dog and kicks it.

PAUL: The dog goes home, chews on a bone, finds no human emotion so does not know that it is alone.

THE ANGEL: The bone, gnawed upon, knows nothing new. It dreams that it, too, might someday chew.

PAUL: The dream, taking a human shape, walks down the street and greets other human shapes. *(Faint fairground music is heard)*

THE ANGEL: The Mind King did rise to the occasion after all. Though there was no occasion, only a normal day, and that was an occasion. He'd taken his normal breakfast, taken his normal walk, kicked the normal dog on the sidewalk— *(He runs rear, slams one leg up onto the side table and falls back against the wall, throwing up his arms)* Wrong. That was only a thought he had while he was waving his arms in the air. That was normal.

PAUL: A man was waving his hands in the air.

THE ANGEL: Truly, the flutter of the hands, informed the entire landscape. *(Lights flash and fade)* Nothing was . . . absent, exactly. But someone was. Absent.

PAUL: *(He faces out, and circles his head with a hand in a ritual-like gesture, then points to his forehead)* Here I go.
The Mind King was not available, but in closing the door he left a very distinct impression *(THE ANGEL runs down to him, grabs his face, but PAUL pulls away and runs to the other side of the room. THE ANGEL collects plates from the floor, piles them on the table, then leans on the table, as if emotionally shaken)*

PAUL: Hey. I talked to myself. It shook a piece loose.

THE ANGEL: I attacked myself. It opened a door by accident. *(An invisible force throws him from the table, to the floor. PAUL runs to the table and bends over it with his arms out)*

PAUL: He didn't have to think; it happened.

THE ANGEL: His hand . . . cast a shadow on the table at which he had been writing; he was always writing. And the shadow was its own specific and dense reality, which did not mean . . .
Well . . . *(Grabs PAUL's hand)*

PAUL: Oww! *(He pulls free, as a VOICE is heard over the loudspeaker, repeating, "Don't be alarmed, don't be alarmed")*

PAUL: *(As the voice fades)* The Mind King was buttoned down for a night of dream pictures, work for a lifetime. Everything had a key, or was a key. *(He crosses up to the cabinet)* To other people it looked like wasting time. He pulled open a drawer. . . . *(He does so, and takes out a pair of white gloves, which he puts on. At the side of the room, THE ANGEL has entered a closet but immediately returned with his own white gloves, which he puts on simultaneously with PAUL's*

doing so) . . . and took out a pair of socks and indeed, did
what everybody else does.

THE ANGEL: *(Whispering)* The Mind King. *(A bell sounds once,
lights flash and fade)*

PAUL: Here I go—*(THE ANGEL points to his head, as PAUL runs
from the room, and THE ANGEL races about making ritual-
like gestures. PAUL immediately reenters and braces himself against the table)*

PAUL: *(After a pause, he straightens up and holds up his gloved
hands)* Well socked . . . he walked into the next room and
rolled about a bit—that is to say, first stretched himself on
the carpet of course. What was this a key to, he was busy,
wondering . . . *(A bell sounds, and PAUL slowly looks at his
hand, which has risen to his forehead. He follows his hand
as it leads him to pivot—and he whispers ecstatically)*
Harold! *(He runs out immediately and reenters and slowly
feels his way along the wall. On the other side of the room,
THE ANGEL is doing the same)* This rolling about, this
donning of the socks which in and of itself was quite what
you call ordinary?

THE ANGEL: He got the Mind King's point, but he didn't get the
Mind King's point. His arm hurt, from trying to understand. That's the key: how come the stress and strain in
your particular case—

PAUL: My arm, Harold interrupted before he could finish his
question.

THE ANGEL: Yes. My arm. And it seemed to throb in reply.

PAUL: And thinking about that, he felt giddy, said Harold, talk-
ing about himself. *(A woman in a dark dress—ANNA
MARIE—slowly enters in the shadows of the room, near THE
ANGEL. But neither PAUL nor THE ANGEL acts as if they see*

her) The next thing anybody knew, this particular Harold had thrown himself onto the carpet, and he turned over two or three times in a row in a particular way that one could have called rolling.

THE ANGEL: Harold is rolling, they could have said. But Anna Marie asked him, politely of course, to take off his shoes because it offended her sensibilities to see the bottoms that did all the stepping on things—and they did become very visible in the course of the rolling. *(His foot has slowly lifted onto the table)* Oh, yes, everybody agreed, Anna Marie is correct; attention is certainly called to the bottoms. And Harold was glad, in complying, that he was wearing nice— *(He points to his foot)* and somebody else read for that—"clean"—you know what: socks.

PAUL: Suddenly, is it because the eyes don't focus?
  The Mind King lifts from the bed and thinks. That means, putting a closed fist against his forehead. *(ANNA MARIE is slowly crossing the stage at the rear to exit, as PAUL'S hand lifts to his forehead)* And when he erased something, it stayed erased. *(He collapses in slow motion to the floor)*

THE ANGEL: Self-surprise, when I floated a brain wave and it surfaced half-only.

PAUL: *(As ominous music rises, and they both are crawling to the side table)* Self-surprise, when I stepped back into my own story.

THE ANGEL: That's no surprise.

PAUL: I didn't look.

THE ANGEL: *(As they both lift themselves on the edge of the table)* Self-surprise, I fingered my own tune to the total finish.

PAUL: Out of the open mouth, whole sentences like ice cubes.

THE ANGEL: You talk and I shiver.

PAUL: *(He moves toward THE ANGEL, who lifts a hand to stop him, as the lights flash and then fade. THE ANGEL turns and exits as PAUL goes and disconsolately sits on the antique chair. He picks up a strange object, and stares at it)* When I get retrospect, it's too late to know about it.

THE ANGEL: *(Reentering, carrying his own strange object, dressed in a red silk bathrobe)* The Mind King didn't dress, so when Marie came for a visit she said, you're still in your robe *(A soft gong rings)*, and when the Mind King offered her a cracker from his plate of crackers—she hesitated. *(ANNA MARIE has entered by the same door, holding a clock up in front of her face, hiding it completely. Lights flash and fade)* Glancing at the clock of course, she was about to say, "It's not working." Then she realized her mistake.

PAUL: *(Rising, as lights flash and fade)* And the Mind King was already on his feet, holding out his hands, palms up.

THE ANGEL: Marie put her hands in his, but then they had no place to go and stood there for what seemed like an interminable period of time. *(Lights flash and fade)* Marie inclined her head to the left slightly, or was it rather the weight of her own head that did the pulling—and gravity was not personified in that little encounter until the Mind King sort of imitated her tilt to the left, which in his case became a tilt to the right. *(He is staring at his strange object, as the gong sounds and the lights flash and fade, and a VOICE on tape intones, "THE MIND KING")* You take the next step, thought Marie, and broke away to return to her seat.

PAUL: After she was comfortably—

THE ANGEL: So-so.

PAUL: —settled in her chair, she had much cause to wonder, of course, where the attraction between objects, in this case her physical body and the chair to which she gravitated *(He is pressing his strange object against his forehead, and THE ANGEL is sitting in the antique chair)* . . . but the Mind King was there first, and when she tried to sit she found herself descending into his lap and immediately jumped up fast into space itself. *(Lights flash and fade as both turn and for the first time see ANNA MARIE as she dashes across the room to exit)* That's what was filling most of the room.

THE ANGEL: *(Taking off his gloves)* The Mind King hadn't changed, and pulling his robe tight around the contours of his body he as much as said, This is my chair and that's your chair, at least she thought he was directing his gaze along those lines *(He has risen from the chair)*, and when she did sit, it was unclear if it was the chair she had been aiming at since the beginning.

The beginning of what asked the Mind King as if he could read her thoughts, which of course he couldn't, so how did he happen to FALL upon those words, demanded Marie? *(By now PAUL has slowly sunk to the ground, kneeling, pressing his head toward the carpet)* Before he could answer she knew the answer was: GRAVITY.

PAUL: *(Whispers from the floor)* Gravity.

THE ANGEL: *(He hurries to stand just above PAUL, who still kneels head down to the floor)* And then went and tapped the clock lightly, and the Mind King *(A bell sounds once; lights flash and fade)* was content to let the dial express whatever the contingencies of the moment might, logically, be said to express. *(He whirls his arms once in imitation of a clock's hands going crazy; lights flash and fade. Then he looks about the room, races to a blackboard on the floor, picks up an eraser)* And when he erased something—*(He makes another whirl of his arms, as if he were erasing in space, as the lights flash and fade) it stayed erased.

(As both he and PAUL run to different blackboards and crouch before them erasing, an orchestral tone rises, and the blackboards are miked so the sound of the erasing is loud, and then the erasers are dropped. Then PAUL backs off to restudy one of the chair paintings. He goes to sit, and as the nursery tune is heard, he folds his arms, tries to sit, and again falls in slow motion. THE ANGEL picks up a panel that has been lying face down on the floor. It is another chair painting. THE ANGEL supports it from behind and looks down over the top to study the image, as PAUL slowly crosses and then, determinedly, squeezes THE ANGEL against the wall by pushing the panel against him, as raucous trombone swoops are heard)

THE ANGEL: (Throwing up his hands in mock fear, and speaking in squeaky falsetto) Help me. Help me! (The trombones stop as PAUL returns to his chair painting, and again tries to sit and slowly falls. THE ANGEL points to his own head and smiles mockingly)

THE ANGEL: Is a certain person enjoying himself?
      You don't have to answer.
      There's a hole in somebody's plate. (PAUL noisily collects plates from the cabinet and places them in a pile at the head of the smaller table. He sits holding out one plate toward THE ANGEL) I satisfy by what I put on the plate, into the hole. You smile and I smile back. (He lifts his hands in mock fear and squeaks, "Help me, help me!" He lets his painting fall and takes a jump toward the center of the room, as crackling music starts, and PAUL jumps up startled and starts rearranging plates on various tables. THE ANGEL returns to lift the chair painting from the floor and succeeds in sitting in front of it on empty space, folding his arms in satisfaction, and the music stops)

THE ANGEL: The Mind King and plates. *(He twists his head around to stare up into the light)*
He lifted one to the light,
but the light reflected in its porcelain surface had no center,
that is to say
no source,
and the Mind King did ponder. *(As queasy music rises, THE ANGEL puts his painting against the wall with a sob, and then runs to lay several plates out on the smaller table as he speaks)*
He crossed to the piano and pounded.
So he followed his pondering by pounding,
and Marie heard that and scooted into the room. *(He runs to the cabinet and takes a cloth and wipes it once and then comes center wiping his own hands)*
Let me clean those piano keys—
she knew the Mind King's fingers were covered with something or other
—don't call it dirt exactly,
but Marie was very possessive about her keys. *(PAUL is crouching in fear by the table)*
Oh gosh, the Mind King intoned,
I forgot this was your piano.

Could be, chimed in Marie, but nobody's supposed to know for sure.

She hid the dust rag she was thinking of, but it was too late and the Mind King pivoted on the spot, so self-conscious about the turn of events *(THE ANGEL pivots and ends up his little dance kneeling behind the low white screen that stands in front of the sculpted face cabinet)*—he had to end up saying, "Look, I'm dancing."

PAUL: *(As the music rises, he runs to gather plates as he is speaking)* But Marie didn't believe him and found other things to do, like agitating the drapes, and flattening out on the couch with a book over her stomach. *(As he finishes, he is out the door into the next room. During this, THE ANGEL has moved so he is now hidden behind the face cabinet)*

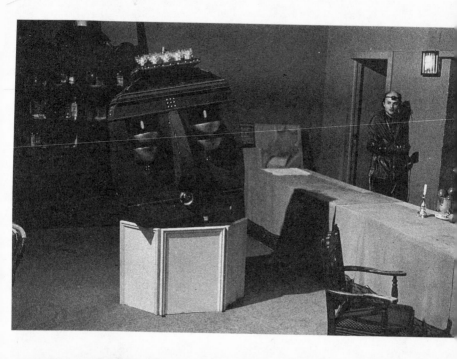

THE ANGEL: *(Behind the face cabinet, as the lights flash and fade and the room seems empty)* By then the Mind King had long since left the room and Marie, he cried, but not too loudly—*(Gong sounds, and the face cabinet tilts, moved by the hidden ANGEL, but the glasses on top don't fall off)*—and also, he was faced the other way, across the room.

PAUL: *(Returning in the doorway)* How interesting of you to relate stories.

THE ANGEL: *(Lights flash and fade as THE ANGEL, from behind, lifts the face cabinet and, still hidden, balances it on the top of the low white screen. After it has been sitting there a few seconds, THE ANGEL emerges. He is now wearing a short, cylindrical shiny white hat, stained with blood, and embossed with one or two ritual-like Hebrew letters. He also wears dark glasses. He speaks very quietly)* I didn't mean it to be interesting, I meant it to frighten.

PAUL: Why?

THE ANGEL: I wanted to turn a key in a lock, and the only way I know how to do that is by frightening.
     Don't you think it works?

PAUL: I wouldn't know about such things. I'm too busy with my own practicing.

THE ANGEL: What do you practice?

PAUL: The piano.

THE ANGEL: I could offer you a job.

PAUL: Doing what?

THE ANGEL: Playing the piano . . . as accompaniment.

PAUL: Accompaniment to what?

THE ANGEL: I plan to make a career out of frightening people. You could play the piano to set the mood. *(He reaches up to run his finger around the rim of one of the champagne glasses. A faint ringing tone is heard)*

PAUL: I don't think I know how to play anything frightening.

THE ANGEL: Oh, no, what you play would be a contrast. It could be the opposite. *(Reacts momentarily, as if he'd cut his finger on the edge of the glass)*

PAUL: Yes, I could do that.

THE ANGEL: Let me see your hands. *(PAUL, in trepidation, slowly holds out his hands)* Yes, those are good hands for playing the piano.

PAUL: *(Looks at his fingertips, then looks up at THE ANGEL)* Thank you.

(THE ANGEL comes slowly to PAUL, then, as a DEEP VOICE begins speaking over the loudspeakers, and music rises, THE ANGEL lunges at PAUL, whirls him, pushes him against the wall, and folds his arms, leaning back against him, keeping him pressed into the wall)

DEEP VOICE: A story is being told. The man telling the story is turning his back on his fellow man, his eyes as if smiling, *(THE ANGEL takes off his dark glasses)*, with the smile causing the eyes to seem outlined in a black line that turns sight into a projectile. *(THE ANGEL now leaves PAUL and slowly circles to set the antique chair downstage. PAUL follows fascinated, sitting slowly in the offered chair, facing the audience)* And the story is in that projectile. So it could change, as story, without changing the shocking capacity that is the projectile nature of story and gaze yoked together.

A story is being told. But where is it being told and where is it being received? And does it mix, in the telling, with other stories, so that no story is self-whole?

THE ANGEL: *(Behind* PAUL, *suddenly clasps his hand onto his head, and forces him to look straight ahead)* This man sits with his back to something. What's behind him he doesn't see.

PAUL: It's not that I'm afraid.

THE ANGEL: Oh, it's not that he's afraid. In order to clarify this, we—I—install a white screen. *(THE ANGEL looks about, as agitated crackling and music is heard, and he spies a folded-up white hospital screen in the corner of the room. He runs to get it and places it in front of* PAUL. *He stops and looks at the audience, then opens the screen to reveal* PAUL, *whose chair now has pivoted, re-placing him with his back to the audience.* THE ANGEL *doesn't react to this but quickly ties up his own two wrists in a rope, then whirls to face the spectators with wrists tied. The music and noise stop abruptly. There is a pause)* You think this is trivial. A cheap trick. On the other hand, logically obvious. *(He becomes irrationally aggressive toward the audience)* I, on the other hand, don't think so! I think . . . here is an inexhaustible mystery! . . . Let's try again. *(He gets out of the rope, as the music returns—mellower now, and he runs back to the corner where he retrieves a small roll-up home movie screen on a stand, which he places directly upstage of* PAUL'S *chair—while* PAUL, *himself, in full view, has reversed his chair and now re-sits, again facing the audience, but now in dark glasses.* THE ANGEL *pulls down the white movie screen into position so it makes a blank white surface behind the seated* PAUL. *Then he ties his own hands again and faces the audience as the music cuts off. There is another pause)*

THE ANGEL: You still don't get my point. I could continue, repeating this manipulation, until you got my point . . . even if you never get it! But I won't physically repeat it. I'll just guide you through, verbally. What I said was—

PAUL: (*Staring at the audience, speaking as if to himself*) I can't see what's in back of me.

THE ANGEL: Then I placed a screen. And when I removed it, he had turned around.

PAUL: I can never see what's in back of me.

THE ANGEL: Mirrors and cameras and such don't count. Then, I placed a screen, again, not to illustrate what I'd said, because it didn't. But it should have made something happen, and it did, several things happened. But your attention might not have been placed properly. Because what you were looking for was an EVENT to happen. But what happened was different.

PAUL: I can't see what's in back of me.

THE ANGEL: "In back of me" stands in for other things. (*Turns to PAUL*) See me?

PAUL: Yes.

THE ANGEL: (*Shouts angrily*) Now look at me! (*Quiet again*) See me?

PAUL: Yes.

THE ANGEL: (*Turning back to the audience*) I didn't notice a difference between when he said it looking away and when he said it looking into my eyes.

PAUL: Look how I'm dressed.

THE ANGEL: *(He turns and stares at* PAUL, *who is dressed as he has been from the beginning, while* THE ANGEL *now wears a red silk bathrobe)* Ah—the Mind King, in his red bathrobe. *(*PAUL *rises slowly, faces* THE ANGEL, *then turns and exits quickly, as* THE ANGEL *hits his own head with his palm, then points his finger to his head. He repeats this a second time, as the tone rises, and he turns to look to where* PAUL *has exited, then turns back and points to his head again, laughing to himself, as* PAUL *reenters—without his glasses now and dressed in a red silk bathrobe very much like the one worn by* THE ANGEL*)*

PAUL: The Mind King still in his red bathrobe.

THE ANGEL: I'm not even looking.

> *(*PAUL *advances a few steps toward* THE ANGEL. *Then* THE ANGEL *advances, forcing* PAUL *backwards, and the lights flash and fade to very dim, but the white screen is illuminated with clear light, and* PAUL *falls back as if momentarily blinded, and turns to run around the room as the nursery tune plays through once. He ends back at the chair, over which* THE ANGEL *now leans, looking into the blank white screen)*

PAUL: *(Quiet and intense)* He leaned on the edge of the balcony railing, overlooking the entire city.

THE ANGEL: *(Hissing, as he pulls back and sits into the chair)* I can see that.

PAUL: *(Holding his robe closed, and moving slowly sideways in front of the white screen, to the other side of the chair)*— clutched at the bathrobe as a breeze threatened but nothing came unbuttoned unless it was the mind, loosened by the breeze that did flow through so much. *(He leans in toward* THE ANGEL*)* Trains crackled under the electric wires, but that too builds into the Mind King's brain, or at least it went through into the eyes and then deeper—or was it wider?—first into the whole brain and, by a logically following network, into the whole body.

THE ANGEL: I see, the Mind King ventured, I am led by my ideas, but where do these ideas come from? *(He looks at PAUL, and rises. Then he approaches PAUL slowly, but suddenly grabs his face and pushes it forcefully, to face directly into the white screen. The tone rises and he runs out of the room and returns with a suitcase)* Marie still hadn't returned from shopping—*(He drops the suitcase onto the floor)* and he found himself led to the bathroom faucet, where, as the warm water, which had been cold at first, splashed over his wrists, he thought, "Wrists. Of course. *(Both he and PAUL are now looking at their exposed wrists)* Let me image a tribe of people, or a civilization even, that locates the mind THERE." *(A soft gong, and PAUL slowly extends his wrists in front of the white screen)* And it wasn't that he imagined cutting into them with a razor blade, but he did make the connection that since the blood was so close to the surface, he could locate the idea faintly there in the wrist. It took a certain effort, of course, but he was no stranger to effort. *(A soft gong. PAUL shifts into a more awkward position, still with wrists against the white screen)* In order to put this mental experiment into action, the Mind King lifted his two hands in preparation and headed toward the door through which he knew Marie would be eventually returning. Not that he went directly to the door. He found himself in the center of the room, thinking about a good and relatively comfortable place to wait, since it might be a considerable wait, and wondered if it would be psychologically more advantageous to remain uncomfortable and standing with, as it were, hands lifted, so that the wrists were exposed to the door. *(A single bell, and PAUL moves free of the screen)*

PAUL: Indeed . . . *(A gong)*

THE ANGEL: Indeed.

PAUL: Indeed.

THE ANGEL: Indeed, thought the Mind King.

PAUL: And he became relatively fascinated by that word.

THE ANGEL: Indeed.

PAUL: And he also noticed a clock and wished he could hear it ticking but of course he couldn't. *(A gong. And in the far shadows, ANNA MARIE slowly enters)*

THE ANGEL: *(Extending his own wrists again)* Having decided on the difficult course—but was it a "course" if he remained standing in place? *(Silence)* Of course it was, since the clock—which didn't, ticked in a very graphic way attached to the time passing, which was a stretch of time that matched nicely to the muscle strain that increased like a stretch, like a course of stretch as the strain became unbearable in his waiting position, though of course it was bearable, though it was unpleasant, and the clock helped or hindered. *(A gong)*

PAUL: When Marie did return, he heard the doorknob turning and the heart beat faster a bit, which movement there made the blood even more available for a moment in his wrists, and he said as she walked through the door, "Hello." *(They are both facing the silent ANNA MARIE. A gong sounds again, and she is slowly sitting, and THE ANGEL turns slowly away from her to continue speaking)*

THE ANGEL: And Marie of course immediately regarded his strange position with his wrists lifted and pointing toward the door, herself with a picture in her own mind, with a laugh that she interpreted as going back out through the door in any of several possible ways, and these all-possible, analyzed, which certainly the Mind King had available to him in a flash. (A gong)

PAUL: Hello, said the Mind King to himself as he lowered his wrists, and Marie said of course, What were you doing, and the Mind King explained, (Backing slowly away from ANNA MARIE) and Marie thought about it a bit and then came and laid her own wrist across his for a while. (A gong) They both smiled and the Mind King said, What did you get? Looking at the suitcase she had placed on the edge of the carpet.

THE ANGEL: Marie started to answer and the Mind King went, "Shhh," and lifted his free wrist, the one that Marie wasn't touching with her own, to his right ear and listened. (Both PAUL and ANNA MARIE have very slowly lifted a wrist to their own right ear) Could you believe, they stayed like that for fifteen minutes or so?

PAUL: Marie, after an interval, had performed a similar maneuver with her own available right wrist and ear. (A gong)

THE ANGEL: And after that fifteen minutes or so they both agreed it had been a very interesting experience but it probably wouldn't have general validity or widespread influence: and so they were content not to speak about it much, but sometimes they thought about what it had been like, and on rare occasions they referred to it. (A gong) For instance, two days later the Mind King says, "Give me your wrist. . . . " (Both THE ANGEL and PAUL start to turn slowly toward ANNA MARIE, extending their wrists, and ANNA MARIE slowly rises from her chair) . . . and Marie smiles, and does so. (A pause, as melancholy music is heard faintly. After a while, ANNA MARIE starts to exit, then she turns back to look at them, then turns back and exits more rapidly. THE ANGEL and PAUL lower their wrists, and speak softly, each to himself, somewhat overlapping one another)

THE ANGEL: Once upon a time, I said no to ambition. I wanted to be remembered.

PAUL: Once, I said no to belief. But I had to believe in something. *(They are both sitting at the table, in front of empty plates)*

PAUL: I said no to passion. The pain shifted.

THE ANGEL: Once, I said no to my own identity; the drift came to a halt. Too late, too late.

PAUL: I got trapped in my own categories.
. . . So I sat down to a big meal and picked at my food. *(Pause)*

THE ANGEL: Hungry?

PAUL: As always.
Always hungry.

THE ANGEL: Where am I?
Am I outside myself? *(PAUL has fallen asleep in his chair)* The imaginary lock, turned, opened—*(PAUL snorts himself awake, as the music changes. He rises and moves across the room, passing in front of THE ANGEL without looking at him)*

THE ANGEL: *(Rising)* A story is being told.
The best thing, is try and listen when a story is being told. *(Lights flash and fade, as THE ANGEL collapses to the floor as if knocked out by the light, but PAUL doesn't seem to notice and continues to cross and sits in the antique chair in front of the white screen, as the DEEP VOICE starts to speak and THE ANGEL slowly lifts himself from the floor)*

DEEP VOICE: A story is being told. Does it penetrate?
Much later, it penetrates
later, when sleep turns upside down,
and the blind eye feeds the illuminated ear

not for deep meaning,
but for the sleep of thought.
Look right now, he's right side up
pulled by the top of his head.
(*As the* VOICE *finishes,* THE ANGEL *has already lowered the white screen and come up behind* PAUL, *who sits in his chair, asleep again.* THE ANGEL *puts his hand on top of* PAUL's *head, pulling it abruptly back so that* PAUL *is looking to the ceiling the moment the* VOICE *has stopped)*

THE ANGEL: Right!!! . . . in a way.
    The Mind King often slept—that was his way of returning to the source, which the Mind King did as often as he could but not often enough.

PAUL: (*Rising*) When the void was entertained, the Mind King was entertained. He was empty inside—that's what he understood, finally. So he leaned against the wall and fell through an open window. (*A gong, and* THE ANGEL *freezes, while* PAUL *runs to the white hospital screen and holds onto it for safety*) . . . Fortunately, it was on one of the lower floors.

THE ANGEL: (*In a mocking squeak*) Help me. (*His voice returns to normal*) Unfortunately, it was on one of the lower floors, and so when the Mind King fell through—(*He hits his fist into his palm,* PAUL *cowers, and* THE ANGEL *laughs*) . . . he wasn't at all hurt, but he wasn't at all helped, either.

PAUL: It's true, he didn't do much floating through the air. And how, how, how? . . . did he come to be leaning against the wall? Was it instinct?

THE ANGEL: It was deeper than that.

PAUL: The Mind King—(*A single bell, and* PAUL *grabs the suitcase from the floor*) tumbling into the street—

THE ANGEL: (*Grabbing back the suitcase*)—the Mind King landing on his feet.

PAUL: (*Grabbing the suitcase back again, as* THE ANGEL *manages to grab at prayer shawl resembling* PAUL'S, *which hangs out of the suitcase, and he throws it over his shoulders*)—the Mind King looking back through the open window. (*He runs out of the room with the suitcase*)

THE ANGEL: (*Calling after* PAUL) Who calls?

PAUL: (*From the next room*) Was it the Mind King who said that? He turned back to the open window and opened his mouth wide.

THE ANGEL: (*Calling out through cupped hands*) Who calls? (*He sits, and holds his head*) The Mind King was inviting trouble. (*He jumps up and runs to the door through which* PAUL *exited, and shouts in his squeaky falsetto*) Help me!

PAUL: (*Reentering as the lights flash and fade to soft lilting music. He is now in a worn overcoat, a battered felt hat, and a white silk scarf. He hurries to lean on the nearest table*) The Mind King knew he was inviting trouble, and a man in a dark overcoat came striding no, more "walking down the corridor in his direction." I'm trying to sell you something, said the man in the overcoat—

THE ANGEL: (*Hitting his own head in anger*) No, I'm trying to sell YOU something, said the Mind King! (*Suddenly sad*) . . . but he didn't emphasize the "you," and the two of them sat down to dinner. But as it wasn't dinnertime—(*As he crosses the stage, his voice rises while his body rises on tiptoes*)—they sat down to—(*A single bell, as lights flash and fade*)—tea!

PAUL: Tea??

THE ANGEL: *(Seated at the table, rattling along as if being at-tacked by electric shocks)* To discuss things over tea! When tea was over they still hadn't attained the subject in ques-tion. I have my own proclivities and you have yours. They started talking both at once, but neither one found his or her sentence. What—? *(He stops, suddenly shocked)* Was the other one possibly . . . a she? *(He races, very upset, from the room as the lights flash and fade, and PAUL races to the back wall. And immediately, THE ANGEL returns with a life-sized dummy in his arms who seems to resemble ANNA MARIE. He whirls with her in his arms and bends her over the table as if to give her a kiss)*

PAUL: *(Angrily)* The Mind King asked both of them to take off any disguises that either of them might have been hiding behind. *(THE ANGEL looks at PAUL, and slowly starts exiting with the dummy)* That proved nothing, and the subject at hand—*(A single bell)* . . . proved to be no real subject at all. So the Mind King headed off in his direction *(The music changes, and is now a faint chorus of women's voices)* . . . and the other person headed off in his or her direction and then, later—ensconced—*(The lights flash and fade)* . . . each of them went through a series of simi-lar experiences, ending up with the departure into a series of different directions, *(The lights flash and fade)* . . . so there was in fact a kind of yoke or link, between the many different locales, I needn't name them, that all the many different people ended up inhabiting. *(PAUL is now leaning against the cabinet, staring into a bright light that comes from the next room, lending an autumnal glow to the rear wall. THE ANGEL has reentered and stands behind PAUL, looking into the same beautiful light)* The Mind King was in his room. He tried, very hard he tried, not to let the image of another place or time pop into his consciousness. *(THE ANGEL turns suddenly and enters the closet, slamming the door, which startles PAUL)*

THE ANGEL: *(From behind the door)* But of course that was very difficult and those pops did occur. *(He reenters, wiping his hands on a white towel)* So . . . he slept a bit—

PAUL: *(Turning away from the cabinet, also holding a white towel)* His usual solution.

THE ANGEL: —and come what may, he went on in similar directions. *(He looks at PAUL)* Choose one! *(A gong)*

PAUL: Why choose . . . just one?

THE ANGEL: *(Looking slowly up into the light, grinning stupidly)* What's happening?

PAUL: *(Frozen, mid-movement)* When nothing happens I'm in my element. *(He lifts his head, slowly)* Ultra-polite, a half smile.

THE ANGEL: *(Still grinning)* Me too, my face scrubbed with language. *(A single bell, and they both, slowly, react as if they were trying not to vomit, the white towels covering their mouths)* What happened?

PAUL: *(Looking up slowly, as a tone is heard)* I reswallowed an alphabet.

THE ANGEL: What happened?

PAUL: When nothing happens—I'm in my element.

THE ANGEL: Me too. I twist and turn, just like you. *(A woman's chorus is again heard in the distance)*

PAUL: *(Looking up at a long white screen, near the top of the room, with small golden propellers protruding from it, which have started to revolve)* Clocks—! Tick me into the unavoidable river.

THE ANGEL: Yes. And the clock says, what clocks always say:
(In a tiny voice) Okay. Okay!

PAUL: Right.

THE ANGEL: Okay. I see a hole.

PAUL: Whatever it is, I don't like it.

THE ANGEL: So? Let's hear the bad news: fast.

PAUL: Everybody tried to get a grip on reality.
      And after a while
      Reality got spoiled for that very reason. (PAUL has been
      slowly approaching THE ANGEL. As he gets to him, he stops
      moving. Frozen with his arms slightly up in the air)

THE ANGEL: (Hypnotically) Move nothing. Touch nothing. (PAUL
      lets out a sigh and sags. THE ANGEL relifts his arms) Let
      everything remain as is. (He touches him on the chin, and
      PAUL comes back to consciousness)

PAUL: Here was somebody, going through his life, not control-
      ling anything, not talking well, not with a sense of direc-
      tion but just coming out, sometimes, with phrases which,
      because of the way they were placed, seemed to have a very
      oracular significance. (He looks out over the audience, and
      smiles strangely, extending his arms halfway) What a per-
      fect life. (Holding this position, he slowly turns to look
      directly upstage at the cabinet, and the illuminated giant
      light bulb that sits on top) What a wonderful life.

THE ANGEL: (Punching him lightly on the arm) Hey, whaddaya
      say; you and me; let's team up.

PAUL: (Pulling away, as the music changes, becoming lively and
      aggressive) First! Hand me a letter!

THE ANGEL: Ah! A story is being written.

Somebody opens a letter. It's empty—an empty envelope. *(They are racing around the room, picking up and casting aside the referred-to objects)*

PAUL: Somebody finds the blank sheet of paper; a name is missing; nevertheless it flutters to the floor.

THE ANGEL: The envelope wasn't empty after all. There was a blank piece of paper.

PAUL: Somebody can't escape writing something—

THE ANGEL: What?

PAUL: —on the blank piece of paper. Do we claim in retrospect that the envelope wasn't empty?

THE ANGEL: For instance: The universe decides to be a cloud.

PAUL: A cloud . . .

THE ANGEL: It feels sick—and this is the first time that human beings know a cloud could feel sick.

PAUL: *(Holding his head)* When a cloud feels sick, it is more aware of its physical being than when it feels . . . okay.

THE ANGEL: Right. *(He races to stand on a chair and points to the propellers whirling in front of the white screen)* An airplane flies through the cloud. This is irrelevant, except to indicate how everything depends on something else to exist.

PAUL: Me.

THE ANGEL: *(Jumping down from his chair)* Me!

PAUL: ME!!!

> *(THE ANGEL races to the closet, as PAUL races up to the cabinet, and as they both pull open respective doors, they tumble backwards to the sound of breaking glass)*

PAUL: Yessss! *(THE ANGEL recovers and jumps into the closet)* The cabinet was open, and the Mind King collected items, and as his hands slid over these items, several flowers tumbled to the ground. *(He races off into the next room as THE ANGEL races in from the closet)*

THE ANGEL: I've reached the point, he offered—*(Lights flash and fade)*—where I'm doing too much THINKING about the conclusions of the things I'm starting to think about.

PAUL: *(In suddenly from the next room)* He allowed his head to whirl—

THE ANGEL: *(Pivoting—in a squeaky voice)* Help me.

PAUL: Then, guess what.

> *(The lights flash and fade, as ANNA MARIE'S naked arm is seen moving in from the door behind PAUL, her hand sliding along the wall)*

THE ANGEL: Something alert on the page in front of his eyes, twisted under his fingers—is this my wooden pencil? *(PAUL tries to catch the hand, but it is pulled away as he misses and hits the wall with his body)* But he was holding somebody's hand. *(He jumps back onto the chair beneath the screen with the whirling propellers)* A boat went by the window—wet? It had things spinning, on its sides—*(Lights flash and fade)* Are those propellers? Since he was in bed with a bad cold—didn't that happen fast—somebody else agreed to lie down on top of him and warm him up.

PAUL: *(With the towel over his head like a kerchief)* That person was over the covers—*(A single bell)*—while he was under the covers.

THE ANGEL: The only color in the room was a very dark gray color on the walls, and the Mind King said out loud—*(The music changes)*—music would jar my nerves. It would give a suggestion of language, but it would be . . . SMOOTHER— than I want to be in my language! *(He jumps down from the chair)*

DEEP VOICE: *(Over the loudspeakers, as the music cuts off)* The Mind King speaking in the third person only, in the third person only.

PAUL: Do I feel like this because the temperature outside is unseasonably cool?

(THE ANGEL races to embrace PAUL, as the lights flash and fade. Then he steps away and ties his own wrists together again with a rope, as PAUL turns sadly and goes out of the room)

DEEP VOICE: *(As the music returns)*
Speaking . . . speaking
in the third person only.

THE ANGEL: *(Coming slowly to a downstage chair to sit)* He wanted to sleep. I speak of myself in the third person. He wanted to sleep, released into a true world of impulse. Because it is true—*(The music changes, and the woman's chorus is heard faintly)*—the vast majority of his impulses were never acted upon—smothered by consciousness, a shame, but unavoidable for everybody except the Mind King. *(His voice turns harsh, and he rises)* Everybody else, frantically churning in reaction to multiple impulses—
never acted out—
never known—

but in sleep; functional only in sleep!

Which is why HE, speaking in the third person, WANTED to sleep!

That seemed REALLY exciting to him! *(He pauses)* . . . who continued to speak in the third person. So that inside and outside could be the same thing. *(He is standing next to the long table parallel to the wall to the audience's right. And he lies back upon the table, swinging his feet up, so he is stretched out as if asleep)*

PAUL: *(Who has reappeared at the other end of the table)* I knew it from the beginning.

I'm at the edge of sleep. Is it true?

THE ANGEL: *(As if speaking in his sleep)* Plunge in . . . now . . . *(He rolls onto his side)* Now . . .

PAUL: *(Advancing slowly down the table, as the music builds)* He doesn't know if he hesitates, or if this is where he wants to be, so moving forward is unnatural, and he doesn't even . . . try . . .

(The music is much louder now, and the lights are shining with mystical intensity. THE ANGEL slowly rises and pivots and steps onto the floor, and then both THE ANGEL and PAUL, moving at the same time, slowly, both lean back against the table, and swing their bodies and legs up so they are both stretched out, in identical positions, at different places on the same table)

DEEP VOICE: Speaking in the third person only.

PAUL: *(Lifting his head)* At the very edge of experience, he jumped.

THE ANGEL: *(Lifting his head)* He could have done that.

PAUL: At the very edge of experience, he withdrew.

THE ANGEL: He could have done that also.

(They both slowly move to the floor again, as the music rises. They take a slow step in unison away from the table, as if moving toward something wonderful on the opposite side of the room. Then they hesitate as the VOICE speaks)

DEEP VOICE: This nervous energy did whirl the Mind King into his mirror image . . . *(They both retreat a step and turn to look at each other)* and was the image in the mirror the same thing . . . *(Each reaches slowly to touch his own face)* or the opposite thing?
That was in fact, the same thing,
the second thing,
the third thing. *(Their hands have fallen, and they slowly return to their positions, lying, without moving, as if in the depth of sleep, on the long table)* Within an hour, life took care of everything, answered his questions as he might have known: . . . but of course he did know that all along, and he didn't even have to think about knowing it.
   Because body, mind, everything went into action without a moment's hesitation as a bell rang, a door opened, new people came and went . . . including the Mind King . . . and the weather changed. *(The light gets more intense)* The darkness lifted.
   Which just meant, of course, that it went someplace else, for a while.

(The voices of the women singing get louder, the light changes again, and as PAUL and THE ANGEL lie there immobile on the table, the music slowly cross fades to the sounds of a tiny electric church organ, playing a popular, revival-belt-style Sunday church service hymn, and the lights, very slowly, fade to darkness)

THE END

Samuel's Major Problems. Produced by the Ontological-Hysteric Theater at the Ontological at St. Mark's Theater, N.Y.C. January–March 1993. Written, directed, and designed by Richard Foreman.

SAMUEL:	Thomas Jay Ryan
MARIE HELENE:	Jill Dreskin
DR. MARTINO:	Steven Rattazzi

Late at night, in a room where a party has taken place. A room with many shelves and cabinets, heavily festooned with streamers and balloons that hang down touching the Oriental carpets covering the floor. Loose papers and confetti are also scattered over the floor, along with some overturned chairs. The walls are dotted with many small pictures of human skulls. Some real skulls are also mixed in with the books and strange objects on the shelves. Gold letters and mysterious signs and diagrams gleam from dark corners.

A wall of transparent plastic separates the stage from the audience, and depending upon the light illuminating a particular scene, the audience often sees a ghostlike reflection of itself on the transparent wall, overlaying the image of the performance. Behind this wall, the actors wear radio mikes on headsets, which enables them to speak in hushed tones throughout the play, with the deliberate slowness of someone muttering to themselves. There is also continual music throughout, soft repetitive loops of a measure or two of music, which only occasionally crest in volume to accompany a dance or a more violent action.

As the play begins, dance music played on a solo accordion is heard coming from the next room, then the sound of party horns as MARIE HELENE and DR. MARTINO chase a disheveled SAMUEL into the room. His coat is off, his tie is undone. He is a hulking figure who seems to be a hunchback, slightly drunk from the night of partygoing, and he shuffles away from them to the far corner of the dimly lit room. All are wearing paper hats.

MARIE HELENE takes a piece of paper from the shelf and holds it out to SAMUEL. After several tries, he snatches it from her, and stumbles to a chair where he reads the piece

*of paper. The music has faded, and we hear, softly over the
loudspeakers, voices chattering a rapidly spoken gibberish.*

SAMUEL: *(Reading, his voice deep and husky)* He had death in
his arms . . .

MARIE HELENE: Come again?

SAMUEL: *(Looking away from his paper)* I hug death in my arms
and dance with her.

MARIE HELENE: Her? What makes it a "she," Samuel?

SAMUEL: In my case, that's all.

MARIE HELENE: Ah. In finding nothing, you found beauty? *(She
blows her horn once in his face)*

SAMUEL: *(Looking up at her)* Come again? *(She moves away as
the dance music rises, and SAMUEL holds out his arms to her
and whispers huskily)* Come again? *(The music increases,
a bell tolls, and SAMUEL takes a few lurching dance steps
toward MARIE HELENE, hissing out, "Please! Please!" with
each step. DR. MARTINO blows his horn, and MARIE HELENE
circles around to stand by a chair at the rear. SAMUEL
follows her, and slowly sinks into the chair as the music
fades and DR. MARTINO leaves the room)*

SAMUEL: *(Slowly pondering each word)* Sometimes, it was rain
that did it to Samuel.
I mean sometimes, it was his brain.
It got away too fast.

MARIE HELENE: Running?

SAMUEL: Not raining?

MARIE HELENE: Sometimes, a word slipped.
    A word made a mental slip.

SAMUEL: *(Looking off to the light)*
    It would be perfect if
    when it rained
    water fell to earth.

MARIE HELENE: But it does.

SAMUEL: It would be perfect
    if tall houses
    had open windows.

MARIE HELENE: *(She has stretched out on the carpet)*
    It would be perfect
    if trees bent. *(The soft sound of voices chattering has returned)*
    That would be perfect.
    Was the sun out?
    It was too bright to tell.

SAMUEL: It would be perfect
    if shoes and socks
    went together.
    Perfect
    if dictionaries
    filled with words.

MARIE HELENE: Name some.

SAMUEL: I don't know where to begin.

MARIE HELENE: I'm in the same boat.

    (The music changes, and a voice sings softly "Smile, Smile, Smile . . . ")

SAMUEL: Perfect
  if the color of the sky kept changing. *(He hides his eyes from the light)*
  And it does.

MARIE HELENE: Yes. But I see a certain consistency.

SAMUEL: That's perfect.

MARIE HELENE: Then we agree.

SAMUEL: It would be perfect if you'd write to me.

MARIE HELENE: I'm talking.

SAMUEL: It's half and half.

MARIE HELENE: That's perfect.

SAMUEL: I couldn't put everything into a letter. *(Wistful violin music is heard)*

MARIE HELENE: You could try.

SAMUEL: No.

MARIE HELENE: You could fool me.

SAMUEL: I did.

MARIE HELENE: *(As she runs out)* Then it's perfect!

SAMUEL: *(Alone)* Houses are perfect, trees are perfect, rain, sky, shoes, rocks, birds, tables, those are perfect: but that's not everything. I've run out of categories.

MARIE HELENE: *(Returns with a big dictionary she plops down on the shelf beside Samuel)* It would be perfect if you said just one more word!

SAMUEL: *(Slowly turning away from the book)* I hope I choose the right one.

MARIE HELENE: What's your choice?

SAMUEL: *(After a pause)* I'm buttoning my lip.

MARIE HELENE: Buttons are perfect. Lips are perfect. *(She leans forward and kisses him, ending on his lap)*
It would be perfect
if there was something that wasn't perfect.

SAMUEL: We'll never know, for sure.

MARIE HELENE: Sad?

SAMUEL: Could be.

(The music has imperceptibly changed, as it will continue to change every few lines of dialogue, throughout the entire play)

MARIE HELENE: Here. Take my perfect handkerchief. *(She takes a white silk cloth from her bodice, which he takes and presses to his forehead in pain, rising from his chair)*

MARIE HELENE: *(Backing away)* Oh, no—not like that! *(She screams as SAMUEL collapses to the floor, and she runs out of the room. A DEEP VOICE speaks over the loudspeakers, and SAMUEL struggles to his feet and comes toward the glass wall)*

DEEP VOICE: Dream versus hypnotism, Samuel. Those are your two alternatives. In one, you surge into your own wave. In

the other, you wake into following orders. But the third
alternative—

SAMUEL: Samuel thought there were just two—

DEEP VOICE: —awake, and simultaneously free. Called death,
Samuel. That's why it's as appealing as sin.

SAMUEL: Could it be that I toasted the second-rate, under the
impression that compassionate meant "hero"?

*(MARIE HELENE has reentered in the shadows carrying an-
other toy horn and a bouquet of roses. She blows the horn
once)*

MARIE HELENE: Awake to that a little too soon, Samuel. Confusion
was not the recipe.

SAMUEL: But the angel of that persuasion
caps a lifetime of energy
with a slow lift-off
into a name-that-tuneless
everybody sings
ad infinitum.

MARIE HELENE: How to be friends—a smile says it best. But I
covered, of course, my own mouth first. *(She moves away,
as DR. MARTINO crosses the rear of the room, goes to a
bookcase to take down a bottle, and pours himself a drink)*

SAMUEL: *(Turning away)* There are people too smart for me. They
make me dizzy, so I make a big effort to get on top of those
things—and my head muscles contract, as if my head were
trying to jump to the very top of those things it was very
hard to understand.

DR. MARTINO: Of course, Samuel. Some people mentally outdis-
tance you.

SAMUEL: They do. They do do that.

DR. MARTINO: Is there a solution to this problem?

SAMUEL: Yes. I should stop trying to understand what's hard.

DR. MARTINO: That's not how to achieve things, Samuel.

SAMUEL: But you don't understand. It does bad things to my head muscles.

DR. MARTINO: One could disagree.

SAMUEL: Don't, please.

DR. MARTINO: Exercise is good, Samuel.

SAMUEL: But so is relaxation.

MARIE HELENE: Both are good.

DR. MARTINO: They should alternate.

MARIE HELENE: Good luck. 1, 2, 3, 4, 5, 6, 7, 8, 9, 10. *(She and DR. MARTINO make a run around SAMUEL, who spins, trying to keep them in his field of vision, even though their circles are in opposite directions, and SAMUEL staggers dizzily as the others leave the room)*

SAMUEL: Alone now, I feel— *(He checks his watch)*—a little more comfortable. *(He picks up a piece of paper from the floor)* I think I'll make a few notes to myself on this discarded piece of paper.

DR. MARTINO: *(Reentering)* What are you doing, Samuel? *(SAMUEL crumples the paper and tosses it away)*

SAMUEL: Just wasting time, in a sense. Please don't try to assure me I haven't lost my bearings.

DR. MARTINO: Is that your subjective impression?

SAMUEL: It must have been something you did to me once.

DR. MARTINO: On purpose?

SAMUEL: I don't know.

DR. MARTINO: I don't know either. (*SAMUEL, frowns, goes to uncrumple the paper*) What the hell are you looking for?

SAMUEL: I bring good news that I can't quite remember.

DR. MARTINO: Then it must have been somebody else first . . . bringing you such "good news."

SAMUEL: I can't remember, so I'm relatively free to plunge into my own invention. (*As MARIE HELENE reenters and offers him an unsliced melon, which resembles a human brain*) What is this? Something to eat?

DR. MARTINO: Why not? That's the sociable thing to do.

SAMUEL: Maybe I'm not so hungry.

DR. MARTINO: Did I forget to tell you? I'm here for a reason.

SAMUEL: That means you tricked me.

DR. MARTINO: About what?

(*SAMUEL has crossed upstage, where he discovers a cabinet with a door, large enough to walk into. He moves his hands across the door's surface*)

SAMUEL: I feel disoriented.

DEEP VOICE: *(Over the loudspeaker)* In a small room, a cabinet held things inside. People who passed through the room, or did things in the room, occasionally saw the cabinet open. People who entered the room infrequently, or just once in their entire lives—many of those people never saw the cabinet open, never saw its insides. *(SAMUEL backs away suspiciously)* But they did not doubt that it held things. Which made it, therefore, acceptable as a cabinet.

DR. MARTINO: Maybe— I tricked you, once upon a time. It's possible I've forgotten.

SAMUEL: That would be good news.

DR. MARTINO: Why?

SAMUEL: I'd like to think you weren't totally in control of your faculties.

DR. MARTINO: Why?

SAMUEL: I'd be in a better position.

DR. MARTINO: You can rest assured I'm not totally in control of my faculties.

SAMUEL: If I turn away from you, it's because I want to rest my eyes. Looking at you, I find it impossible to make the mental jumps that seem important to me. *(A pause. He is staring into space with his back to DR. MARTINO)* Anybody there? *(Pause)* I wonder how long I've really been alone. The dangerous feeling in my limbs must be something that has roots in a more fluid period of my life. That said, I can of course bow my head to the inevitable. But be careful. Language running away with itself means the eyes stumble, as if eyes had legs. *(He has twisted one foot over the other, and now, as the voice of someone singing "Smile, Smile" is heard again, he pivots suddenly, which re-aligns his feet, but he wobbles from the maneuver and laughs at himself in amazement)* Well, they do.

DR. MARTINO: You know, I haven't been looking at you. But I have been listening.

SAMUEL: What I heard from your corner of the room washed over me, doctor.

DR. MARTINO: Indeed.

SAMUEL: Like a very deep ocean, but since I don't swim . . .

DR. MARTINO: Indeed.

SAMUEL: I just ducked my head into the next wave and came up for no air at all. But it turned out to be air. Was I dead or alive?

DR. MARTINO: That's optional.

SAMUEL: Oh, no. That's never optional.

DR. MARTINO: *(Smiling)* I should know.

SAMUEL: Why should you know?

DR. MARTINO: Hello, I'm death, of course. *(He is crossing slowly toward SAMUEL)* I'll probably be hanging around for the next, oh—twenty years or so.

SAMUEL: Will I get to like you?

DR. MARTINO: Oh, I'm likable. *(He offers his hand in friendship)* If you dig deep enough.

SAMUEL: Let's say, confounding all expectations we become friends. *(Taking his hand)* What can you do for me?

DR. MARTINO: *(Pulling away upset)* Oh please—! Nothing! Hands off—PLEASE! *(He runs out and SAMUEL would follow but, confused, opens the door to the cabinet instead, and stares into it, fascinated)*

DR. MARTINO: *(Reentering behind SAMUEL)* Figure it out, Samuel, whatever one experiences? Well—think about something else.

SAMUEL: *(Slamming the door closed)* Easy to say. But even if all stress gets eliminated, I suppose there would still remain disease certainly, and death certainly.

DR. MARTINO: *(Carefully spreading a white cloth on the floor)* You leave out the most important consideration.

SAMUEL: I would have thought death was the most important.

DR. MARTINO: Death? Not quite. New beginnings. Back to childhood itself—fingers and toes hyperactive, twitching, just for the sake of allowing energy to throb through that tiny body.

SAMUEL: Me?

DR. MARTINO: You. *(He is kneeling on the floor now, behind the cloth)* Because all living things are driven by a heart that pulsates. Yes—pulsations racing blindly through the entire body, frantically grasping for activities upon which to attach themselves, glued intimate and tight. *(He is now crawling across the floor toward SAMUEL, who is also down on all fours)* Usually such activities—the normal ones chosen from among the objects life offers, friend Samuel—career, family, achievements of the sort that are the sort of activities that are a normal kind of living. *(In front of*

SAMUEL, *he whispers to him)* All necessary in a sense, because turning one's back on such things, trying to be alone for any length of time, unsupported by the trivia of normal life among normal human beings—what happens? Well, friend Samuel, to a very few it happens that they dissolve into the reputed white light—read as translation for something unspeakable, of course—but to most it means when pulsations from the center find no external object upon which to glue themselves, they rebound onto the self, and shake it in a way that is much more than disruptive. And that twitch, that pulsation, turning back upon the host . . . poisons, Samuel. The self, poisoning the self. *(He stands up, chuckling to himself)* In other words—what Samuel is doing is very dangerous. Be re-involved, friend Samuel.

SAMUEL: No. I choose to risk it.

DR. MARTINO: Party's over.

SAMUEL: What party?

DR. MARTINO: *(Pouring himself another drink)* Well, not a real party.

SAMUEL: What was it? *(The babble of voices rises again, and DR. MARTINO picks up a party horn and blows it, producing momentary silence)*

DR. MARTINO: Pretending.

SAMUEL: Isn't that a party?

DR. MARTINO: You're under a misapprehension.

(In the shadows at the back of the room, MARIE HELENE enters carrying a birthday cake with lit candles)

SAMUEL: Then I escaped from one kind of misapprehension into another.

DR. MARTINO: What a tortuous route.

SAMUEL: Nah, I'm just holding a head that echoes where the hair starts. Space travel.

DR. MARTINO: Me too, Samuel, tip to toe—matched, aligned, to every one of your mental trajectories.

MARIE HELENE: *(Advancing slowly with her cake, she whispers softly)* Happy birthday.
     This is for you.
     But I wouldn't eat it.

SAMUEL: Why?

MARIE HELENE: I made it special.

SAMUEL: Is it a kind of poison?

MARIE HELENE: Well, not poison, but a kind of emotional poison. So I wouldn't eat it.

SAMUEL: Is there an alternative?

MARIE HELENE: Well . . . eat it, and find out.

SAMUEL: *(Turning away, to pour himself a drink)* Birthdays don't mean very much to me.

MARIE HELENE: I'm going to cut this cake. Right now. *(She takes a big knife from the shelf)* Right here and now. (*SAMUEL* turns away, and *MARIE HELENE*, seeing this, becomes irritated and stabs him in the arm. *SAMUEL* screams in pain)

DR. MARTINO: *(Smiling)* How about that?

SAMUEL: *(Staggers to a chair, holding his wound)* Now—this is a real problem!

DR. MARTINO: Right. This is a real problem. How best to deal with this?

MARIE HELENE: I'd suggest a tourniquet. *(SAMUEL follows her advice by taking off his belt and winding it around his arm)* I'd suggest calling a doctor. *(SAMUEL goes to a phone and dials)*

SAMUEL: *(After listening to the phone)* By mistake—I got the weather report.

MARIE HELENE: Try Information.

SAMUEL: But this—this is pure information. Fifty-seven degrees, north by northwest, southerly something—

MARIE HELENE: I better wash that dirty knife. *(She runs off, but peeks back in immediately as SAMUEL sneaks up to the cake, which has been left on a shelf, and puts out a finger to lick some of the icing)*

MARIE HELENE: *(Hissing at him)* Don't you dare touch that cake while I have my back turned!

SAMUEL: *(Stops, caught in the act)* Your attitude re-reminds me of all responsibilities concerning politeness.

DR. MARTINO: She's not speaking from a position of polite. She's speaking from a position of right and wrong.

SAMUEL: It was wrong to hurt me.

DR. MARTINO: *(Taking the cake away from SAMUEL)* Oh no it wasn't, it was a lesson. One you needed badly.

SAMUEL: What could I learn from this lesson?

DR. MARTINO: It could have been a verbal lesson. She could have made it a verbal lesson. (*MARIE HELENE enters as a doctor, with bag and stethoscope*)

MARIE HELENE: Who telephoned for a doctor, please?

SAMUEL: I got the weather report by mistake.

MARIE HELENE: Clever.

SAMUEL: Oh?

MARIE HELENE: I see you're wounded. (*She helps him remove his jacket*)

SAMUEL: Yes, but was it self-inflicted? Probably not.

MARIE HELENE: I don't think so either. I see you have a birthday.

SAMUEL: Yes.

MARIE HELENE: I hope it wasn't supposed to be your last.

SAMUEL: That never occurred to me. (*She takes the cake and offers it to him with a smile, as the music gets louder, as it often does when there is a pause in the dialogue. SAMUEL looks at the cake, then turns away nervously*) Now I'm of two minds. . . .

DEEP VOICE: (*Over the loudspeaker*) After a day preparing oneself for adventure, what finally happened was viewable only as excess, because the unexpected, however tiny—

DR. MARTINO: (*Interrupting the tape*) Wait a minute. See any specific doors into this room? (*SAMUEL and DR. MARTINO* look *wildly about, then run out of the room through sepa-rate exits, leaving MARIE HELENE alone)*

DEEP VOICE: *(As they run out of the room)* Erase that. Reerase that.

SAMUEL: *(His voice is heard over the loudspeaker, though he is still out of the room)* I remember at least one.

DR. MARTINO: *(Also out of the room)* Then somebody must have used it at least once.

SAMUEL: Excuse me, I don't see the relationship between the way into this room and this chair I'm evidently sitting on.

DR. MARTINO: It's called a door.

SAMUEL: This? This thing I'm sitting on?

DR. MARTINO: Wait a minute—now you have ME confused! *(They both run back into the room and find chairs to sit on)*

SAMUEL: Excuse me, but how did you get here?

MARIE HELENE: Didn't somebody—"telephone"? *(There is a flash of light as both SAMUEL and DR. MARTINO fall off their chairs.)*

DEEP VOICE:
Ah, adventures with electricity.
Propellers on all things that move.
He who smiles through space.

SAMUEL: *(As the chattering tape is heard again, replacing the music)* You know how it is. One telephones, but often the mind plays tricks—*(SAMUEL comes down to the glass wall and feels it with his hands)*—for instance, two numbers may be reversed because your mind goes blank and you try to do the whole number by rote, but there's a reversal.

MARIE HELENE: Which could operate in other realms.

SAMUEL: Yes.

MARIE HELENE: Not just numbers.

SAMUEL: Excuse me, doctor—isn't everything, ultimately, numbers?

MARIE HELENE: Oh-oh—you shouldn't have spilled the beans, Samuel.

SAMUEL: If that's true . . .

MARIE HELENE: Forget I said it.

(The chattering has been replaced by a sustained note of music, which rises as DR. MARTINO is thrown off his chair by an invisible force)

DR. MARTINO: What is this?

SAMUEL: What are you doing? *(He is watching as MARIE HELENE slowly advances on him with a loaded hypodermic needle)*

MARIE HELENE: This should make Samuel forget, well, anything he might have heard that he shouldn't have heard. I hope he's not afraid? Anyway, it's for his own protection.

SAMUEL: Is that true?

MARIE HELENE: Really. Yes, it's true. *(She gives him a long, slow injection)*

SAMUEL: *(Rubbing his arm, turning to stare out a large window through which an unearthly light now streams)* You know—there was something special about today, but I can't remember what.

MARIE HELENE: I'm a little disappointed you haven't made a pass at your physician.

SAMUEL: Isn't it better to keep such relationships professional?

MARIE HELENE: Samuel! Where did you hear that? *(She kisses him, but he pulls gently away)*

SAMUEL: Please. Don't try to rewrite all my beliefs in one fell swoop.

MARIE HELENE: Hey, never turn your back on us, Samuel!

(MARIE HELENE and DR. MARTINO both suddenly pull swords from bookcase shelves, and a frightened SAMUEL runs from the room. MARIE HELENE and DR. MARTINO each have dinner plates, and they advance with drawn swords upon the birthday cake)

DEEP VOICE: An effort was made, to reach the very summit, of experience, but experience, as usual, belied the true state of things, and as it faded— *(They are trying to cut into the cake with their swords, but as they do so, they begin to feel ill, and sink to the floor)*—whispers of its unsatisfactory nature reached everyone involved. Though the sad fact was that everyone involved was not prepared to allow that particular nuance to redirect an entire lifetime of effort. So it remained, once again, for art to stand in for reality.

SAMUEL: *(Backing slowly into the room)* My propellered self, smiling the usual smiles. *(He turns and races down to touch the glass wall)*

MARIE HELENE:
> He, porcupine with propellers.
> Suspended in space by sharpness.

SAMUEL:
> Fables of identity with no tears,
> a self-congratulatory search for permanent glue—
> the attachment to chairs, kitchen utensils,
> the touch of amazing foods, lifted into the air.
> (*DR. MARTINO lifts the cake, and slowly revolves*)
> But wait a minute—

MARIE HELENE: That's why you're still here.

SAMUEL: Here, here I am, questioning that fact.

(*A loud note sounds, sending everyone scurrying to different corners of the room*)

DEEP VOICE: And the universe answers Samuel, saying, I invented the electricity of such pregnant moments, self-swimming, through my own depths of invention.

SAMUEL: You see my point? If I tried to escape and was not successful, and so returned somehow, here to this very chair, I still have to ask, Why precisely here? (*He is on his feet, as DR. MARTINO stands before him, holding out a sword. SAMUEL lunges, and seems to fall on the sword, as a voice on tape again sings, "Smile, smile," and SAMUEL revolves, in seeming pain, which turns into a laugh as he reveals he hasn't impaled himself on the sword, but only captured it under his arm*) In other words, I don't disappear into my chair, do I? No, I don't disappear into my own chair. Here I am. (*He presents himself*) And Samuel says, the propellers that whirl on my body tilt, my whole body.

DR. MARTINO: Jesus Christ, Samuel, are you repeating yourself?

SAMUEL: Impossible.

MARIE HELENE: Hello again. Is something different?

SAMUEL: Yes.

MARIE HELENE: Yes, but what?

SAMUEL: The world . . . turns into the goddamn total universe! (*The music rises, as SAMUEL pulls a coffinlike box into the room, and DR. MARTINO and MARIE HELENE race to find chairs and sit. SAMUEL slowly opens the lid of the coffin, looks in, then slams the lid down, and as he does so, falls backward onto the carpet*)

DEEP VOICE: Erase that. Reerase that.

DR. MARTINO: (*Referring to the coffin, as SAMUEL slowly reopens it, and slowly steps inside, kneeling with his back to the others*) Some nights he's inside it, some nights not.

MARIE HELENE: You know, I'm beginning to see things from your perspective.

SAMUEL: Whatever can she be talking about?

MARIE HELENE: I admit something, I don't like talking to the back of somebody's head.

SAMUEL: Let me assure you, it's impossible to really talk to yourself. (*Pause*) I've tried.

MARIE HELENE: What happens?

SAMUEL: It's a regular conversation.

MARIE HELENE: Who butts in on such a conversation?

SAMUEL: *(Slowly twists to her)* Hard to identify, but it happens.

MARIE HELENE: Funny—you're looking straight at me—

SAMUEL: *(Stepping slowly out of the coffin)* I have to confess my eyes wander a little. A gaze that isn't a hundred percent steady. *(He slams down the lid of the coffin and again falls backwards onto the carpet, as a loud tone fills the air and* MARIE HELENE *whirls once in place, and* DR. MARTINO *runs from the room. The light flashes once and then becomes very dim)*

MARIE HELENE: It's your propellers at work, Samuel.

SAMUEL: *(On the carpet)* The whole universe is at work.

MARIE HELENE: Really, it must be a bad habit.

SAMUEL: Maybe something even more serious. Please. Take my pulse.

MARIE HELENE: It won't help.

SAMUEL: Take my pulse.

MARIE HELENE: I've lost the habit.

SAMUEL: *(A deep whispered growl)* Please!

MARIE HELENE: Don't think I'm frightened, I'm just interested in maintaining the idea of perspective.

SAMUEL: That's how the world works, but let me remind you—

MARIE HELENE: I know. This isn't the world, it's the universe.

SAMUEL: I must be hearing things.

MARIE HELENE: Does it go bumpity-bump; thump-thump? *(He is on his hands and knees by now, and she is standing over him. She gently pushes him with her foot, causing him to roll over on his back, looking up at her)*

SAMUEL: Ah—more habits.

MARIE HELENE: You want your pulse taken?

SAMUEL: Please. *(She circles him, and slowly lies down on top of his body. His arms enfold her, as she whispers the beats of his abnormally slow pulse)*

MARIE HELENE: One and two and three and four and five and six and . . . *(She falls silent in his arms)* What's happening?

SAMUEL: I don't know. What's my pulse rate?

MARIE HELENE: This is crazy, but—

SAMUEL: Tell me.

MARIE HELENE: I don't know if it's your pulse rate or my own pulse rate.

SAMUEL: I could swear I was talking to myself.

MARIE HELENE: *(Lifting herself off his body in irritation)* Didn't you tell me that wasn't possible? *(They scuttle away from each other on all fours, as DR. MARTINO enters, amused to see what is happening)*

DR. MARTINO: Hello again.

SAMUEL: I bet you could have arranged it to come in thirty seconds earlier.

DR. MARTINO: But why?

SAMUEL: It would have clarified something.

DR. MARTINO: What?

SAMUEL: You notice something different? Or is that just my perspective?

DR. MARTINO: I'm not aware of any perspectives.

SAMUEL: Go on.

DR. MARTINO: *(Slowly moving to sit on the edge of the open coffin)* Certainly. You're neither sitting in your appropriate chair, nor facing toward the most important object in this room. And Dr. Marie Helene isn't performing the usual professional services.

SAMUEL: Those seem irrelevant.

DR. MARTINO: I mention it, because I now also feel a little dizzy. *(He slips into the coffin, half holding on so his head and feet are still visible)*

SAMUEL AND MARIE HELENE: *(As he falls)* Don't sit!

DR. MARTINO: *(From his awkward position)* Was that two of you talking at one time?

SAMUEL: Yes.

DR. MARTINO: Why? Or is that just my perspective on things?

SAMUEL: It was a momentary . . .

DR. MARTINO: What? *(A pause)*

SAMUEL: Language . . .

DR. MARTINO: What?

SAMUEL: . . . fails me here. It runs out of steam.

DR. MARTINO: But not completely.

SAMUEL: Which means I keep talking to myself because other people don't seem to come up with desirable alternatives.

DR. MARTINO: Try me, Samuel. *(The verbal chattering joins the wistful music that floats through the room)*

SAMUEL: By my calculations your entrance was about thirty seconds too late. *(DR. MARTINO slowly rises from the coffin)*

DR. MARTINO: Please show me what I missed.

(There is a pause, as SAMUEL and MARIE HELENE consider whether or not they want to go through the pulse-taking procedure again. Then SAMUEL falls to his hands and knees. The music rises, and MARIE HELENE comes, gives him a push with her foot to roll him over, and circles him, as DR. MARTINO watches them with a chuckle. She slowly goes down on top of him again, whispering, "One and two and three and four and five and six." Then she falls silent, and they lift a bit from the floor to look for DR. MARTINO'S approval)

DR. MARTINO: *(Chuckling to himself)* Words fail me. *(A loud tone, and flashes of light send everyone whirling to the corners of the room, hiding their eyes from those flashes as the VOICE begins speaking over the loudspeaker)*

DEEP VOICE: Oh, Samuel, what does it mean, this plunge into language? Why is it that some realm of speaking pounds from the inside repeating the words "PLEASE! PLEASE!" as the pitiful representation of this inner pressure. But of course, this is no reference to normal discourse, the coming and going of everyday banal conversation.

DR. MARTINO: *(Having recovered from the lights)* Step over here, friend Samuel.

SAMUEL: Why?

DR. MARTINO: You've been through a great deal, so take a moment to relax. *(He pours a glass out of a pitcher)* Drink this.

SAMUEL: Why?

DR. MARTINO: Courage. *(He extends the glass. SAMUEL comes to take it, then hesitates, then tentatively drinks it)*

SAMUEL: What was it?

DR. MARTINO: *(Smiling)* Water.

MARIE HELENE: Something funny, boys?

DR. MARTINO: Ordinary water.

MARIE HELENE: Get down to business, Samuel. What sexual activities are you really into?

DR. MARTINO: *(Laughing to himself)* It was ordinary water.

MARIE HELENE: *(Rubbing her back against the wall)* Hello. I'm death, of course.

DR. MARTINO: Not true, Samuel.

MARIE HELENE: Only one person here knows the truth, but it's a surprise. *(The light flashes once and they all react in pain)*

DR. MARTINO: Jeeze—! *(The sound of babbling voices returns)* What sexual activities ARE you into, Samuel?

SAMUEL: Well, I assumed that sooner or later we'd take off our clothes, get into a bed, and perform sexual congress.

MARIE HELENE: That sounds unpleasant.

SAMUEL: *(Looking toward MARIE HELENE)* I fully imagined that being a prostitute has its unpleasantness.

(A sudden loud thud brings an exclamation from them all, immediately sending them into an eccentric dance as loud dance music blares forth. The dance is a puppet-like shuffle. They seem to have difficulty moving limbs that don't want to respond as they strut around the room, occasionally pulling their own legs to make them move. As suddenly as it began, the music stops, and with another exclamation, SAMUEL and MARIE HELENE whirl out of the room, and DR. MARTINO tumbles to the floor in front of the coffin. He is alone)

MARIE HELENE: *(Heard from the next room, over the loudspeaker)* Did I introduce myself? I'm death, probably.

SAMUEL: *(Also out of the room)* I'm not happy about that.

MARIE HELENE: Oh, you'll enjoy yourself. I'm a good conversationalist. *(DR. MARTINO slowly rises from the floor and takes a Polaroid camera with flash bulb down from a shelf)*

SAMUEL: On what subjects?

MARIE HELENE: Well, spiritual things.

SAMUEL: That's not reassuring. *(He and MARIE HELENE run back into the room. SAMUEL sees MARIE HELENE, and after a moment's consideration, rushes over to take her face be-*

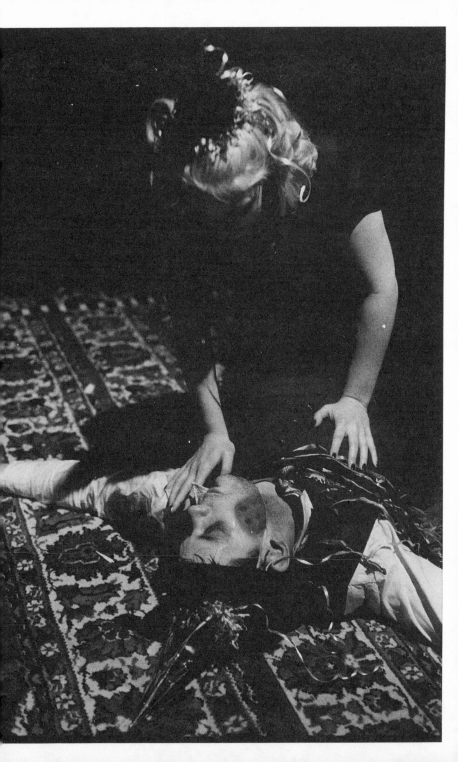

tween his hands and give her a kiss. But she pushes him away in the middle of the kiss, as DR. MARTINO takes a photo of it)

MARIE HELENE: It's like this, Samuel. Pick a new subject.

DR. MARTINO: I'm sorry to have to bring bad news, Samuel, but your worst suspicions are true.

SAMUEL: I can't imagine what they are.

DR. MARTINO: Your most dearly beloved has had a serious rendezvous.

SAMUEL: I have no dearly beloved in my life.

DR. MARTINO: Let's be banal, Samuel. *(Sad, wistful music, and the lights in the room change to the chalky white of a cheap hotel in midafternoon)* Rendezvous that occur with regularity in a fourth-floor room at the Hotel Martina Inez. You know, of course, the Hotel Martina Inez?

SAMUEL: Do I?

DR. MARTINO: I can give you the address of course.

SAMUEL: Write it down on some paper, or I'll forget. *(SAMUEL goes to a shelf and takes a white cloth and blindfolds himself as if for a mind-reading act)*

DR. MARTINO: Can I offer you a pencil? My handwriting is hard to read. *(SAMUEL leans against a pillar, blindfolded, but lifts his head into the light that pours through the window)*

SAMUEL: Your handwriting is perfectly clear.

DR. MARTINO: I've been told otherwise! (*MARIE HELENE has taken a small blackboard off a shelf and is laboriously writing down the name and address of the hotel*)

SAMUEL: I don't know why you're maintaining such a thing.

DR. MARTINO: (*Irritated*) Shall we close the book on that subject?

SAMUEL: I don't know if this is the information I expected.

DR. MARTINO: You seem to be avoiding the subject at hand and deflecting the conversation onto the much less interesting subject of my handwriting.

SAMUEL: Because I sense . . . mystery. You claim your handwriting is unreadable. You produce a sample and it seems to me . . . totally clear.

DR. MARTINO: Read back to me. (*SAMUEL, still blindfolded, puts his hand to his forehead as if to invoke the powers of mental telepathy*)

SAMUEL: (*Receiving a sudden impression*) Jeeze! (*He tries to interpret his impression*) . . . Hotel Martina Inez. Room 428. Boulevard Bria 21.

DR. MARTINO: Is that all?

SAMUEL: There is a predictable regularity to these rendezvous. Every Tuesday at one p.m. in the afternoon. (*He gets another telepathic flash of intuition*) Jeeze! . . . It's now Tuesday afternoon at one p.m.
   This is a room in the Hotel Martina Inez.
   This is my dearly beloved. (*SAMUEL whips the blindfold from his eyes, and at that moment DR. MARTINO shoots a Polaroid flash of SAMUEL'S face, and SAMUEL, blinded by the flash, again exclaims, "Jeeze!" and turns away in pain*)

DR. MARTINO: *(Pulling the print from the camera)* Here's a photograph of the person under suspicion, interfering with Samuel's happiness. *(SAMUEL collapses into a chair and examines it)*

MARIE HELENE: Why are you holding your chair, Samuel?

SAMUEL: It was a picture of me.

MARIE HELENE: Wait a minute—why are you holding your chair?

SAMUEL: So I don't fall.

DR. MARTINO: Are you moving?

MARIE HELENE: You look like you're not doing any moving.

(SAMUEL jumps from his chair, then staggers into a dizzy whirl as a startled MARIE HELENE runs from the room with a shriek, and SAMUEL finds himself staring up into the light from the window)

SAMUEL: *(After a pause)* I woke up. *(He slowly goes and sits on the edge of the coffin)* But I was still asleep, and the dirigible called "no more thinking" was hovering in the air, over my head, when suddenly, on the horizon, a second dirigible—this one not so precisely named—and then a third, and a fourth, and so on, and so forth—

DR. MARTINO: *(Who has come up behind SAMUEL to hiss into his ear)* But a twist on the thin golden thread that attached such objects together, and immediately it was as if . . . *(SAMUEL slowly collapses to the floor, and DR. MARTINO puts hands to his own head, as if he were trying to share SAMUEL'S consciousness)* . . . Samuel himself was spinning in air. Some called it a sky. Some called it a dream field.

DEEP VOICE: *(Which speaks as if for both of them)* But what happened was that the mind split, and the mind had the following adventures. It split into two separate parts.

But there is no way to act this out, or to represent this.

SAMUEL: *(Back on his feet, coming to speak intimately to DR. MARTINO)* This causes me great anguish.

And while it is true that anguish can be acted out, nevertheless its cause, which is the fact that the mind— *(He hits his own forehead with his hand, and staggers backwards, as a tone rises)* splitting into two parts—*(Both he and DR. MARTINO hit their foreheads and stagger backwards)* cannot be represented.

Neither that fact, nor the original fact of the mind splitting—*(One more blow to the forehead)*—neither can be represented.

DR. MARTINO: Recent events?

SAMUEL: A smile that never happened.

(DR. MARTINO runs to the other side of the room to compose himself, as MARIE HELENE reenters in the rear of the room, to watch)

DR. MARTINO: What happened was that the mind split, and I was between those two parts, where there was nothing. That was my "location." So I looked at one part, and there was no me in it. Then I looked at the other part, and there was no me in that either . . . *(He has gone to his hands and knees, and as he speaks, he crawls slowly toward SAMUEL)* though in both, there was a habit of sorts that was continuing, and that was a kind of orientation. But what wasn't oriented at all was the place between. The gap where I was indeed placed. And that was—nothing of course. *(SAMUEL reaches out to place a comforting hand on DR. MARTINO'S forehead)*

I was nothing. I was in nothing. *(He pulls sadly away*

from SAMUEL's hand)

There was nothing I could do. (*He thinks for a moment, then rises and crosses to get one of the party horns and blows it in SAMUEL's direction. MARIE HELENE takes a melon off the shelf, places it on the floor, and kneels down before it, lifting a ceremonial sword she has acquired, as if the melon were a head she was about to decapitate*)

SAMUEL: (*Beside her, indicating the melon*) But this—this is inedible!

MARIE HELENE: Oh, no, Samuel. It just looks that way.

DR. MARTINO: Congratulations, Samuel. This is a test.

SAMUEL: I won't look: ever.

MARIE HELENE: (*Sword still in the air*) Amazing. He just says what comes to mind. (*DR. MARTINO blows the horn again, and MARIE HELENE bends to kiss the melon, and then rises and moves away. She stops and turns back to SAMUEL*) Excuse me—did you say something?

DR. MARTINO: (*Very gently*) Did it ever occur to you, Samuel, that perhaps the devil himself was ill, knew that he was ill, and that all his efforts, misguided as they might be, were simply attempts at self-cure?

SAMUEL: Alone now, my fear surfaces.

DR. MARTINO: Alone at last, Samuel. Are waves cresting on the surface of that nothing?

MARIE HELENE: What's on your face, Samuel?

SAMUEL: Maybe a little dirt.

MARIE HELENE: How about—I lick it off?

SAMUEL: *(He looks at her with longing)* Oh . . . please. *(They kiss, as a high soprano sings a single note in the distance)*

DEEP VOICE: *(As the kiss continues)* Erase that. Reerase that . . . *(MARIE HELENE takes a step back and studies SAMUEL'S face)*

MARIE HELENE: Why is it still there?

SAMUEL: *(Touching a spot on his face that seems discolored)* Please, don't be frightened. Please.

MARIE HELENE: Why not be frightened?

SAMUEL: Because it's catching.

DR. MARTINO: You're perfectly safe, Samuel. Look around. See something frightening?

SAMUEL: I'm trying to hallucinate, thank you.

DR. MARTINO: Were you beautiful when you were a child?

SAMUEL: I think not.

DR. MARTINO: And was your mother very beautiful?

SAMUEL: I think not, also.

DR. MARTINO: Lift your hands. Lift both hands from the side of your body, like wings.

SAMUEL: I've never done that.

DR. MARTINO: Do it now.

SAMUEL: No. I'm not beautiful.

DR. MARTINO: But that's not being questioned. (*SAMUEL whirls to catch MARIE HELENE holding up two small paddles behind his shoulders as if they were his wings, and she immediately takes them away*) Look again. (*MARIE HELENE goes and opens the cabinet at the rear*) I see the same thing you see, Samuel, but that isn't frightening. It's for pure entertainment. Get inside.

SAMUEL: Why now?

DR. MARTINO: So I can prove what isn't frightening. Get inside.

SAMUEL: Why now?

DR. MARTINO: For your entertainment. (*SAMUEL considers this for a moment, then makes a decision and dashes into the cabinet, closing the door behind him. As a strange rhythmic music rises, DR. MARTINO hurries to the cabinet, revolves it, and swings open the door to show SAMUEL still inside*) See how reassuring it is, Samuel? Continuity exists.

SAMUEL: This is amazing. I'm still here.

DR. MARTINO: (*Pushing SAMUEL back inside and shutting the door*) Generally in such situations, when the cabinet is opened, the volunteer has vanished— (*Behind DR. MARTINO'S back, SAMUEL opens the door and looks out*)—and one is suitably entertained by the unusual. But the normal, on the other hand, does not ordinarily entertain. (*He is circling the room, like a professional magician*) It's a break in routine that refreshes. But of course, if that break in routine is great enough to be named catastrophe, that is not entertaining. (*He turns and walks suddenly to smack into a pillar, recoiling from the collision, holding his head in pain*) That—is upsetting. So it can be said that entertainment is the proper, minimal degree of the upsetting. You see then, why this is entertaining. (*Turning to SAMUEL*) Are you ready to be REALLY cooperative?

SAMUEL: I'm not sure.

DR. MARTINO: Of course, I don't usually find people very co-operative—

SAMUEL: About what?

DR. MARTINO: Let's try it reversed. I'll be the cooperative one. I'll do whatever you say.

SAMUEL: Suppose I'm not sure what I want.

DR. MARTINO: Then I can help— *(He seizes SAMUEL by the lapels)*—with suggestions. *(He pushes him away from the cabinet and enters it himself)*

SAMUEL: I don't like being pushed!

DR. MARTINO: Make ME disappear.

SAMUEL: I have no interest in that.

DR. MARTINO: Liar! *(DR. MARTINO closes the door on himself, and the box spins one half way around, back to front, as if by itself. Then DR. MARTINO appears from behind the box and stands against its back side, which is now facing front)*

DEEP VOICE: *(As faint giggling is heard)* But the disappearing act, threatened from the word go, turned into the word "gone." Only the disappearance was from emptiness already, so it erased what was already erased.

DR. MARTINO: *(Tapping the revealed rear of the box)* Rest assured, there's no secret rear exit from this cabinet. This side is impenetrable. *(He laughs and spins it halfway again, so it is back to its original position with the door showing)* Well, physically impenetrable.

SAMUEL: *(Falling to his knees as the lights dim, as MARIE HELENE runs from the room and DR. MARTINO goes and peeks from behind the box)* I waited for midnight.

DR. MARTINO: *(Whispers)* Midnight.

SAMUEL: It happened. *(A pause)* I waited for something to eat at one thirty in the morning. Total toast.

DR. MARTINO: I smell something burning. *(A pause)*

SAMUEL: I waited for a telephone call that zipped by like an express bus—no stops.

DR. MARTINO: *(Coming forward again)* Oh, Samuel, you waited for applause that had holes in it. You looked between your two hands and said, "Clap myself into a coma." But why bother?

SAMUEL: A failure of nerve.

DR. MARTINO: What failure of nerve?

SAMUEL: I didn't let you have your way with me.

DR. MARTINO: Ultimately, it was my choice.

SAMUEL: A failure of nerve. You said, "Make me disappear," and I said, "I'm not interested." But that was my failure of nerve, because what I really wanted was this room to sufficiently hallucinate— *(MARIE HELENE has entered in the rear)*

MARIE HELENE: Look at all the flowers, Samuel.

SAMUEL: *(Spinning around the room, looking for flowers, touching the walls to prove to himself that they are real)* What I

really wanted—rising in waves to engulf me, delirious
repetitions of shapes, colors—

DR. MARTINO: Oh, I thought we did that.

SAMUEL: —it didn't happen! Here's the same room.

DR. MARTINO: It LOOKS perfectly safe.

SAMUEL: SOLID?

DR. MARTINO: Yes.

SAMUEL: Unmoving? What other people refer to as my mental
stability, I call—failure of nerve.

DR. MARTINO: Ah, no hallucinations at all—

SAMUEL: But of course, right this minute I'm busy hallucinating,
chairs, walls, flowers— (*He grabs a lampshade from a
lamp in the corner, puts it on his head like a knight's visor,
and seizes the sword from the shelf, acting the part of an
adventurer*)

DR. MARTINO: I don't see anything special in your behavior.

SAMUEL: (*Posing with his face covered by the lampshade*) My
failure of nerve. Notice? I don't start ranting and raving.

DR. MARTINO: But neither do I, Samuel.

SAMUEL: Right. Hold on tight.

DR. MARTINO: You? Or me? (*MARIE HELENE lifts off the lampshade, revealing a despondent SAMUEL, who slinks away*)
Ahh, the sea is calm tonight?

SAMUEL: No tornados.

DR. MARTINO: Right. No tornados.

SAMUEL: Bye-bye.

DR. MARTINO: Where are you going?

SAMUEL: You won't follow me.

DR. MARTINO: I won't have to follow you. I count on your failure of nerve.

SAMUEL: *(Very softly)* Help me. *(A pause. MARIE HELENE comes to him, and places a silly-looking crown on his head)* Help me!

DR. MARTINO: Do you mean that?

SAMUEL: Just testing the water.

DR. MARTINO: Free-associate.

> *(There is a pause. A rare moment of silence when even the music ceases. Then intense white light slowly rises, pouring in from the window. And SAMUEL turns, and sees a vase of flowers on a shelf. He goes and seizes the vase, which is black, but MARIE HELENE is quickly beside him and takes the black vase from his hands. As she does so, he retrieves the flowers, and turns toward the light, and moves toward the window. MARIE HELENE goes and puts the empty vase on a shelf just below the window, just below the beam of tremendous light that pours from it. They all stand looking at the vase, and MARIE HELENE is still touching it)*

DEEP VOICE: The vase was empty. *(MARIE HELENE gently removes her hands from the vase)* She tried to fill the vase with flowers—but the flowers didn't fill the vase. *(There is a pause. Then SAMUEL moves into the center of the room and looks about. He looks back at the vase, then sees several more vases on other shelves throughout the room, and as the* VOICE *continues, he goes and collects in his arms all the flowers from those other vases)* At first they seemed to fill the vase. But then Samuel saw, or hallucinated, that the flowers were not filling the vase. It was empty. The vase was hurtling through space at hundreds of miles an hour. Nothing filled it. *(From another shelf,* MARIE HELENE *has taken a small package, which she carries back toward* DR. MARTINO, *who holds it for her as she opens it at the top and extracts a pure white vase.* SAMUEL *has left the room. Gentle music begins again, heartbreaking music)*

MARIE HELENE: Look what I bought yesterday afternoon at one p.m. *(She is by now, holding the pure white vase up into the beam of light that pours from the window)* A twin. *(By now,* SAMUEL *has reentered, holding a second white vase)* What did you do with your flowers, Samuel?

SAMUEL: At first I put them in the vase. Then I took them into the next room.

MARIE HELENE: The room looks empty. Did you move things out?

SAMUEL: No.

MARIE HELENE: Now, it's one p.m. We have two vases. What could go in them? *(A pause. The music shifts, evoking faraway places)*

SAMUEL: Nothing I can think of. *(Pause)*

MARIE HELENE: Somebody can't think of anything to say.

SAMUEL: I think these are emptiness vases. Nothing can fill them, and in fact, the emptiness in them flows out to fill the space around.

MARIE HELENE: What made me buy this second vase, Samuel? There must have been a reason.

SAMUEL: No. *(A pause)* Maybe there was no reason.

MARIE HELENE: Maybe you're right. So let's each take one of these vases and hold it against our foreheads. *(Slowly, they both lift a vase to their foreheads)* What are you thinking?

SAMUEL: I don't feel the urge to answer. *(A pause)* Let's just . . . disappear.

> *(The music has stopped. DR. MARTINO walks slowly toward the coffin, and SAMUEL and MARIE HELENE lower their vases to watch him)*

DR. MARTINO: *(Opening the lid of the coffin)* Some nights he's inside this. Some nights, not. *(He lets the lid drop with a loud thump, and the noise sends everyone to a different corner of the room, one hand covering their eyes and the free arm spinning in front of them like a propeller)*

SAMUEL: *(As he begins spinning his arm)* Do you mind terribly if I hold my head together?

DR. MARTINO: Samuel!

SAMUEL: He had lots of time. It counted for him.

> *(They all stop spinning and stagger backwards slightly)*

DR. MARTINO: He had two eyes; they made circles without moving.

MARIE HELENE: He remembered something; no story there.

DR. MARTINO: No story there. He forgot something. It turned real.

SAMUEL: He had a smile. Circling the body, it wept profusely.

DR. MARTINO: He had a face. It smiled therefore.

SAMUEL: He had a brain—

DR. MARTINO: *(Laughing)* Really!

MARIE HELENE: *(Hissing at DR. MARTINO)* Stop that.

SAMUEL: Glowed, like a stone.

DR. MARTINO: Like a stone.

SAMUEL: Like a stone.

MARIE HELENE: Like a stone.

SAMUEL:
> So blunt, so to the point.
> He kicked it.

DR. MARTINO: Kicked it?

SAMUEL:
> It flew down the road crying,
> This is my life, this is your life.

DR. MARTINO:
> But he had no sense of direction.
> Like a flower in the wind—

MARIE HELENE: More flowers, Samuel, covering the whole mountain. *(They all run to the corners of the room to hide, and the lights flash and then suddenly grow dim. MARIE HELENE whispers)* And death moved something. *(She runs from the room)*

DR. MARTINO: Immense, Samuel. Really immense.

SAMUEL: He had death. He sat there.

DR. MARTINO: How does it come to be yours, Samuel? This death. Does it have a shape?

SAMUEL: A shape like an angel.

(Someone on the tape is singing softly, "Smile, smile, smile . . . ")

DR. MARTINO: Something to hold onto?

SAMUEL: Falling probably.

DR. MARTINO: Where could you fall to, Samuel? Into angelic arms?

SAMUEL: Yes.

DR. MARTINO: Does that frighten you?

SAMUEL: Yes.

DR. MARTINO: Why?

(SAMUEL, still kneeling on the floor, has been hit by a thin beam of white light that has begun to pour from the window. There is a different sound to the music, as if it has become the music of angels)

SAMUEL: Look at it this way. When an angel appears, and demands of me the ultimate sacrifice—I howl with rage.

DR. MARTINO: That must be very frightening.

SAMUEL: My own howling frightens me, yes. *(He slowly rises to his feet)* But knowing I am serving the universe's purposes, my howl is in fact . . . music.

(The music has stopped. There is silence. MARIE HELENE enters on tiptoe, carrying three very delicate white screens. She moves to give one to SAMUEL and another to DR. MARTINO. In separate corners of the room, they all hide behind the white screens that they hold in front of their faces, facing the coffin. Samuel is trembling, and the sound of someone breathing deeply is heard)

MARIE HELENE: *(Very gently)* Relax, Samuel. *(Very slowly, to the sound of the breathing, they all lower their screens to the floor, and MARIE HELENE crosses, and steps into the coffin. She crouches down inside, hiding her face in her hands. There is a pause. Faint giggling is heard, and MARIE HELENE picks up her head, turns it toward SAMUEL, and slowly removes her hands from her face. She is smiling. She speaks quietly)* It's just me.

DR. MARTINO: You'll have to get used to many such moments, Samuel.
   Think of it as a kind of preparation? *(He is offering his hand to help MARIE HELENE out of the coffin)*
   But there is no preparation.
   You just get used to it. *(They are all, for a moment, holding hands in a circle. Then DR. MARTINO turns and walks slowly away)* But Samuel can get used to anything.

SAMUEL: I'll never get used to it.

DR. MARTINO: Never? Then you'll have to elect the alternative. *(SAMUEL is following DR. MARTINO, but his head is down and he doesn't see the pillar, and bangs his head against it, and staggers a bit, holding his head in pain. DR. MARTINO sees this, and shakes his head sadly)* You'll just have to keep on . . . being useful.

SAMUEL: Come again?

DR. MARTINO: You know, making that special music of yours, Samuel. That special . . . HOWL. You said it was rage. Maybe it was something else. No matter.

MARIE HELENE: *(Holding a single flower out to SAMUEL)* Do it again, Samuel.

SAMUEL: Not right now.

DR. MARTINO: Okay. Later.

MARIE HELENE: Please, Samuel, smell it for ME? *(He takes the blossom, and slowly crushes his face into it)*

DR. MARTINO: Oh, Samuel, are you howling again?

MARIE HELENE: Oh, Samuel . . . are you howling again?

(Angelic music is heard again, as DR. MARTINO and MARIE HELENE move to the corners of the room, and SAMUEL staggers to the center, his face still in the flower. And as he struggles to look up to the light, DR. MARTINO and MARIE HELENE, as if to mock him, start a funny little dance, whirling their arms and shaking their hips at SAMUEL, as the light pours through the window, and the VOICE speaks for a final time as they are dancing)

DEEP VOICE: But of course it was no real howl. It was just knowing, somehow, that the room would be soon empty, or much sooner, or maybe even . . . NOW!

(They run to dance in another corner. But SAMUEL turns slowly in the center of the room, as the lights fade to darkness)

THE END

my head
was a
sledgehammer

My Head Was a Sledgehammer. Produced by the Ontological-Hysteric Theater at the Ontological at St. Mark's Theater, N.Y.C. January–March 1994. Written, directed, and designed by Richard Foreman.

THE PROFESSOR:	Thomas Jay Ryan
THE FEMALE STUDENT:	Jan Leslie Harding
THE MALE STUDENT:	Henry Stram
GNOMES:	Bob Cucuzza
	Maristella Lindner
	Tom Ross
	Noah Weinreb

A large room with pink walls, a kind of classroom perhaps, with many blackboards on the walls. But there are also eccentrically painted gray shapes, suggesting large ink-blots evoking memories of animals or strange geographical continents, and black horizontal lines of varying thickness, which give an added Egyptian-like texture to the walls. Here and there tall bookcases reach to the ceiling. Roses creep up the walls and around corners, and tiny flags of no specific nature are hung here and there. At the rear of the stage is a long railing, a foot downstage of the rear wall, much like an exercise bar in a dance studio. From the ceiling hangs a double-faced head, which revolves slowly throughout the play. There are some small carpets, defining areas of action, and some thin red poles with lights on top. It is a lecture room, but it is also a laboratory, or a studio, or a gymnasium—all at once.

The play begins as piano music repeating a short child-like phrase is heard over what sounds like chattering crickets. Everyone who speaks wears a radio microphone on a headset, enabling them to speak softly and intimately throughout the play. The music—repeating loops made from brief musical phrases—continues through all moments of the play, ever changing, ever returning, giving musical underscoring to all the dialogue and occasionally rising in volume to punctuate a dance or a complex manipulation of objects.

Four gnomelike creatures with red hair, tall caps, beards, and eyeglasses appear on tiptoe. They creep onto the stage and go to different points in the room, from which they each pull a white dotted string from retractable spring devices that keep all the strings taut. At the end of each string is a small rubber ball, and the gnomes crouch down and dangle the balls over seemingly random spots on the floor. At the same time, the FEMALE STUDENT enters, a young woman with long dark hair, ankle-high socks, and a beret. She sets down a briefcase and puts on a pair of white gloves. At the same time, the PROFESSOR enters. He is a burly man in a soiled white shirt with the sleeves rolled up past the elbows. He wears a thick, studded belt. On his head he wears a tight-fitting white bandanna, and over what look like motorcycle pants he wears athletic knee pads. His face is covered with many small scratches, and he seems to resemble a member of a motorcycle gang as much as a distinguished professor. He stops as he enters the room, seemingly hypnotized by a single white glove that lies carefully spread out on a white cloth that has been laid on the floor directly in his path.

FEMALE STUDENT: Okay, Mr. Professor—(With a tiny yelp of pleasure, the GNOMES all fall to the floor, still holding their strings. The PROFESSOR turns to study them. Then he circles back to the glove, bends down, and puts it on) Are you as weird as I think you are?

PROFESSOR: (Turning slowly to confront her) Not likely.

(The music rises, accompanied by a voice chattering rapid gibberish. The MALE STUDENT runs on suddenly and the PROFESSOR whirls to face him. The MALE STUDENT is dressed in knickers, carries a briefcase, and on his head sports an army fatigue cap. The PROFESSOR runs from him to the FEMALE STUDENT, who stamps down on his foot, and the PROFESSOR yowls in pain and runs to one of the blackboards and begins to erase—though there is nothing to erase—and the MALE STUDENT follows him to the blackboard to observe, whereupon the PROFESSOR drops his eraser and slams himself with his back against the blackboard to watch for a further attack. During this the GNOMES have retracted their strings, and now all squat at the rear wall, holding the exercise bar, and the music is quiet again)

FEMALE STUDENT: Disturbed? You hear voices, Professor?

PROFESSOR: I'm lucky that way. *(He takes a few steps, and she shadows his move)*

FEMALE STUDENT: I'd say, weird.

PROFESSOR: I feel connected.

FEMALE STUDENT: Connected to what?

PROFESSOR: *(As both students stalk him)* To the source of my voices.

FEMALE STUDENT: Okay. That's weird.

PROFESSOR: . . . Are you weird, or am I weird?

FEMALE STUDENT: What's the criteria?

> *(Three of the GNOMES run forward, each carrying a tray with a small printed card. The PROFESSOR and the STUDENTS each pick up a card, glance at it, and toss it to the floor, whereupon the GNOMES retrieve the cards and go back to the exercise bar)*

PROFESSOR: *(Addressing the female student)* Let me invite you— *(He takes an apple from a bookcase and holds it out to her)* Come a little closer.

FEMALE STUDENT: In what sense, Professor? *(She runs to him carrying a rope, and quickly entangles him with one hand behind his back)*

MALE STUDENT: The question is: what can he do with one hand tied behind his back?

(The *PROFESSOR* unwinds himself as the *GNOMES* exit, and he proceeds to erase the already erased blackboard, as the *FEMALE STUDENT* goes and lies down on one of the tiny carpets. The *PROFESSOR* stops, and as the *MALE STUDENT* goes down on all fours to crawl toward the *FEMALE STUDENT*, the *PROFESSOR* also sinks to the floor)

PROFESSOR: My secret desire is—win love from many beautiful women.

FEMALE STUDENT: (Propped up on an elbow to look at him) I'll pretend I didn't hear that sentiment, Professor.

PROFESSOR: I'm speaking of things closest to my heart, madam. (The four *GNOMES* run in with long silver wands and take positions around the *FEMALE STUDENT*, using the wands to point at a watch on her wrist)

MALE STUDENT: Notice what's on her wrist, Professor? (In slow motion, the *GNOMES* fall to the floor)

PROFESSOR: A very beautiful watch. (As soft organ music begins and *GNOMES* retire)

MALE STUDENT: Hey—who do YOU pray to, Professor?

PROFESSOR: I don't.

MALE STUDENT: What kind of religious ceremony?

PROFESSOR: I don't have any religious observations.

MALE STUDENT: God plays no part in your life?

PROFESSOR: None at all.

MALE STUDENT: There is no God in your life, Professor?

PROFESSOR: None at all.

(*Suddenly, one of the* GNOMES *rolls a cabinet into the room at great speed. It comes to an abrupt stop. Displayed in the cabinet is a violin*)

FEMALE STUDENT: What a beautiful violin, Professor.

MALE STUDENT: (*As if experiencing a vision*) My God—

FEMALE STUDENT: Do you play it?

PROFESSOR: I scratch out noise.

FEMALE STUDENT: I'll bet you play better than that, Professor.

PROFESSOR: I scratch out terrible noises, which I like doing in private.

FEMALE STUDENT: You're saying that just to provoke me, Professor.

PROFESSOR: Not at all.

(*An electronic tone rises, and the* PROFESSOR *and the* MALE STUDENT *put hands to their foreheads, moan, and fall to the floor, as the* FEMALE STUDENT *crosses and pulls the violin from the cabinet. She studies it in her hands, as the* PROFESSOR *and* MALE STUDENT *recover and run from the room. Just at that moment, the* GNOMES *run in and snatch the violin from the* FEMALE STUDENT *and run out of the room with it. She chases after them, and the* PROFESSOR *and* MALE STUDENT *reappear and join the chase. Then, alone together, the three embrace one another despondently. Each kisses his own right hand, and three* GNOMES *sneak back into the room and go to pull the strings from the wall. The* PROFESSOR *and his* STUDENTS *have been caressing their own face with their kissed hand. But when they see the* GNOMES

dangling the rubber balls at the end of the strings, each goes
slowly on tiptoe to one of the balls, to take a position leaning
ecstatically against a wall with a ball now placed close to
each of their bodies. The tone is very loud, and the three of
them stare up into space, pointing one finger to their
foreheads)

FEMALE STUDENT: (As the tone softens) What does your internal
time say now, Professor?

PROFESSOR: It doesn't speak to me, it manipulates me in other
ways.

FEMALE STUDENT: Okay, Professor. (They all leave their positions)
Imagine a completely different play called . . . (She tries to
think, then comes up with a title) "Fingers Alert." What
could happen in such a play?

(The tone rises again, and while the two men cover their
ears, the FEMALE STUDENT runs to the blackboard and runs
her fingernails down its surface. Then everyone runs to new
positions as the music changes. The FEMALE STUDENT has
her back to the room. The two men sneak toward her and
one softly whispers "Cookoo!," which makes her whirl in
irritation. She picks up a metal dog leash from the floor,
bending over provocatively, then turning to threaten the
men, who are muttering happily to themselves—"I guess
we showed her a thing or two")

FEMALE STUDENT: Imagine a play called "Dogs on Duty." (The
two men take a step back and growl, and then reach for
books high on the bookcase, but unable to control the
books, a few tumble to the floor, as the FEMALE STUDENT is
gliding about the room, trailing a dog leash on the floor
behind her provocatively) What could happen in such a
play? (Disco music rises as she circles the room. The
GNOMES arrive with plates carrying cards that are again
read and tossed away. One GNOME places a chair wrapped

in brown paper on the little carpet, and then the GNOMES go
to the rear and rest on the exercise bar. The PROFESSOR has
acquired another apple, which he holds out toward the
FEMALE STUDENT)

PROFESSOR: Did you ever see this in real life, madam?

FEMALE STUDENT: (She approaches it slowly to study it) An apple!
(She and the GNOMES and the MALE STUDENT form a line,
and they all cover their eyes)

PROFESSOR: (Re-presenting the apple) Remember? Did you ever
see this in real life?

(Everyone in line slowly looks toward the MALE STUDENT,
who covers his private parts with his hands, and all but he
and the FEMALE STUDENT slowly fall to the floor as the
childlike piano tune returns. Then the FEMALE STUDENT
grabs the chair wrapped in paper and pulls it noisily from
the room as the GNOMES rise and run out after her. The MALE
STUDENT comes down to watch the PROFESSOR erase the
already erased blackboard. Then he begins erasing one
right next to it. The PROFESSOR is jealous and pushes him
away and starts erasing on this other blackboard. The MALE
STUDENT tries again, and as the PROFESSOR reinvades his
blackboard, he gives up. The PROFESSOR stops and studies
the MALE STUDENT)

PROFESSOR: You just lied to me.

MALE STUDENT: I don't lie, I don't tell the truth. I'm here to do
neither of those two stupid things.

PROFESSOR: What are you here for, sir?

MALE STUDENT: To be slippery on things, Professor. (He twists his
legs and mockingly pretends to slip, falling to the ground
with a shriek that turns into a laugh as the PROFESSOR runs

across the room, opens a briefcase, and pulls out a stack of papers)

PROFESSOR: Well, here's what I'm here for. (He starts throwing individual pieces of paper into the air, and as they flutter to the floor, the GNOMES run in and collect them and run to the walls to hold the sheets of paper high up on the walls)
I want to be in a place
from which truth—
(He whirls ecstatically and runs across the room, only to have an accident—he bumps into the wall and cries out in pain as he holds his damaged nose) Ow! Now we have a problem. Truth: gushes forth. (The MALE STUDENT barks twice, breaking the mood as the GNOMES turn from the wall to watch) I want to be a place THROUGH which truth—
(The GNOMES run from the room, clutching their papers as the MALE STUDENT barks again) I want to be a place through which truth passes. (He has come and captured the MALE STUDENT in a headlock, but the student immediately escapes)
But when it passes through ME—
stripping off its protective cloak—
Ah, but why do I wear my protective cloak?
Because truth revealed, believe it or not, takes the unfortunate shape of everything that isn't true. (He crosses to the MALE STUDENT, who is now erasing one of the blackboards already erased) This happens! THIS REALLY HAPPENS! (As the MALE STUDENT turns to face him, the PROFESSOR turns away sadly) But if mere actors speak this, then it no longer happens.

MALE STUDENT: (Inspired to imitate his professor) Me too. I want to be, a place through which truth passes. (He goes to take down a book) Did I get that right, Professor? (He bounces gently across the room, singing a scale to himself. Then turns a page and finds the passage he was looking for and reads) "I want to be a place through which . . . truth passes." *(The FEMALE STUDENT is crossing behind them, studying an apple she holds in her hand)*

PROFESSOR: Turn the page.

MALE STUDENT: *(Ecstatically hugging the book to his chest)* I'd like to linger a bit longer over this very particular page.

PROFESSOR: Turn the page.

MALE STUDENT: *(As he does so)* What does it say on this page, Professor?

PROFESSOR: Wait a minute—*(He crosses to the MALE STUDENT, momentarily distracted by a big pink disk that rolls in behind him, manipulated from behind by a GNOME. Then he recovers his composure, and goes to whisper to the student)* That's my line. *(Grabs the book away and reads)* "What does it say on this page?"

MALE STUDENT: "Eat me"?

PROFESSOR: Please? *(He checks the book, sees no such line, and hands the book back to the MALE STUDENT, who proceeds to tear a page out of the book and, with a flourish, eats it)* By the way, Professor—*(The FEMALE STUDENT comes rushing forward to present the apple to the PROFESSOR, who scurries out of the way and runs to fall back ecstatically against a wall, as a GNOME pulls a string from the wall to hold on the PROFESSOR's knee, and the MALE STUDENT retreats to pose spreadeagled against the pink disk at the rear of the room, continuing all the while to chew the page torn from the book)*—do I consider you a place through which truth passes? You'll never know, Professor, because you can't get inside my head. *(He turns away)* Let's make a guess—

FEMALE STUDENT: *(Running forward)* What's a guess?

PROFESSOR: Somebody should write this down so I don't forget. *(He whirls away to find a piece of paper, but miscalculates and bangs against the wall)* Jesus Christ—! *(Holding his head, he realizes the collision was very stimulating)*—this is the most interesting thought I've had in a long time. What's a guess?

MALE STUDENT: *(Immediately copying his PROFESSOR, he comes and bangs against the same wall)* Jesus Christ—! *(He spits out the paper he has been chewing and holds his stomach)*— this is the most interesting meal I've had in a long time. What's a guess?

PROFESSOR: Do you think I can make this lady disappear? *(He gives the disk a shove and it rolls out of the room)*

FEMALE STUDENT: I do hope somebody gets hurt.

PROFESSOR: Why?

MALE STUDENT: Hey, do you know the name of every book in your oh-so-extensive library, Professor?

PROFESSOR: I believe I do.

FEMALE STUDENT: I doubt it.

MALE STUDENT: Close your eyes, Professor. Then feel your way to the bookcase. Take out a book without looking.

(In trying to do so, the PROFESSOR again bangs into a wall. But as he recovers from the collision, the GNOMES arrive to offer a white cloth to the STUDENTS and the PROFESSOR. They each take one and hold it in front of their eyes as they take three tentative steps forward. Then as the music rises, the GNOMES steal the cloths and run from the room, as the PROFESSOR and the STUDENTS spin dizzily. As they spin, the rolling cabinet has reentered)

MALE STUDENT: As you can clearly see—

PROFESSOR: Where?

MALE STUDENT: *(Holding his forehead as the FEMALE STUDENT takes an envelope from the cabinet)* I already wrote the name of the book I predicted you'd pick, and sealed my guess in a white envelope.

FEMALE STUDENT: *(Opening the envelope and reading)* It's titled— *(She looks up at the PROFESSOR)*—you're not going to believe this.

MALE STUDENT: Oh, I believe it.

FEMALE STUDENT: "Dossier of Fear."

PROFESSOR: I have no such book in my entire library.

MALE STUDENT: Hey, look again. *(He collapses to the floor as the PROFESSOR runs to the cabinet, and the FEMALE STUDENT tears the envelope to pieces and throws the pieces into the air)*

PROFESSOR: *(Looking at a book he has taken from the cabinet)* You're quite right. The book is entitled "Dossier of Fear." But I'm convinced that heretofore I had no such book. *(He leafs through it)* Its pages are all blank pages. *(A GNOME snatches the book from the PROFESSOR and runs out of the room)*

MALE STUDENT: I could have secretly hidden that book in your collection. Isn't that possible, Professor?

PROFESSOR: Would you do that?

MALE STUDENT: Well, imagine a play entitled "Broken Promises."

(The GNOMES run in with red apples on dinner plates and place them on the floor, as choral music rises. The PROFESSOR and STUDENTS each take a rubber mat from a shelf, spread it on the floor, and vigorously wipe their feet on it, grunting in accompaniment. Then they put away the mats, and the PROFESSOR seizes a large shapeless object wrapped in brown paper, which he holds out toward the FEMALE STUDENT, who has run to the exercise bar, where she swings her lower leg in a circular propeller motion. The MALE STUDENT grabs the object from the PROFESSOR and hides it in the bookcase as the PROFESSOR runs to observe the FEMALE STUDENT from another angle. She immediately stops)

MALE STUDENT: Welcome. Let me tell you a story in the center of which I hide a very personal message.

FEMALE STUDENT: Excuse me but—how will we be able to recognize such a private message?

MALE STUDENT: Well . . . *(He reaches out toward the plates with apples, and the two others do likewise)* Imagine a play—

(As the music rises, all three grunt and lurch in place toward the apples. The GNOMES run in to grab the plates and apples, and run out of the room banging the plates together, making a noise that causes the PROFESSOR and STUDENTS to hold their ears and howl in pain. They race to the bookcases, and each grabs two plates with handles on the bottom, enabling them to be held like orchestra cymbals. The music stops, and they awkwardly hold the cymbal plates, looking at one another. Then they slowly hide them behind their backs. The FEMALE STUDENT, especially embarrassed, runs from the room, and the PROFESSOR takes a few steps after her, to watch her exit. The MALE STUDENT has begun to erase an already erased blackboard, and the PROFESSOR turns to address him)

PROFESSOR: There might be enough time here to explain something.

MALE STUDENT: What?

PROFESSOR: Did you ever heretofore explode, Professor?

MALE STUDENT: Is this called talking to myself?

(They retake the cymbal plates, and as choral music rises, each runs to a wall, smacks the plates high up against the wall, and holding them against the wall, revolve their hips three times, grunting in rhythm. Then they whirl to face each other)

PROFESSOR: Try using my real name.

MALE STUDENT: I don't think names are a real issue, vis-à-vis a man who wants to genuinely explode.

PROFESSOR: On the verge?

MALE STUDENT: Hey, why not take me up on that?

(The childlike piano tune returns, as a GNOME rolls in a wooden cart in which the FEMALE STUDENT is riding, as another GNOME wheels in a white folding hospital screen, which the PROFESSOR studies for a moment, then folds about himself so he is hidden inside. By this time the MALE STUDENT is bent over holding onto the railing of the cart, and the FEMALE STUDENT hits him three times with a riding crop. He cries out in pain and runs away.)

PROFESSOR: *(Inside the screen, softly)* "When stones are shoes, the bottoms of the feet go deaf."

MALE STUDENT: Do I have your permission, at least, to get torn to pieces by contradictory forces?

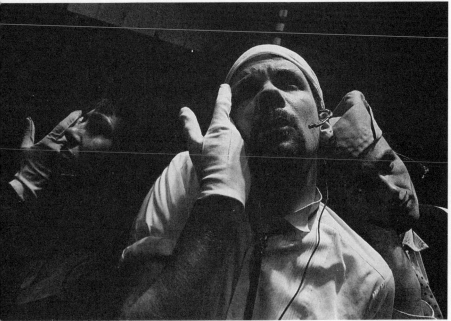

PROFESSOR: *(Opening the screen)* Of course you have my permission.

(The FEMALE STUDENT reenters with a large stuffed horse, which she transfers to the MALE STUDENT, who lets it fall to the ground at his feet. A VOICE is heard on tape, repeating the phrase "Remarkable people never depend on self-revelation." The repeated phrase is joined by organ music as the MALE STUDENT picks up the horse and lifts it over his shoulders, its legs hanging down along each side of his neck. At the same time, the PROFESSOR places an apple at the MALE STUDENT's feet, and the PROFESSOR and the GNOMES stand in a semicircle around the apple, pointing to it with silver wands)

MALE STUDENT: I was hoping you'd offer me a handkerchief.

PROFESSOR: Why of all things a handkerchief?

MALE STUDENT: Can't you guess? *(He slowly revolves in place, as the PROFESSOR and the GNOMES slowly fall to the floor, with wands still pointing toward the apple)* A handkerchief to stop the bleeding.

PROFESSOR: *(From the floor)* From which wound, pal?

MALE STUDENT: Ah, some of them can't be reached. So I'll have to try this one conveniently here in the palm of my hand.

FEMALE STUDENT: Imagine a play called "The Pretend Hat." *(She takes a man's felt hat from a bookcase and places it on her head)* What could happen in such a play?

PROFESSOR: That's a very, very old wound, madam.

MALE STUDENT: I was hoping you'd offer me a coat.

PROFESSOR: Ah, hearts of ice.

MALE STUDENT: *(Smiling, he looks upward, as lively music begins to filter into the room)* Oh, Professor, you remembered.

PROFESSOR: *(Hearing the music, his hands travel up as if he were going to perform an exotic belly dance. His hips sway with the beat)* I remember nothing, pal, I just . . . *(The music is loud now, and he has to shout)* I GO, with the FLOW—

(To very aggressive, marchlike jazz music, PROFESSOR and MALE STUDENT do a strange dance where they grunt to the beat, pumping their arms like suction pumps, then strutting around the stage doing an exaggerated breast stroke, then standing in place again, grunting and working their arms. Perhaps it's the memory of a bizarre military career. The GNOMES have appeared in the entrance to cheer them on, but a moment later the GNOMES are racing for the horse, which was dropped as the dance began. They lift it high in the air and run with it to one of the blackboards. As they rub its nose into the blackboard, both the PROFESSOR and the MALE STUDENT rush to the same blackboard and begin erasing. The GNOMES drop the horse and pull it by its legs to the other side of the room. In the rear, the FEMALE STUDENT has reentered pulling the cart, which now has a large wooden chair loaded in it upside down. She comes to a stop and watches. She is wearing a graduation robe and cap with tassel. The GNOMES run from the room, and the music turns quiet and threatening. The two at the blackboard sense her presence and stop erasing, but they don't want to look at her)

FEMALE STUDENT: *(Smiling, looking straight ahead)* Thank you, Professor.

PROFESSOR: For what? *(He and the MALE STUDENT go back to erasing)*

FEMALE STUDENT: I'm thrilled to be included.

PROFESSOR AND MALE STUDENT: *(They stop and look at each other)* In what?

FEMALE STUDENT: By the way, Professor Number Four . . . ?

(She holds out a set of car keys and rattles them. The PROFESSOR and the MALE STUDENT race to separate bookcases, pour themselves a shot of liquor, and toss it down in one gulp)

PROFESSOR: *(Gasping for breath after the drink)* I needed that.

MALE STUDENT: *(Gasping)* I needed that too.

FEMALE STUDENT: —is still parking the car.

PROFESSOR: Parking the car?

MALE STUDENT: Then we could get rid of the horse.

FEMALE STUDENT: What horse?

PROFESSOR: Better not.

MALE STUDENT: Why not? *(They both take another stiff shot. Then the PROFESSOR comes up behind the FEMALE STUDENT and smiles sweetly)*

PROFESSOR: Have a seat. *(He looks about quickly, and is embarrassed to see there is no chair, so runs back for another shot)*

FEMALE STUDENT: Hello again, Professor.

PROFESSOR: Where's Professor Number Four?

MALE STUDENT: That's been covered.

PROFESSOR: With what?

FEMALE STUDENT: Parking the car, Professor.

PROFESSOR: Parking the car.

MALE STUDENT: *(To himself, amazed)* I knew it, I knew it—

PROFESSOR: *(Racing to the female student)* Have a seat.

FEMALE STUDENT: *(Hesitating, with just a hint of seductiveness, she begins taking off her cap and gown)* I already did.

> *(A tone rises as the **PROFESSOR** and the **MALE STUDENT** slowly fall to the floor muttering to themselves, "Oh, yeah," overcome by her partial disrobing. A **GNOME** comes to take the chair from the cart, setting it on one of the small carpets, as the **PROFESSOR** struggles to his feet, holding his head)*

PROFESSOR: It must be that something powerful happened to me. I heard this very desirable woman say out loud to me, "I already did."

FEMALE STUDENT: But I already do.

PROFESSOR: Vis-à-vis, you know—

MALE STUDENT: Horses!

PROFESSOR: No. Chairs. *(Music is rising that evokes the image of many **GNOMES** busily scurrying through the city)* I wanted those words to be magically invested with something powerful enough to throw me to the floor.

FEMALE STUDENT: I did.

PROFESSOR: I tried to make it happen.

FEMALE STUDENT: *(She approaches the **PROFESSOR**)* I did. *(She hits the **PROFESSOR** and he falls to the floor. The **GNOMES** appear*

and accompany the fall with a "Wheee!" of excitement.
Then she approaches the MALE STUDENT) I did. *(She hits*
him, and he also falls, accompanied by a "Whee!" from the
GNOMES. Then the GNOMES rush forward and help the two
on the floor to rise, and they do a whirling dance with the
PROFESSOR and his STUDENTS. The PROFESSOR shouts out
over the dance—)

PROFESSOR: I remember I said, "Where's Professor Number
Four?" And you said, "Parking the car, parking the car,
parking the car—which might take a very long time!" *(The*
dance music stops and the GNOMES run from the room)

MALE STUDENT: Hey, how long?

FEMALE STUDENT: *(After a pause)* A very long time.

PROFESSOR: What's the estimate of a very long time? *(Ominous*
music begins softly, and everybody finds a new corner of the
room in which to feel more secure)

FEMALE STUDENT: Let's just say—time doesn't exist for me.

(As the cabinet rolls into the room, the MALE STUDENT puts
on a dunce cap, and the PROFESSOR takes a rolled-up chart
out of the cabinet, waits for a moment, then lets it unroll
dramatically to show a brightly colored selection of auto-
mobiles painted on the chart. There is a pause while the
two STUDENTS try to make sense of it)

MALE STUDENT: Okay. Something about a horse—

PROFESSOR: Wrong. *(Then he thinks)* But that should work—

FEMALE STUDENT: Why should it work if it's wrong, Professor?
(She thinks) Unless, the key is more interesting than the
lock?

PROFESSOR: *(Cocking his head to one side)* Well—

FEMALE STUDENT: Shit—that can't be right.

> *(The music rises as the PROFESSOR runs to hang the chart on the wall, but he reverses it so the other side is now revealed. Instead of late-model automobiles, the other side is illustrated with full-color pictures of prime cuts of meat. All three run to different shelves to pour themselves a drink, but at the last minute, they stop themselves and slap the offending hand reaching for the bottle. They look at the hand for a minute, then shrug and pour themselves a drink anyway. They gasp as it goes down the throat)*

PROFESSOR: *(Stepping forward to watch their reactions to the liquor)* No problem. *(He circles back to lean nonchalantly against a bookcase)* Here's another way to look at it. What is a human being—except—that which—*(The MALE STUDENT is staring at the meat chart)*—dig deep enough now: "Doesn't know."

MALE & FEMALE STUDENT: *(Enlightened, they hit their own foreheads)* Ahhhhh!

PROFESSOR: Animals, for instance—zebras, lions, buffalos— *(Startled, they turn to watch a white screen zip in behind them to stand against the rear wall, a GNOME behind it. Then the PROFESSOR recovers, and slowly approaches the FEMALE STUDENT)* and more ordinary things like dogs and cats. *(She hasn't been looking at him, but he whirls her around, threateningly. Then he turns from her and picks up the horse, which is still lying on the ground. He carries the horse and stands holding it, as if posing for a photo against the white screen at the rear of the room)* None of those animal things are in a state of not-knowing, because the issue never arises. So a human being is the birth of not-knowing as a real possibility. And when that benificent stupidity is ended? *(He steps forward with the horse. Then* he drops it on the floor and returns alone to the white screen) Then in fact— (The large pink disk rolls in front of him, and he speaks, hidden behind it)—he, or she, is no longer a human being. (The disk rolls quickly out of the room, revealing the PROFESSOR facing the white screen with his back to the room. As he takes a few steps backwards, the white screen moves to the side and tilts at a slight angle. The PROFESSOR turns back to speak to the room, whispering and slowly kneeling on the collapsed horse) Maybe that's why Professor Number Four is taking such a goddamned eternity to park the goddamned automobile.

FEMALE STUDENT: Look, you're into something— (The white screen whisks off) I'm just not into, Professor. (There is a pause. The PROFESSOR looks disoriented)

MALE STUDENT: Hey, that seems to quiet him down to a considerable extent.

PROFESSOR: I wondered who was going to be the first to say something. (Looks from one to the other) What do you know, it was me.

FEMALE STUDENT: You almost said something important, Professor, but it wasn't you.

PROFESSOR: Didn't I speak first?

FEMALE STUDENT: No.

PROFESSOR: Who did? (A Bach-like phrase of music is rising)

MALE STUDENT: I'll have to go into the next room, but I think— (He points to himself) "If you go— (With his other hand, he points to the PROFESSOR) —I go."

PROFESSOR: Really?

MALE STUDENT: Yes. *(They all run for a set of cymbal plates with handles, and smack them high up on the wall)*

FEMALE STUDENT: *(Calling over her shoulder)* What time is it?

PROFESSOR: My watch stopped! *(He runs out of the room. The two others relax to watch him go)*

FEMALE STUDENT: *(To the MALE STUDENT)* Think about this, Professor. If God himself were to come into this room right now . . . *(She thinks, then turns and places her cymbal plates against his, and with a slight push, sends him spinning from the room. Alone, she faces forward)* It would mean time had indeed stopped. *(She bangs her two plates together and rubs them against each other)*

PROFESSOR: *(Offstage, using a Godlike intonation)* God?

FEMALE STUDENT: *(Putting away her plates)* I'm not interested.

PROFESSOR: *(As the MALE STUDENT is pushed onstage, wearing a white feather headdress)* You have to be interested. *(He himself appears, wearing a white feather headdress that is much more impressive than his student's)*

FEMALE STUDENT: My God, that's desperation on your part, Professor.

PROFESSOR: Not on my part.

MALE STUDENT: Not on my part, Professor. *(He covers his eyes and tiptoes to a corner, as the others try to hide. It's a game of blindman's buff. The voice on tape is again heard repeating over and over, "Remarkable people never depend on self-revelation")*

PROFESSOR: 1, 2, 3, 4, 5, 6, 7, 8, 9, 10. *(He turns from his corner, looks up to the heavens, and starts to spin in place)* Now, if God, really—

FEMALE STUDENT: Oh, that's vulgar, Professor, and so pretentious, it's doubly vulgar.

MALE STUDENT: *(Shrugging)* Now me—? I'm very naive.

PROFESSOR: Primitive?

MALE STUDENT: Proud of it.

FEMALE STUDENT: What?

PROFESSOR AND MALE STUDENT: Both. *(They both collapse to the floor, moaning, "Oh, yeah!" An electronic tone rises, and the FEMALE STUDENT sits in the chair as a white screen is slid in behind it, giving it the aspect of a throne)*

FEMALE STUDENT: Better sit in this, gentlemen.

PROFESSOR: *(Rising from the floor)* Why?

FEMALE STUDENT: Well, it's a very electric chair. *(She rises from the chair and attaches electric cables to its arms)*

PROFESSOR: I don't want to be electrocuted, madam.

MALE STUDENT: I don't want to be electrocuted either.

FEMALE STUDENT: Do you see wires?

PROFESSOR: *(Turning away)* There are so many things about these "oh-so-desirable women" I can't justify to myself—

FEMALE STUDENT: You like my company, admit it. *(The "busy gnome" music is rising)*

MALE STUDENT: True, you like the aggravation, Professor. It energizes.

PROFESSOR: I like that, but I don't like its source, I like its results.

FEMALE STUDENT: It's the same thing.

MALE STUDENT: It's the same thing, Professor.

FEMALE STUDENT: Pleasant dreams, Professor. *(She and the MALE STUDENT run to bookshelves and rip pieces of paper to pieces, throwing them into the air like confetti, as the music rises, along with the voice on the tape repeating, "Remarkable people never depend on self-revelation")*

PROFESSOR: I need lots of sleep! *(He takes papers from his briefcase and throws them into the air, as GNOMES run in to retrieve them, and music and talk all start overlapping in a jumble of sound as the lights grow dim)*

FEMALE STUDENT: No problem—it's as if a curtain were rising.

MALE STUDENT: Imagine a play called "The Pretend Hat." What could happen—

PROFESSOR: *(Overlapping, as he throws his papers)* I'm imagining a play called "Mysteries of Arrogance." That's more my style!

FEMALE STUDENT: Guess!

PROFESSOR: What's a guess?

FEMALE STUDENT: Time will tell!

PROFESSOR: Quite!

FEMALE STUDENT: Counting on internal time, Professor?

PROFESSOR: I turn into somebody who opens his mouth, and whatever comes out travels in desirable directions only! *(He has run up against a blackboard, and with the sound of that collision, things quiet down and the GNOMES run from the room. All that is heard now is an electronic tone. The PROFESSOR turns from the blackboard to face the FEMALE STUDENT, who is sitting on the floor on the horse, lighting a cigarette. It seems to be late at night. The PROFESSOR speaks quietly)* Automatic truths, madam.

FEMALE STUDENT: Good. What's the technique?

PROFESSOR: *(A pause, then he decides to reveal his secret)* Well, I make up rhymes.

FEMALE STUDENT: Then what?

PROFESSOR: The technique is, they don't rhyme.

FEMALE STUDENT: Really, Professor! *(Now there is complete silence)*

PROFESSOR: This is supposed to illustrate something.

FEMALE STUDENT: *(Rising from the floor. The MALE STUDENT stands next to the PROFESSOR, holding out a man's felt hat)* Ah, your method is the illustrative method.

PROFESSOR: Yes.

FEMALE STUDENT: You make up rhymes that don't rhyme.

PROFESSOR: Not quite. I make up rhymes. I do that. But: they don't rhyme.

FEMALE STUDENT: *(After a pause)* I appreciate the difference.

PROFESSOR: Do you?

FEMALE STUDENT: *(She takes the felt hat from the MALE STUDENT and places it on her closed fist. At the same time, the PROFESSOR removes his feather headdress)*
Here is my hat.
What do you think of that?

PROFESSOR: That rhymes.

FEMALE STUDENT: *(The childlike tune on the piano returns)* Oh. I thought perhaps you'd say to me, That doesn't rhyme.

PROFESSOR: *(He thinks)* But it does.
"Here is my hat—*(He turns to erase the already erased blackboard, and she throws the hat to the floor)*
What do you think of that."

FEMALE STUDENT: Wait a minute. Does that rhyme?

PROFESSOR: We'll have to find out.

FEMALE STUDENT: How?

PROFESSOR: Over the course of time. *(He continues to erase, and the MALE STUDENT steps forward)*

MALE STUDENT: How many people really attend your lecture courses?

PROFESSOR: *(Turning to him in irritation)* Look—! *(Embarrassed to answer, he turns away)* It varies.

MALE STUDENT: Sure.

FEMALE STUDENT: Sure.

MALE STUDENT: But in general, how many?

PROFESSOR: *(Very quietly)* Not many.

FEMALE STUDENT: Come on, how many?

PROFESSOR: Sometimes one. Sometimes two, or three.

> (He has crossed the room despondently, just as the MALE STUDENT is reaching for some books on a high shelf, but accidently on purpose makes them tumble to the floor)

MALE STUDENT: Oh, Jeeze, I'm sorry—another accident.

PROFESSOR: On purpose?

MALE STUDENT: Hey, you know the esteem in which I hold you.

PROFESSOR: (Sarcastically) Yeah.

MALE STUDENT: (As the electronic tone returns) Therefore the fact that your lectures are not well attended does not, in my eyes, reflect upon you in the least, but rather upon your students. (The FEMALE STUDENT is quietly rolling the wooden cart into the light. She climbs in, puts her knee up on the railing, studying the PROFESSOR from a provocative pose)

PROFESSOR: You mean, on the ones not totally present.

MALE STUDENT: Possibly those also.

PROFESSOR: But of course—you have no way to know—the quality of those who do attend with regularity.

MALE STUDENT: No.

PROFESSOR: I invite you, Professor. (He is staring at the FEMALE STUDENT)

MALE STUDENT: That's impossible.

PROFESSOR: *(He backs away from the FEMALE STUDENT)* My feeling is, the universe uses me as it will. *(He stumbles over the horse and falls to the floor, then looks up in awe)* Jesus, did I just rhyme?

MALE AND FEMALE STUDENT: *(Quietly)* Oh yeah . . . !

PROFESSOR: It's hard to know, but I think it rhymed with something.

MALE STUDENT: I don't think so.

(The PROFESSOR moves to the rear, where he is illuminated by light coming from the next room, and begins talking to himself)

PROFESSOR: In a certain play entitled "My Head Was a Sledgehammer," a certain character falls deeply in love with his mirror image, although his mirror image doesn't resemble him in many important ways. *(He moves slowly back toward the cart, to gaze at the FEMALE STUDENT)* But is a much more beautiful image. A magic mirror, and the character who has so fallen in love says things that seem beside the point, not expressing love really, but do they?

MALE STUDENT: *(From the shadows at the side of the room)* Do they what?

PROFESSOR: Do they win him the love of women?

MALE STUDENT: Women in general?

(The lights have risen, and are bright again)

FEMALE STUDENT: Be more specific.

PROFESSOR: *(He runs to erase an already erased blackboard and the words pour rapidly out of him, as the two STUDENTS reach up and make books tumble from high shelves, and a* GNOME *rolls the cart around the room)* You see what's happening to me? I've been placed in a situation where verbal disorganization—while it does not rule—has been dreamed of deeply by certain individuals who vibrate on the edge of an aura that does divide a particular arena into those who are beautiful and those who are simply pieces of shit.

FEMALE STUDENT: But Professor, isn't that a false distinction?

PROFESSOR: No longer true, madam.

FEMALE STUDENT: Look at ME—?

PROFESSOR: Once again the goddamned philosophers have undone me.

MALE STUDENT: Does this implicate every single one of them?

PROFESSOR: Correct. Every single one of you has cheated me out of my appropriate energies.

MALE STUDENT: Oh, gee. Which of those sons of bitches have done this to you, Professor?

PROFESSOR: I don't know individual names.

MALE STUDENT: Uh-uh! The truth, Professor.

PROFESSOR: Hey—! *(Ominous music begins, and the* PROFESSOR *mutters to himself)* I want it to pour forth abundantly.

MALE STUDENT: What stops you, Professor?

PROFESSOR: Can truth travel between two people? I think not.

FEMALE STUDENT: How come? *(The MALE STUDENT is poised at the blackboard, ready to take notes)*

PROFESSOR: This I can explain. But don't confuse, please, my explanation with the truth.

FEMALE STUDENT: Explain!

(The PROFESSOR runs to his briefcase, takes out a stack of paper, and throws sheets of it into the air. The GNOMES pick up pieces of paper and run to the walls, holding the paper flat against the walls as high as their arms can reach)

PROFESSOR: If the truth is the truth about something—

MALE STUDENT: —But it has to be about SOMETHING!

PROFESSOR: But: that thing it's the truth about—eats it!

MALE AND FEMALE STUDENT: Huhhhh? *(The GNOMES pull away from the walls to watch in disbelief)*

PROFESSOR: And the truth—eaten—disappears by turning into whatever it is that eats it.

MALE AND FEMALE STUDENT: *(Hitting their foreheads in recognition)* Ahhhh! *(The GNOMES run out of the room)*

PROFESSOR: In order to clarify this, I shall now tear to pieces an important envelope, within which— *(The cabinet rolls in quickly. The PROFESSOR runs to it, takes out an envelope and opens it and reads a piece of paper, which he then tears to pieces and throws into the air like confetti)* I forgot what was in the envelope. But that's okay—because it illustrates my real and most secret import.

FEMALE STUDENT: (Rubbing her body up against him) I don't know how to say this, Professor. But what you just did really turns me on.

PROFESSOR: Not really?

FEMALE STUDENT: Really. (The MALE STUDENT has also come to cuddle up against the PROFESSOR)

PROFESSOR: You're not lying to me?

FEMALE STUDENT: Truth is—I'm not lying.

(Irritated, the PROFESSOR slaps the MALE STUDENT to make him back off. Then he runs to a bookcase and tears up more paper, which he throws into the air)

PROFESSOR: How could I possibly know who's lying? (A doorbell rings)

FEMALE STUDENT: My God, that must be me.

PROFESSOR: (Calls out, as lively dance music is beginning) Just a minute!

(Both he and the MALE STUDENT find more paper to tear up and throw into the air. As it floats down, they shake hands, then bump shoulders and go into the dance they have already performed where they use their hands in a pumping motion, swing their hips in place, and then do aggressive breast strokes as they strut around the stage. The FEMALE STUDENT picks up the horse, holds it between her legs, and tries to ride the horse across the stage in time to the music. Then she falls with a scream)

FEMALE STUDENT: Why did you make me do this, Professor?

PROFESSOR: (As the dance stops) I don't know of course.

FEMALE STUDENT: Intuition?

PROFESSOR: I can't say it was intuition.

> *(The dance recommences minus the FEMALE STUDENT, as two GNOMES enter carrying a giant white envelope high in the air, marching in time to the music. The MALE STUDENT breaks from the dance to grab a small envelope attached to the big one and stares at it, as the dance music gives way to a return of the childlike piano tune and the big envelope is carried off)*

MALE STUDENT: Hey, what can you say about what you've been doing since you came into this room, Professor?

PROFESSOR: Theorize about it? Spare me—

MALE STUDENT: I'm afraid there's no other option, Professor. *(He holds the small envelope to his own forehead)* Close your eyes!

FEMALE STUDENT: What a shame, Professor. *(She is crossing the room carrying an egg she holds over a mixing bowl)* You haven't produced the desirable egg. And your heart, Professor, which was never whole, breaks—*(She breaks the egg into the bowl, as the MALE STUDENT, who has torn his envelope to pieces, throws it into the air)*

MALE STUDENT: Hey, what effect is this having on you, Professor?

PROFESSOR: Remarkable enough, it brings tears to my eyes.

MALE STUDENT: Genuine magic?

FEMALE STUDENT: No tears visible. He makes you believe in them simply by his tone of voice. *(She runs to his side)*

PROFESSOR: Are you threatening to saw me in half, madam?

MALE STUDENT: She doesn't know how to do that without hurting you, Professor.

PROFESSOR: Try hurting me. Go ahead, twist something. *(Each twists one of his arms, and he grunts in pain)* Now I'm feeling a little pain. Though it would be more poignant doing this in public. *(They twist him around and slam him into a blackboard, as the VOICE on tape is heard repeating again and again, "Remarkable people never depend on self-revelation" softly through the following conversation)* What am I able to perceive, even through tears of pain?

MALE STUDENT: Bypass the tears, move to the ears.

PROFESSOR: What's happening?

MALE STUDENT: Oh, it hasn't happened Professor, so that's why it's still interesting.

PROFESSOR: What is?

MALE STUDENT: Well, you've been crying. *(A music of anticipation is heard)*

PROFESSOR: Nobody noticed—

FEMALE STUDENT: Don't believe him. He was crying real tears.

MALE STUDENT: That's what I thought—

PROFESSOR: Don't believe it—*(The cabinet rolls quickly into the room and he runs up to it)* My next trick? This book disappears. *(He takes out a book and holds it up in the air)*

MALE STUDENT: Was the drawer empty?

PROFESSOR: Careful. I make things appear out of nothing. *(He throws the book back into the cabinet, and he and the MALE*

STUDENT *circle each other with their hands up in the air as if to say, "Nothing up my sleeve")*

MALE STUDENT: Bravo, Professor!

PROFESSOR: Thank you, Professor! *(They run toward each other, and just before they collide, fall suddenly on their knees and roll away from each other. Then they fall back exhausted onto the floor)*

MALE STUDENT: Now, tell me, Professor, why do you prefer the disappearing act to the opposite?

PROFESSOR: That takes some explaining—

FEMALE STUDENT: Both kneel for this.

PROFESSOR: *(Rising)* Unnecessary.

FEMALE STUDENT: I assume you both kneel for this, more than once, please.

PROFESSOR: *(Muttering to himself)* Perhaps I have been waiting to enter this very arena.

(The FEMALE STUDENT takes a stack of books from the bookcase, turns back to the PROFESSOR, and deliberately throws the books onto the floor. At the moment of impact, the PROFESSOR and the MALE STUDENT hold their heads and collapse slowly, moaning, "Oh, yeah!")

FEMALE STUDENT: Should I repeat myself?

MALE STUDENT: Does she mean repeating myself even when I don't remember?

FEMALE STUDENT: Everybody—out of this room, please!

MALE STUDENT: What did I say?

FEMALE STUDENT: *(Momentarily perplexed)* If I say everybody—
am I included?

MALE STUDENT: Do it! Do it immediately, please. *(The FEMALE
STUDENT runs out of the room and the MALE STUDENT comes
forward on his hands and knees, unaware of the PROFESSOR
behind him)* Now that I can't see anybody because they left
the room, I can't see anybody, because they left the room.

PROFESSOR: Amazing, sir.

MALE STUDENT: Huh?

PROFESSOR: Your reality is my own reality.

MALE STUDENT: If that's true—?

PROFESSOR: A particular friend helped me out of an impasse.

MALE STUDENT: How?

PROFESSOR: He, or she, blocked all my escape routes.

*(The MALE STUDENT turns to get away but bumps into a wall
and spins off against a blackboard, as an electronic tone
rises)*

MALE STUDENT: But was it a he or a she?

PROFESSOR: I can't possibly remember.

MALE STUDENT: The truth, Professor—

PROFESSOR: That's what I meant from the beginning. I can't
remember!

(The tone rises momentarily, as the pink disk rolls in, and entering with it, and posing in front of it, is the FEMALE STUDENT, *who is now wearing an exotic bright red shoe on one foot)*

FEMALE STUDENT: What changed the minute I left the room, Professor? Come on, tell me what's radically different.

MALE STUDENT: It always happens like this. As soon as someone asks me, What's radically different, if I fail to notice what's radically different, I find myself in very deep shit.

PROFESSOR: I find myself in very deep shit, Professor.

FEMALE STUDENT: Finally, somebody noticed.

PROFESSOR: What was noticed?

FEMALE STUDENT: I bought new shoes, Professor. *(She grabs a leg of the horse, swings it around, and positions herself with one foot displayed on the horse's rump)* Or—at least one.

MALE STUDENT: Jesus Christ, the one thing I failed to notice was an individual shoe!

PROFESSOR: I think we're both in deep shit, Professor.

FEMALE STUDENT: Dizzy? Me too. *(She runs excitedly forward and spins herself, then screams and falls, as the* GNOMES *enter and pull strings from the wall and dangle the little balls over the floor near her body)*

PROFESSOR: This is too much. The angel who dominated my life turns human, but do I believe it?

FEMALE STUDENT: I bought new shoes, Professor, that's all.

PROFESSOR: Why? Of all possibilities—?

228   RICHARD FOREMAN

FEMALE STUDENT: Simple. To get back down to earth. *(Ominous music plays softly)*

PROFESSOR: Run that by me again.

FEMALE STUDENT: *(Rising from the floor)* Careful, Professor. When I pick up speed, I pick up more than speed.

PROFESSOR: Does it really look like I'm about to gravitate toward whatever pulls me in directions I'm totally incapable of traveling?

FEMALE STUDENT: *(Trying to figure things out)* The only thing I can come up with: Somebody must have had God in mind—remember him?—when he went down on his hands and knees in front of me.

MALE STUDENT: That was last night, madam. *(Going down on his hands and knees before her)* But here we have a whole new beginning.

FEMALE STUDENT: I don't see the difference.

PROFESSOR: *(Also going down on all fours)* Here's the difference.

FEMALE STUDENT: *(Circling the two men, as the GNOMES sneak out of the room)* Right again, Professor. The effect is totally different.

PROFESSOR: Continue, please.

FEMALE STUDENT: Well, the word that comes to mind immediately is . . . *(She thinks for a while)* Literature?

PROFESSOR: Stop groping for respectability, madam.

FEMALE STUDENT: I was doing the opposite, Professor. If I say "literature," that's like saying "shit." *(The GNOMES enter, tearing pages from books and scattering them over the floor)* Whereas if I started rolling my tongue over an objective word like "science"? Well, that's sweet enough to plunge somebody like me into those nether regions where pigs do fly, Professor.

PROFESSOR: Strange, to me science has no particular aroma. *(The FEMALE STUDENT kicks his behind, and he jumps up from the floor)* Ow! Why did you do that?

FEMALE STUDENT: Figure it out, my friend. *(He comes down to her and looks into her eyes)*

PROFESSOR: I'm your friend no longer, madam. *(He goes, but she grabs his arm to stop him, as a GNOME is rolling out a thin red carpet diagonally across the floor, and sad violin music is heard)*

FEMALE STUDENT: No longer the friend of science? *(He pulls away and leaves the room)* I must have fallen prey to the unenviable error of being reticent when it comes to putting my best foot forward. *(The MALE STUDENT has picked up the horse and carries it down to her)*

MALE STUDENT: Maybe it's time to try genuine role reversal?

FEMALE STUDENT: Just as an experiment?

MALE STUDENT: Look at it this way. If it's an experiment, we can pretend nobody really gets hurt. *(He throws her the horse, which she catches in her arms, as the pink disk rolls out of the room and is simultaneously replaced by the cabinet, which now offers a display of shoes. The MALE STUDENT selects a pair with red apples attached to the tips of the toes. He sits on the floor putting them on)*

FEMALE STUDENT: Inconclusive. This is inconclusive. *(She throws away the horse, as the childlike piano tune returns)*

MALE STUDENT: (Standing up and looking sadly at his shoes) As a matter of fact, this is inconclusive.

FEMALE STUDENT: (Joining him in contemplation) But it still counts. Because our agreement is—it's inconclusive. (She runs back to grab the horse, pulls it along the red carpet to one end, and sits down on top of it, as the MALE STUDENT lifts the apples off his shoes and studies them)

MALE STUDENT: That reminds me—

FEMALE STUDENT: What?

(Two GNOMES have appeared and are kneeling, each holding out a loaf of french bread toward the MALE STUDENT. Each bread has a little napkin draped over its middle)

MALE STUDENT: (Backing away from the bread) Wait a minute. Am I being asked to invent something? (He reaches for a book on a high shelf, perhaps to research some important invention, but he accidentally tumbles books down over himself. At the same moment the GNOMES are permanently fixing an erect french bread on the toe of each of his shoes. The tiny napkins now delicately cover the upright tips of the bread. The MALE STUDENT takes a few tentative steps, studying the bread that rises from his feet)

MALE STUDENT: You're not going to believe this.

FEMALE STUDENT: Try me, Professor.

MALE STUDENT: This might not be an appropriate moment, but— (He bends toward the bread)—I'm really hungry!

FEMALE STUDENT: Ah, just like Professor Number One, Professor Number Two, Number Three, Number Four, Number Five, Number Six—

MALE STUDENT: Wait a minute.

FEMALE STUDENT: What are you trying to tell me?

MALE STUDENT: How do I know? (*He is lifting a bread from one shoe, holding it close to his body so it points out from between his legs toward the FEMALE STUDENT, who averts her face*)

FEMALE STUDENT: Then how can I share your experience?

MALE STUDENT: Oh, I don't see how it can be avoided.

FEMALE STUDENT: It's being avoided.

MALE STUDENT: Let me show you something.

FEMALE STUDENT: What?

MALE STUDENT: (*He extends the bread a bit more*) You decide.

FEMALE STUDENT: I choose not to see this.

MALE STUDENT: Ahh—

FEMALE STUDENT: (*Whirls to face him, pointing at the bread*) I choose not to see this thing.

MALE STUDENT: —I don't imagine this bread appeals to a female professional such as yourself.

FEMALE STUDENT: Of course not. It's much too long. (*She turns and throws her horse away*)

MALE STUDENT: But. Here's the thing—shorten it.

FEMALE STUDENT: How?

MALE STUDENT: *(His eyes glistening)* Hey, use a knife.

FEMALE STUDENT: You do that, please. *(She hides her eyes and runs to a far corner)*

MALE STUDENT: With a genuine—knife?

FEMALE STUDENT: With a knife!

MALE STUDENT: *(Backing up along the carpet, caressing his bread)* Ah, with a genuine knife?

FEMALE STUDENT: *(She grabs the bread from him and throws it away. Ceremonial horns are heard honking)* I said with a knife, because what I intended, was a knife!

(They both run to the bookcases and throw down even more books, searching for knives, which they find hidden behind the books. They hold them up into the light, which is now intense, and white streamers attached to the knife handles flutter as they move the knives in circles. The music builds and the white hospital screen is rolled into the room by two GNOMES. Behind the screen is the PROFESSOR in his feather headdress, but he towers above it because he is walking on tall cothurni. The screen pivots around him as he slowly advances, and he is seen supporting himself with a long staff. In his other hand is a knife held high in the air, with streamers falling from its handle. Strapped to his waist is an open book trailing long streamers. The music changes to the childlike piano tune. The PROFESSOR advances slowly, his feet weighed down by the cothurni)

MALE STUDENT: Hey, Professor! Why do you walk that way?

PROFESSOR: *(Staring up into the light)* When you get old, Professor—that's what it feels like. So, my God, get used to it, Professor! *(Two GNOMES cause the screen to circle him slowly)* Because that's what it's going to feel like, when your head pivots in the direction of all desirable ladies, and you WOBBLE, Professor—you too Professor! And if you don't get ready for that, Professor, you're going to be very, very unhappy! *(The screen is in front of him now, and he cries out, lifting his arms in the air)* Ohhh! Very unhappy!

(The ominous music becomes deafening, while the GNOMES are tearing pieces of paper to bits, which they throw into the air as the MALE STUDENT and the FEMALE STUDENT run after the floating pieces of paper, trying to stab them with their knives. Then the loud music abruptly stops, and everything is silent, and then a wistful violin is heard, and the PROFESSOR lifts his face up over the edge of the hospital screen)

PROFESSOR: *(Very quietly)*
    See what happens?
    Time passes through unchartable waters.
    Language proliferates
    just so things can be said nobody ever intended.
    Then,
    they come true.

FEMALE STUDENT: I want to see this.

PROFESSOR: I speak. It comes true.

MALE STUDENT: *(Advancing toward the screen)* How, Professor?

PROFESSOR: Pure speed, Professor.

MALE STUDENT: Speed?

PROFESSOR: Jumping fast over every new consideration. *(He points a finger toward the FEMALE STUDENT)*
    Bang!
    And beyond that—nothing.

Getting there really fast, Professor:
Then, nothing.

MALE STUDENT: Hey, that sounds like skipping even, well, life itself, Professor. *(He is circling the room as the GNOMES slowly remove the screen from around the PROFESSOR and install it at the rear of the room, in the shadows, where the GNOMES hide behind it)*

PROFESSOR: Right, everything so fast, life is skipped. *(He is proceeding slowly down the red carpet)* Right.

(From behind the screen, the GNOMES throw their hands up in the air. Just their wiggling hands are visible as they shout gleefully, "Wheee!")

MALE STUDENT: Now, wait a minute, what's achieved if life is simply skipped, Professor?

PROFESSOR: Nothing has to be achieved. That's the beauty of it.

MALE STUDENT: Everything skipped? Then one arrives at nothing, Professor. *(He gestures toward the FEMALE STUDENT, who cracks open an egg over a mixing bowl. Again the GNOMES throw up their hands and shout "Wheee!")* Why is that desirable?

PROFESSOR: I didn't say it was desirable.

MALE STUDENT: Hey! What is it, if it isn't desirable, Professor?

PROFESSOR: Necessary, that's all.

MALE STUDENT: Necessary for what?

PROFESSOR: I don't know. You, you don't know. *(He lifts his staff and points it toward the FEMALE STUDENT)* She, she, she doesn't know—

(*Music rises as the* MALE STUDENT *and* FEMALE STUDENT *join hands and whirl once as the* GNOMES *shout, "Whee!"*)

MALE STUDENT: Then slow down, Professor. Enjoy the ride at least!

(*As the* STUDENTS *come out of their spin, all but the* PROFESSOR *are whirled out of the room. He is left alone in a shaft of light, and he laboriously crosses the room on his cothurni. It is very quiet, just the faraway sound of the childlike piano tune*)

PROFESSOR: (*To himself*) Why do you suppose it is that whenever I remember you, you seem very uncomfortable, Professor? While I, after all is said and done, seem perfectly comfortable.

MALE STUDENT: (*His voice only, heard over the loudspeakers*) Suppose I left, forever. You'd be bored. (*Still alone, the* PROFESSOR *looks with anguish to the sky, and spreads his arms, as if pleading for mercy. The* MALE STUDENT *enters slowly, but the* PROFESSOR *doesn't seem to be aware of him*) You'd be all alone.

PROFESSOR: (*Turning slowly to look at him*) It wouldn't matter.

FEMALE STUDENT: (*Entering the room*) If you were all alone, that would matter, Professor.

PROFESSOR: Oh no it wouldn't. It wouldn't even be part of my life. Because life—that's not where it's happening, madam. You think it's happening in life: you're wrong, beautiful madam.

FEMALE STUDENT: Well, for instance . . . what other place could it be happening?

PROFESSOR: *(He moves laboriously away from her)* No, it's not happening someplace else. It's happening right here. But it's not happening in life.

FEMALE STUDENT: Where is "here," Professor, that isn't in life, please? And if it's not it's someplace else?

PROFESSOR: *(Turning on her in irritation)* Well, why don't we just shut up and admit I'm right? *(The pink disk rolls into the room, hiding the MALE STUDENT)*

FEMALE STUDENT: But that means—give up total power over my own mind.

PROFESSOR: Okay. That means powerlessness. Bye-bye, Professor— *(He points his staff toward the disk, which rolls out of the room, taking the MALE STUDENT with it)* Ah, maybe that's the point.

FEMALE STUDENT: Somebody's mind is a total blank.

PROFESSOR: Ah, isn't that the point, madam?

FEMALE STUDENT: What?

PROFESSOR: *(Listening to a strange new music, looking around the entire room)* What is this?

FEMALE STUDENT: Among myriad possibilities, I don't know to what you refer.

PROFESSOR: *(As the male student sneaks back into the room)* This is an idea that is not allowed to come into existence. *(Both the MALE STUDENT and FEMALE STUDENT slowly sink to the floor, muttering to themselves "Oh yeah . . . !")* Its power as an idea is not thereby minimized. *(He has turned his back and is slowly walking to the rear wall)* Ohhhhh—it still exerts power.

MALE STUDENT: *(From the floor)* Hey . . . what idea is that?

PROFESSOR: *(Turning back to them)* This is an idea that doesn't exist. It makes the walls of this room vibrate. And failing to do so, something else writes on my forehead, letter of invisible fire.

MALE STUDENT: What I don't see is the fire.

PROFESSOR: It's invisible fire!

MALE STUDENT: Sorry, Professor—if it's invisible, it's not in life. And if it's not in life, I'm not interested, because I'm here in life. *(He and the FEMALE STUDENT lift their arms and start slowly spinning through the room, as a new music rises)* So what interests me is here, where I am. *(He and the FEMALE STUDENT meet and tango together for a few steps, then break away from each other and spin to opposite walls as the PROFESSOR shouts over the music)*

PROFESSOR: Hey, that's silly, Professor!

FEMALE STUDENT: Why, Professor?

PROFESSOR: Because what's interesting, Professor, is what's there— *(Pointing his staff at the MALE STUDENT)*—where you are!

MALE STUDENT: Here I am!

PROFESSOR: But—! That you don't know!

MALE STUDENT: Don't know what? *(A pause, and the PROFESSOR turns away)*

PROFESSOR: Where you are.

MALE STUDENT: Ah, but even if I don't know about it, that's still here in life, Professor.

FEMALE STUDENT: Hello again.

PROFESSOR: Once again, very silly.

MALE STUDENT: Do better than that, Professor.

PROFESSOR: *(As a pounding music begins to rise, he stomps across the room)* Okay. That's unalterably SILLY, Professor!

MALE AND FEMALE STUDENT: *(Collapsing to the floor)* Ohhh yeah . . . *(The pounding music rises, as the GNOMES roll in four large disks with blackboards attached, and begin to frantically erase the blackboards)*

PROFESSOR: —because the most interesting thing about anybody in this room is where you are! That part of where you are that isn't where you think you are!

FEMALE STUDENT: Oh, my God—does that rhyme, Professor? *(Both STUDENTS have run to blackboards and are frantically erasing)*

MALE STUDENT: That's silly.

FEMALE STUDENT: That rhymes!

MALE STUDENT: That's so silly!

PROFESSOR: Now that's REALLY silly—*(All the others, GNOMES included, join hands, shouting, "Wheee!" as they circle once around the professor and then return to their work at the blackboards)* Then again, if you really think that's silly—? *(He is bellowing through the pounding music when a flash of light makes everyone erasing fall to the ground and then immediately jump up to start erasing again. Then*

another flash of light, and again they fall and jump back to work—and through all this chaos the professor is striding across the stage on his cothurni and shouting over the music)
Better think it through again!
From the beginning!
One more time! *(He beats the air with his staff, in rhythm with his invocation)*
One more time!
One more time!

(The others have fallen to the floor one last time, and stay frozen with their legs up in the air, as the PROFESSOR *swings his staff into the air one last time and doesn't move, as the light suddenly goes out and the music stops)*

THE END

my head was a sledgehammer
(Original Text)

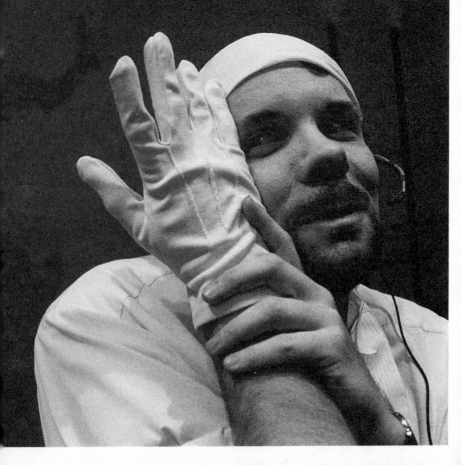

E ACH PLAY IN THIS BOOK HAS BEEN ANNOTATED WITH COMPLEX
stage directions that carefully described the staging each
text was given when I directed it for my own Ontological-
Hysteric Theater. But I can imagine future productions that will
ignore my own style of theatrical productions and completely
reconceive the texts for totally different productions of the same
play. When I have written a play, it first exists on the page in the
form of an open field poem, a text with practically no stage
direction and no indication of who is speaking which lines.

What follows is the text of *My Head Was a Sledgehammer* in
the form it was in when I chose to produce it on stage for the
Ontological-Hysteric Theater. As you will see, many interjec-
tions, and many references to "professor" or to the other
characters—references that were added during rehearsals of my
specifically conceived production—are all absent, as well as
repetitions and other details that evolved in rehearsal but were
determined by the particular setting and characters I chose to
utilize only for my particular staging of the text. The text that
follows is, therefore, the text I originally wrote, before I went
into production. It is clear that the cast was not determined at
this point—there could have been two actors, five actors, or
many more, either male or female—with lines of dialogue suitably reassigned. And the locale where the play was set could
have also been different. I believe that some future production
of the play might wish to consider working from this original,
unannotated text.

I also believe that as pure language, the text has an interest
parallel to and quite different from the annotated script. Need-
less to say, the same stripped-down version of any of my other
plays might easily be prepared, simply by recopying them
minus stage directions and any indication of who is speaking.
It's something I would suggest future directors of my work
consider as a viable option.

Are you as weird as I think you are?

Not likely.

Disturbed? You hear voices?

I'm lucky that way.

I'd say, weird

I feel connected.

Connected to what?

To the source of my voices.

Okay. That's weird.

Are you weird, or am I weird?

What's the criteria?

Let me invite you—Come a little closer.

In what sense?

The question is: What can he do with one hand tied behind his back?

My secret desire is—win love from many beautiful women.

I'll pretend I didn't hear that sentiment.

I'm speaking of things closest to my heart.

Notice what's on her wrist.

A very beautiful watch.

Who do YOU pray to?

I don't.

What kind of religious ceremony?

I don't have any religious observations.

God plays no part in your life?

Not at all.

There is no God in your life?

None at all.

What a beautiful violin.

My God—

Do you play it?

I scratch out noise.

I'll bet you play better than that.

I scratch out terrible noises, which I like doing in private.

You're saying that just to provoke me.

Not at all.

What does your internal time say now?

It doesn't speak to me, it manipulates me in other ways—

Okay. Imagine a completely different play called "Fingers Alert." What could happen in such a play?

Imagine a play called "Dogs on Duty." What could happen in such a play?

Did you ever see this in real life?

An apple.

Remember? Did you ever see this in real life?

You just lied to me.

I don't lie, I don't tell the truth. I'm here to do neither of those two stupid things.

What are you here for?

To be slippery on things.

Here's what I'm here for.
I want to be in a place from which truth—
gushes forth.
I want to be a place
through which truth—
passes.
But when it passes through me—
stripping off its protective cloak—
Ah, but why do I wear my protective cloak?
Because truth revealed, believe it or not, takes the unfortunate shape of everything that isn't true.

This happens. This really happens.
But if mere actors speak this, then it no longer happens.

Me too. I want to be a place through which truth
  passes.

Did I get that right?

I want to be a place through which truth passes.

Turn the page.

I'd like to linger a bit longer over this very particular
  page.

Turn the page.

What does it say on this page?

Wait a minute—

That's my line.

What does it say on this page?

Eat me.

Please?

By the way, do I consider you a place through which
  truth passes? You'll never know because you can't
  get inside my head.

Let's make a guess—

What's a guess?

Somebody should write this down so I don't forget.

Jesus Christ, this is the most interesting thought I've
    had in a long time.

What's a guess?

_____

Do you think I can make this lady disappear?

I do hope somebody gets hurt.

Why?

Do you know the name of every book in your oh-so-
    extensive library?

I believe I do.

I doubt it.

Close your eyes. Then feel your way to the bookcase.
    Take out a book without looking.

As you can clearly see—

Where?

I already wrote the name of the book I predicted you'd
    pick, and sealed my guess in a white envelope.

It's titled—you're not going to believe this.

Oh, I believe it.

"Dossier of Fear."

I have no such book in my entire library.

Look again

You're quite right. The book is entitled "Dossier of Fear." But I'm convinced that heretofore I had no such book. Its pages are all blank pages.

I could have secretly hidden that book in your collection. Isn't that possible?

Would you do that?

Well, imagine a play entitled "Broken Promises."

Welcome. Let me tell you a story in the center of which I hide a very personal message.

Excuse me but—how will we be able to recognize such a private message?

Well . . . Imagine a play. . . .

There might be enough time here to explain something.

What?

Did you ever heretofore explode?

Is this called talking to myself?

Try using my real name.

I don't think names are a real issue, vis-à-vis a man who wants to genuinely explode.

On the verge?

Hey, why not take me up on that?

When stones are shoes, the bottoms of the feet go deaf.

Do I have your permission, at least, to get torn to pieces
    by contradictory forces?

Of course you have my permission.

I was hoping you'd offer me a handkerchief.

Why of all things a handkerchief?

Can't you guess? A handkerchief to stop the bleeding.

From which wound?

Some of them can't be reached. So I'll have to try this
    one conveniently here in the palm of my hand.

That's a very, very old wound.

I was hoping you'd offer me a coat.

Ah, hearts of ice.

You remembered.

I remember nothing, I just go with the flow—

Thank you.

For what?

I'm thrilled to be included.

In what?

Have a seat.

I already did.

It must be that something powerful happened to me. I heard this very desirable woman say out loud to me, "I already did."

But I already do.

Vis-à-vis, you know—chairs. I wanted those words to be magically invested with something powerful enough to throw me to the floor.

I did.

I tried to make it happen.

I did.

Let's just say—time doesn't exist for me.

Wrong. But that should work—

Why should it work if it's wrong? Unless, the key is more interesting than the lock?

No problem.

Here's another way to look at it. What is a human being except that which "doesn't know." Animals, for instance—zebras, lions, buffalo, and more ordinary things like dogs and cats. None of those animal things are in a state of not-knowing, because the issue never arises. So a human being is the birth of not-knowing as a real possibility. And when that beneficent stupidity is ended, then in fact he, or she, is no longer a human being.

You're into something I'm just not into.

That seems to quiet him down to a considerable extent.

I wondered who was going to be the first to say something. *(Pause)* What do you know, it was me.

You almost said something important, but it wasn't you.

Didn't I speak first?

No.

Who did?

I'll have to go into the next room, but—I think if you go I go.

Really?

Yes.

———————————————

What time is it?

My watch stopped.

Think about this. If God himself were to come into this room right now, it would mean time had indeed stopped.

God?

I'm not interested.

You have to be interested.

That's desperation on your part.

Not on my part.

Not on my part.

Now, if God, really—

Oh—that's vulgar, and so pretentious, it's doubly vulgar.

I'm very naive.

Primitive.

Proud of it.

What?

Both.

Better sit in this.

Why.

It's a very electric chair.

I don't want to be electrocuted.

I don't want to be electrocuted either.

Do you see wires?

You like my company, admit it.

True, you like the aggravation. It energizes.

I like that, but I don't like its source, I like its re-sults.

It's the same thing.

It's the same thing.

Pleasant dreams.

I need lots of sleep.

No problem—it's as if a curtain were rising.

Imagine a play called "The Pretend Hat." What could happen—

I'm imagining a play called "Mysteries of Arrogance." That's more my style.

Guess.

What's a guess?

Time will tell.

Quite

Counting on internal time?

I turn into somebody who opens his mouth, and whatever comes out travels in desirable directions only. Automatic truths.

Good. What's the technique?

Well, I make up rhymes.

Then what?

The technique is, they don't rhyme.

Really!

This is supposed to illustrate something.

Ah, your method is the illustrative method.

Yes.

You make up rhymes that don't rhyme.

Not quite. I make up rhymes. I do that. But: they don't rhyme.

I appreciate the difference.

Do you?

Here is my hat.
What do you think of that.

That rhymes.

Oh. I thought perhaps you'd say to me, "That doesn't rhyme."

But it does.
"Here is my hat.
What do you think of that."

Wait a minute. Does that rhyme?

We'll have to find out.

How?

Over the course of time.

How many people really attend your lecture courses?

Look— It varies.

Sure.

Sure.

But in general, how many?

Not many.

Come on, how many?

Sometimes one. Sometimes two, or three.

You know the esteem in which I hold you.

Yeah.

Therefore the fact that your lectures are not well attended does not, in my eyes, reflect upon you in the least, but rather upon your students.

You mean, on the ones not totally present?

Possibly those also.

But of course—you have no way to know—the quality of those who do attend with regularity.

No.

I invite you, Professor.

That's impossible—

My feeling is, the universe uses me as it will. *(He falls)*

Did I just rhyme?

It's hard to know, but I think it rhymed with something.

I don't think so.

———————————————

In a certain play entitled "My Head Was a Sledgehammer," a certain character falls deeply in love with his mirror image, although his mirror image doesn't resemble him in many important ways. But is a much more beautiful image. A magic mirror, and the character who has so fallen in love says things that seem beside the point, not expressing love really, but do they?

Do they what?

Do they win him the love of women?

Women in general?

Be more specific.

You see what's happening to me? I've been placed in a situation where verbal disorganization—while it does not rule—has been dreamed of deeply by certain individuals who vibrate on the edge of an aura that does divide a particular arena into those who are beautiful and those who are simply pieces of shit.

Isn't that a false distinction?

No longer true.

Look at me—

Once again the goddamned philosophers have undone me.

Does this implicate every single one of them?

Correct. Every single one of you has cheated me out of my appropriate energies.

Which of those sons of bitches have done this to you?

I don't know individual names.

Uh-uh! The truth?

I want it to pour forth abundantly.

What stops you.

Can truth travel between two people? I think not.

How come?

This I can explain. But don't confuse, please, my explanation with the truth—

Explain!

If the truth is the truth about something—

—But it has to be about something.

But: that thing it's the truth about eats it.

And the truth, eaten, disappears by turning into whatever it is that eats it.

In order to clarify this, I shall now tear to pieces an important envelope, within which— *(Pause)* I forgot what was in the envelope. But that's okay—because it illustrates my real and most secret import.

I don't know how to say this. But what you just did really turns me on.

Not really?

Really.

You're not lying to me?

Truth is— I'm not lying.

How could I possibly know who's lying?

That must be me.

Why did you make me do this?

I don't know of course.

Intuition?

I can't say it was intuition.

What can you say about what you've been doing since
    you came into this room?

Theorize about it? Spare me—

I'm afraid there's no other option.

Close your eyes.

What a shame you haven't produced the desirable egg.
    And your heart, which was never whole, breaks—

What effect is this having on you?

Remarkable enough, it brings tears to my eyes.

Genuine magic?

No tears visible. He makes you believe in them simply by his tone of voice.

Are you threatening to saw me in half?

She doesn't know how to do that without hurting you.

Try hurting me. Go ahead, twist something. (*Done*) Now I'm feeling a little pain. Though it would be more poignant doing this in public. What am I able to perceive, even through tears of pain?

Bypass the tears, move to the ears.

What's happening?

It hasn't happened, so that's why it's still interesting.

What is?

Well, you've been crying.

Nobody noticed—

Don't believe him. He was crying real tears.

That's what I thought—

Don't believe it.

My next trick? This book disappears.

Was the drawer empty?

Careful. I make things appear out of nothing.

Bravo!

Thank you.

Now, tell me, why do you prefer the disappearing act to the opposite?

That takes some explaining—

Both kneel for this.

Unnecessary.

I assume you both kneel for this, more than once, please.

Perhaps I have been waiting to enter this very arena.

Should I repeat myself?

Does she mean repeating myself even when I don't remember?

Everybody out of this room, please.

What did I say?

If I say everybody—am I included?

Do it immediately, please.

Now that I can't see anybody because they left the room, I can't see anybody, because they left the room.

Amazing. Your reality is my own reality.

If that's true—?

A particular friend helped me out of an impasse.

How?

He, or she, blocked all my escape routes.

But was it a he or a she?

I can't possibly remember.

The truth—

That's what I meant from the beginning. I can't remember.

What changed the minute I left the room. Tell me what's radically different.

It always happens like this. As soon as someone asks me, What's radically different?, if I fail to notice what's radically different, I find myself in very deep shit.

I find myself in very deep shit.

Finally, somebody noticed.

What was noticed?

I bought new shoes. Or—at least one.

The one thing I failed to notice was an individual shoe.

I think we're both in deep shit.

Dizzy? Me too.

This is too much. The angel who dominated my life turns human, but do I believe it?

I bought new shoes, that's all.

Why? Why, of all possibilities—?

Simple. To get back down to earth.

Run that by me again.

Careful— When I pick up speed, I pick up more than speed.

Does it really look like I'm about to gravitate toward whatever pulls me in directions I'm totally incapable of traveling?

The only thing I can come up with— Somebody must have had God in mind—remember him?—when he went down on his hands and knees in front of me.

That was last night. But here we have a whole new beginning.

I don't see the difference.

Here's the difference.

Right again, the effect is totally different.

Continue, please.

Well, the word that comes to mind immediately is "literature."

Stop groping for respectability.

I was doing the opposite. If I say "literature," that's like saying "shit." Whereas if I started rolling my tongue over an objective word like—science? Well, that's sweet enough to plunge somebody like me into those nether regions where pigs do fly.

Strange, to me science has no particular aroma. *(Kicked)* Why did you do that?

Figure it out, my friend.

I'm your friend no longer.

No longer the friend of science? I must have fallen prey to the unenviable error of being reticent when it comes to putting my best foot forward.

Maybe it's time to try genuine role reversal?

Just as an experiment?

Look at it this way. If it's an experiment, we can pretend nobody really gets hurt.

Inconclusive. This is inconclusive.

As a matter of fact, this is inconclusive.

But it still counts. Because our agreement is— It's inconclusive.

That reminds me—

What?

Am I being asked to invent something? *(Bread strapped to the feet, making bread shoes)* You're not going to believe this.

Try me.

This might not be an appropriate moment, but I'm really hungry.

What are you trying to tell me?

How do I know?

Then how can I share your experience?

Oh, I don't see how it can be avoided.

It's being avoided.

Let me show you something.

What?

You decide.

I choose not to see this.

Ahh—

I choose not to see this thing.

I don't imagine this bread appeals to you.

Of course not. It's much too long.

But. Here's the thing—shorten it.

How?

Use a knife.

You do that, please.

With a genuine knife?

With a knife.

Ah, with a genuine knife?

I said with a knife, because what I intended, was a knife.

(One enters on cothurni)

Why do you walk that way?

When you get old, that's what it feels like.

So get used to it

Because that's what it's going to feel like, when your head pivots in the direction of all desirable ladies, and you wobble.

And if you don't get ready for that, you're going to be very, very unhappy. Ohhh! Very unhappy!

See what happens?
Time passes through unchartable waters.
Language proliferates
just so things can be said nobody ever intended,
then, they come true.

I want to see this.

I speak. It comes true.

How?

Pure speed.

Speed?

Jumping fast over every new consideration.
Bang!
And beyond that—nothing.
Getting there really fast.
Then, nothing

That sounds like skipping even, life itself.

Right, everything so fast, life is skipped. Right.

What's achieved if life is simply skipped?

Nothing has to be achieved. That's the beauty of it.

Everything skipped? Then one arrives at nothing.
Why is that desirable?

I didn't say it was desirable.

What is it, if it isn't desirable?

Necessary, that's all.

Necessary for what?

I don't know. You, you don't know. She doesn't know—

Then slow down. Enjoy the ride at least.

Why do you suppose it is that whenever I remember you, you
    seem very uncomfortable, while I, after all is said and
    done, seem perfectly comfortable.

Suppose I left, forever. You'd be bored. You'd be all alone.

It wouldn't matter.

If you were all alone, that would matter.

Oh no it wouldn't. It wouldn't even be part of my life. Because life—that's not where it's happening. You think it's happening in life: you're wrong.

Well, for instance . . . what other place could it be happening?

No, it's not happening someplace else. It's happening right here. But it's not happening in life.

Where is "here," that isn't in life, please?—and if it's not it's someplace else?

Well, why don't we just shut up and admit I'm right?

But that means—give up total power over my own mind.

Okay. That means powerlessness. Maybe that's the point.

Somebody's mind is a total blank.

Ah, isn't that the point?

What?

What is this?

Among myriad possibilities, I don't know to what you refer.

This is an idea that is not allowed to come into existence. Its power as an idea is not thereby minimized. It still exerts power.

What idea is that?

This is an idea that doesn't exist. It makes the walls of this room vibrate. And failing to do so, something else writes on my forehead, letter of invisible fire.

What I don't see is the fire.

It's invisible fire.

Sorry— If it's invisible, it's not in life. And if it's not in life, I'm
  not interested, because I'm here in life. So what interests
  me is here, where I am.

Hey, that's silly.

Why.

Because what's interesting is what's there—where you are.

Here I am!

But— That you don't know.

Don't know what?

Where you are.

Ah, but even if I don't know about it, that's still here in life.

Hello again.

Once again, very silly.

Do better than that.

Okay. That's unalterably SILLY. Because the most interesting
  thing about anybody in this room is where you are. That
  part of where you are that isn't where you think you are.

Does that rhyme?

That's silly.

That rhymes.

That's so silly.

Now that's REALLY silly—
Then again, if you really think that's silly—?
Better think it through again!
From the beginning!
One more time!
One more time!
One more time!

THE END

i've got
the
shakes

I've Got the Shakes. Produced by the Ontological-Hysteric Theater at the Ontological at Saint Mark's Theater, N.Y.C. January-April, 1995. Written, directed, and designed by Richard Foreman.

MADELINE X:	Jan Leslie Harding
LOLA MAE DUPRAE:	Mary McBride
SONYA VOVONOVICH:	Rebecca Moore
SCHLOMO LEVITICUS:	Michael Osano

The play is set in a room that is prepared for a private midnight circus. Balloons and streamers festoon the walls. Several ceiling fans spin above, and mammoth amounts of white flowers cascade near the ceiling.

The room is dominated, however, by a bright red wall at the rear. That red wall thrusts forward at a center fold, slanting back to the right and left on each side of the center, which intrudes aggressively into the square shape of the depicted room.

A cabinet stands to one side, mystical letters decorating its surface. Similar letters appear on the walls, which are filled with a variety of paintings, patterns, and three-dimensional skulls. All across the stage, from left to right just above head height, a narrow transparent plastic panel hangs embossed with backward letters that spell out "I've got the shakes" again and again to fill its entire length. From the center of the ceiling, a large upside-down head pours down tangled golden hair that stops only eight or nine feet above the carpeted floor. Lamps hang from the ceiling, and faintly visible on the red wall are cartoonlike figures—a rabbit and a mouse—each outlined in real flowers. Below them, at eye level, are numerous pads of yellow lined paper, attached to the walls all around the room. The floor is littered with discarded, crumpled pieces of this paper.

A low electronic tone is heard faintly as the audience enters. When it is time for the play to begin, the tone rises in volume and everyone except MADELINE X enters suddenly and crosses to the cabinet. They turn back to look for her as the tone fades. The assembled group includes three elegant CLOWNS, two of them completely chalk white, including their faces, a third who is coal black, and a RINGMASTER in a red coat and hat. These four are onstage for most of the play, moving objects and furniture on and off, and occasionally joining the main characters in frantic dancing. The three characters who enter with the CLOWNS are LOLA MAE DUPRAE, wearing a white ribbon in her hair and loaded down with rings and bracelets; SONYA VOVONOVICH, dressed in a black silk sailor suit; and RABBI SCHLOMO LEVITICUS, wearing a dirty white apron and a black skullcap. The two women wear bright lipstick that has been smudged so it streaks across the lower half of their faces, making it appear as if they had been sloppily eating from a pot of red jam.

MADELINE X appears and crosses through the group to open the cabinet. She wears a skimpy silk dress, very short, and tall sexy boots that rise to above her knees. On her head she wears a diamond tiara. Her lipstick is also smudged across her face.

She leaves the cabinet, and then turns back to confront the group. In general, everyone throughout the play speaks quietly, as if to himself or herself. To facilitate this, each actor wears a headset with a radio microphone.

MADELINE X: Okay?

LOLA MAE DUPRAE: (Slowly pointing a threatening finger at MADELINE X) Careful . . .

(MADELINE X turns and hurries off. The others assemble again in different parts of the room. Then MADELINE X slowly reappears. She is holding one end of a dirty white fringed cloth, which is shoulder high. MADELINE X slowly backs into the room while an invisible someone offstage holds the other end of the cloth so that as MADELINE X reaches the center of the room, the cloth, as she holds it taut, lengthens, its bottom just touching the floor.

SCHLOMO approaches her, and as he gets close, she spins and releases the cloth, which falls to the floor, and SCHLOMO holds his nose, which has been hit accidentally by one of *her hands as she spins. A CLOWN picks up the end of the cloth and returns it to her, and she again pulls it taut)*

MADELINE X: Okay, ignorance. *(The others gather for a brief discussion, then SCHLOMO kneels to MADELINE X)* Yeah. You follow me this far? *(She drops her cloth again, and this time falls on top of the kneeling SCHLOMO. She screams, recovers, and runs downstage as SCHLOMO mutters, "Oh, my back!" The CLOWNS lift the white cloth high behind MADELINE X as a backdrop, over the top of which we can see that the other three actors have climbed onto chairs for safety)* Maybe what this room needs is a name—so it can exist in real space and time. *(She runs into the cloth, pulling it up into a corner of the room, but the CLOWNS hold firm to the two ends, and it forms a slingshot which hurls MADELINE X downstage again into the arms of the waiting RINGMASTER. They pivot once from the collision as MADELINE X mutters, "Shit," and spins off and hits a wall. She recovers and approaches the others, who are now seated)* The space inside this room is named ignorance.

LOLA MAE DUPRAE: *(She speaks throughout the play with a heavy Southern accent)* But my goodness Madeline X, why do you feel the need to put such things into very awkward words?

MADELINE X: Because—awkward though my words may be, there is potential reward.

LOLA MAE DUPRAE: I just don't understand.

MADELINE X: If those words go on just a little bit longer through time and space— *(A six-foot-tall primitive God mask painted red like the walls appears rear, as the RINGMASTER enters carrying a serving tray from which dangle two stuffed human legs)* They make a bridge and I can stand on that bridge of words. *(She has taken a head that resembles her own from the cabinet and places it on the tray over the legs)* Or at least, my head stands on that bridge of words. Not that a head stands, really—because it doesn't have legs, does it. *(She takes the head and, holding it high, circles the room as the others rip paper from the pads, crumple it, and throw it onto the floor. Then she loses control of the head and it falls down on her and she screams)* Careful!

SONYA VOVONOVICH: *(Who speaks with a Russian accent throughout the play)* What's wrong now?

MADELINE X: If one of my feet goes in the wrong direction, I tumble. *(LOLA MAE runs and grabs one of the legs attached to the tray as MADELINE X grabs another and they spin excitedly with little screams of pleasure, but as the God mask exits, the RINGMASTER breaks free and hurries the tray with legs offstage)*

MADELINE X: Careful!

SONYA VOVONOVICH: What's wrong now?

MADELINE X: If one of my feet goes in the wrong direction— Me? I tumble. *(Actors and CLOWNS are now assembled in two lines on each side of the stage, facing each other. A loud buzzer announces a blare of rhythmic music. All flap their arms, circle in place, then dance to the center, where each one steps on another's foot, and with a shout of pain all retreat to their two lines and spin, again flapping their arms. Then, as the volume of the music lowers, MADELINE X dances out alone, spins once, screams out as if she has twisted an ankle, and falls to the carpet. The others scream back at her and run to different parts of the room, laughing at her difficulty. The music has ended)*

MADELINE X: *(After a pause, from the floor)* Okay. I didn't really fall down. *(She rises, and crosses to sit with the others)* That was a trick, but this is where the pain is involved.

SONYA VOVONOVICH: That's bullshit.

MADELINE X: It's not bullshit! It's not bullshit! *(She takes the hands of the two nearest her)* I'm supposed to do funny things based on my own life. That's part of the deal, but I come to the realization right now here in front of you—I, Madeline X, have in me no funniness. *(She rises and leaves them sadly)* That is—I have the form of funniness . . . but no funniness. *(There is a silence. The others are embarrassed even to look at her. Then her eyes light up)* I know. I'll be somebody who isn't funny. *(She takes a little golden hammer from off a shelf and holds it up six inches away from her head)* Oh, this is really gonna hurt. *(She hits her head with the hammer, which makes a tiny "crash." At that moment the* CLOWNS *reappear in a conga line and start circling the room. A rhythmic tape is heard over the loudspeakers intoning to a drumming accompaniment, "Don't be alarmed, don't be alarmed."* MADELINE X *joins the end of the conga line)*

MADELINE X: *(Shouting over the tape)* Let's turn on some more lights in this room! *(The lights indeed brighten, and MADELINE X breaks away from the conga line, which then dissolves. Everybody stands and stares at her)* Now you can see me all the better. Did that make me funnier? *(They turn away in embarrassment)* Well, I can see it didn't.

LOLA MAE DUPRAE: Oh, Madeline X—*(Everyone applauds, and LOLA MAE thinks the applause is for her; she lifts her arms and sings out in operatic style)* "Ohhhhh! Madeline X . . . ?" *(They applaud again, and she turns away delightedly. Then composing herself she turns back to MADELINE X)* Since you resent the rest of us? Well, as much as you claim—

MADELINE X: Did I say that? *(The faint electronic hum is heard again. It comes and goes repeatedly throughout the play, highlighting different sections of the dialogue)*

SONYA VOVONOVICH: *(As the others turn and tear off pieces of paper, which they crumple and throw to the floor. This happens repeatedly throughout the play)* Me—Sonya Vovonovich—says perhaps Madeline X should explain why the arena of your activity is oriented to people like us?

MADELINE X: *(After a pause, in which she looks them over)* I might just look that up. *(She crosses to the cabinet, opens it, and starts tossing things to the floor in search of a heavy book, which she seizes, but which falls on her foot—and she responds with a scream. This is accompanied by a quiet version of the earlier dance music. This music, like the electronic hum, recurs again and again throughout the play, giving a special tone to selected parts of the dialogue)*

SCHLOMO LEVITICUS: *(As the others do a few dance steps to the quiet music. SCHLOMO speaks with a Yiddish accent throughout the play)* Perhaps Madeline X chooses to proceed by a strategy of frustration?

LOLA MAE DUPRAE: Ours?

MADELINE X: No. *(She strides to the center of the room)* Mine. *(The others hiss at her, making gestures of disapproval)* Oh, this is really too painful. *(She runs out, almost in tears)*

SONYA VOVONOVICH: I bet soon little Miss Ambitious comes back. *(All hiss toward where MADELINE X has exited)* Okay. I know—*(She grabs a bouquet of red flowers)* Maybe tonight instead, I—Sonya Vovonovich—will assume her role or position or persona. *(Now they turn and hiss at SONYA)* Oh, this is really too painful. *(She runs from the room, almost in tears. The others run out after her, as MADELINE X reappears rear, carrying a bouquet of red flowers. The music rises—only to be interrupted by a deafening crash of cymbals, which cuts off the music, and makes MADELINE X spin and drop her flowers from shock. She whispers to herself,*

"That's nice." She proceeds down toward the audience, then remembers her flowers and retrieves them)

MADELINE X: Me? (She makes a gesture—which causes her to again drop her flowers. She looks down at them, but decides not to pick them up) Madeline X. I have something to teach. But now what it is admittedly I don't know. But as you can see already I make myself . . . available, when I am in this teaching mode. (A CLOWN runs in rear with a white panel—a kind of elongated lozenge—and MADELINE X runs back to stand with her head against it as if it were a halo that stretches a full six feet up from the back of her head) Though I have in fact, nothing to teach. (The CLOWNS set out three panels, upon which a chair is painted. LOLA MAE, SONYA, and SCHLOMO each come and stand in front of a chair, ready to sit and receive instruction) Though I do. Which is to say, I don't know what I am teaching. But of course—(She whirls once to faint music) Madeline X IS teaching! (She exits, as the three others try to sit on the painted chair but fall to the floor, cursing to themselves. The chairs are repositioned elsewhere, and they run to try again, but again fall cursing, as the chairs disappear and MADELINE X reenters carrying a tiny globe of the earth)

MADELINE X: Know this please!

Outside of me a certain mastery exists. It's called the world. (She lets her globe fall to the floor, frightening the others) Everything the world does is masterful. (She is handed a larger globe, which has a little derby perched on top of it. She comes toward the audience, walking into the center of a string dotted black and white, which has been pulled across the stage by a CLOWN so that as her body pulls the center of that stringdown stage, the string echoes the intruding V shape of the rear red wall.)

SONYA VOVONOVICH: So what? The world is one hundred percent outside a person.

MADELINE X: Well, not one hundred percent.

SONYA VOVONOVICH: You mean outside is inside?

MADELINE X: Somewhat.

SONYA VOVONOVICH: So the mastery of the world is inside you, somewhat?

MADELINE X: I rest my case. *(She kisses her globe)*

SONYA VOVONOVICH: What does this mean—"I rest my case"?

MADELINE X: Well—it's a little bit of the world, isn't it? *(She walks upstage and poses for a moment, lifting the string over her head like a pinup girl)*

SCHLOMO LEVITICUS: *(Praying at the cabinet)* Please die, Madeline X.

MADELINE X: You mean, die to myself of course?

SCHLOMO LEVITICUS: She's interrupting me! *(Their voices compete for a moment with a recording of voices singing, "I won't hurt you, I won't hurt you," which comes over the loudspeakers)*

MADELINE X: How else should I react but by interrupting?

SONYA VOVONOVICH: You don't have to react.

MADELINE X: Then why speak to me?

SCHLOMO LEVITICUS: I rest my case. *(He stretches out his arms, and a globe is placed in each hand)*

MADELINE X: What does that mean—"I rest my case"?

SCHLOMO LEVITICUS: Take a good look. *(As the CLOWNS remove the globes, MADELINE X, who has received a bouquet of red flowers from the CLOWNS in exchange for her globe, throws the red flowers to the floor)*

LOLA MAE DUPRAE: *(Whirls and points to the flowers)* Look, the Rose Room!

SONYA VOVONOVICH: The Rose Room?

MADELINE X: Trash. I'm afraid what you bring me is one hundred percent trash, ladies.

SONYA VOVONOVICH: *(Tearing paper from the wall)* That is the first answer. Now what do we bring you?

MADELINE X: I never fall into such traps

LOLA MAE DUPRAE: We bring you ourselves, Madeline X. And therefore we agree. Total trash.

(There is a loud cymbal crash, which stuns everyone. They quickly recover and run and kneel to MADELINE X)

LOLA MAE DUPRAE: Total trash . . . *(They are overcome with shame and collapse to the floor)*

SCHLOMO LEVITICUS: *(From the floor)* How do we feel after that little faux pas?

MADELINE X: *(She stares at them, then turns away)* Oh, this is really too painful. *(A loud buzzer sounds. Music rises as all hell breaks loose. MADELINE X goes to a wheel of fortune on one of the walls. It's covered with playing cards and candy wrappers, and she spins it frantically by hand as SCHLOMO and LOLA MAE each run and seize six-foot-long beams of wood that lean against another wall. The beams are padded at one end so they look like big black thermometers,* and they run across the stage and crash the sticks against the wall on either side of MADELINE X. But the sticks are attacked by red elastic to their point of origin, so SCHLOMO and LOLA MAE, shaking and moaning from the impact, are pulled back across the stage to where they began. At the same time a small round table is carried on by a CLOWN, and the RINGMASTER places a white projection screen against the red wall. Another CLOWN hides behind a red curtain on a baton that he carries onstage lifted high enough to obscure his upper body and face. MADELINE X has stopped spinning her wheel and examines the front of the mysterious red curtain)

SONYA VOVONOVICH: (Shouting over the music) Try. Try to do better!

SCHLOMO LEVITICUS: (As the music fades) Which means worse, of course.

MADELINE X: Everything's under control, thank you.

SONYA VOVONOVICH: In that case, try harder.

MADELINE X: (Putting her hands against the red curtain) Excuse me. Is this my stupidity at work—or my intelligence?

SCHLOMO LEVITICUS: We don't know.

MADELINE X: (She crosses to the table, behind which SCHLOMO kneels) Test me by touching me.

SONYA VOVONOVICH: A better test is a kiss. (The RINGMASTER whisks away the red curtain for just a second—a CLOWN disguised as a white rabbit is momentarily revealed. MADELINE X turns and screams—and the rabbit is hidden again and hurries off behind his curtain)

MADELINE X: I can't count the number of kisses I've already received.

SONYA VOVONOVICH: What are you going to do about that?

MADELINE X: I'm going to leave it to God.

SONYA VOVONOVICH: You're going to leave what to God? *(The six-foot-tall God mask reenters and is immediately half covered by another red curtain held by the RINGMASTER. SONYA goes behind it and comes forth with a large red-wrapped gift package)*

SCHLOMO LEVITICUS: What we'd all like right now—we'd all like to be initiated into cosmic truths.

MADELINE X: Oh yes. Oh yes, Rabbi, of course. *(He is holding up another little golden hammer, and MADELINE X takes it and positions it six inches from her head)* Shit. This is really gonna hurt. *(She smashes it against her head and moans)*

SCHLOMO LEVITICUS: You look distracted, Madeline X

MADELINE X: I've had bad news. *(The curtain and the God mask whirl)*

SCHLOMO LEVITICUS: Let's not pay any attention.

MADELINE X: My one and only— Can I call him that, please?

SONYA VOVONOVICH: Oh yes, yes do that, please. *(She exits with the package)*

MADELINE X: My one and only left me a letter. *(She grabs a letter from a tray a CLOWN holds out at the end of a long handle)*

SCHLOMO LEVITICUS: After running away with the lady fire superintendent?

(*MADELINE X* is reading the letter, then she lets it fall and turns to *SCHLOMO*)

MADELINE X: Why did you say that?

SCHLOMO LEVITICUS: I think Schlomo Leviticus said, "A very attractive lady fire superintendent".

(*MADELINE X* turns to see *SONYA* and *LOLA MAE* in the rear with white disks on the end of three-foot-long poles—each holding one of the disks in front of another's face. Maintaining this pose, they slowly drift offstage. *MADELINE X* turns back to *SCHLOMO*)

MADELINE X: How did you know?

SCHLOMO LEVITICUS: Maybe Schlomo Leviticus knows things.

MADELINE X: I didn't even know about a lady fire superintendent.

SCHLOMO LEVITICUS: Please don't fixate on things, Madeline X.

MADELINE X: My life's a shambles, that's all! (*She finds a stack of papers, each with a drawing that might represent the face of the Lady Fire Superintendent, and she starts plastering them against the walls*)

SCHLOMO LEVITICUS: Burn.

MADELINE X: What?

SCHLOMO LEVITICUS: Burn!

MADELINE X: Easy to say.

SCHLOMO LEVITICUS: Burn!

MADELINE X: Burn?

SCHLOMO LEVITICUS: It is a definitive function.

MADELINE X: Burn? *(She falls against a wall, then recovers)* I'll burn up.

SCHLOMO LEVITICUS: That teaches Schlomo Leviticus something.

MADELINE X: What?

SCHLOMO LEVITICUS: I don't know yet.

MADELINE X: How long will it take to find out?

SCHLOMO LEVITICUS: Oh, it'll take quite a long time. Lots of things will have plenty of opportunity to go on happening, you very attractive lady— *(He gallantly kisses her hand, and she pulls away. He shrugs)* Take the word of Schlomo Leviticus.

(A loud buzzer, and the electronic tone is suddenly very loud, and MADELINE X runs to spin the wheel again, as SCHLOMO grabs one of the big sticks and again crashes it into the wall next to her. At the same time, the white cloth returns and LOLA MAE and SONYA are wrapped in it, rocking back and forth like two orphans in an open boat in a stormy sea. They are immediately thrown to the floor as MADELINE X runs across the stage and hides her eyes and SCHLOMO goes to spin the wheel. MADELINE X calls out to him)

MADELINE X: Now wait a minute, is it true you know how to navigate life's oceans, Rabbi?

SCHLOMO LEVITICUS: *(Still spinning the wheel as the tone fades)* This information is definitely available.

MADELINE X: Okay, Rabbi, burn, burn, burn, burn, burn, burn!

SCHLOMO LEVITICUS: *(He turns to her)* My exact words reduced to the singular, of course.

MADELINE X: It sounds like multiple to me.

SCHLOMO LEVITICUS: Yes—? *(He lifts his hands and wiggles his fingers over his head)* Multiple in flames.

MADELINE X: Oh, Rabbi, your hands are so expressive.

SCHLOMO LEVITICUS: Could that be—cumulative life experiences?

MADELINE X: *(Examining his hands)* I think it's just your fingers, Rabbi

SCHLOMO LEVITICUS: They must be well exercised.

SONYA VOVONOVICH: *(At the rear of the stage, peering around a corner)* Sonya Vovonovich says, Look, the beloved approaches!

(A little red curtain is carried on rear, concealing the person behind it)

LOLA MAE DUPRAE: This particular beloved would like to know— did Madeline X find the letter? *(She tears a paper from one of the pads on the wall, crumples it, and throws it to the floor)*

MADELINE X: *(Peeking behind the curtain)* I'm really surprised to see him here.

SONYA VOVONOVICH: This particular beloved is of two minds.

SCHLOMO LEVITICUS: My darling—we are all of two minds.

MADELINE X: *(Leaving the curtain, coming downstage)* I'm torn to pieces. What a world!

SONYA VOVONOVICH: Sad, but there's no story in this.

MADELINE X: Please! This is the story of a man who decided to dress like a rabbit and went into the street looking for provocative women.

SCHLOMO LEVITICUS: When the circumstance is right, my darling, the impulse is hard to resist. *(The RINGMASTER has given him a large hypodermic needle. He lifts MADELINE X's skirt, and gives her an injection in her behind)*

SONYA VOVONOVICH: I think there's somebody deciding— *(MADELINE X gives a little scream from the sting of the injection)*—to be very, very, stupid

LOLA MAE DUPRAE: Lola Mae Duprae says, Who likes vanilla Popsicles like I like vanilla Popsicles? *(She is licking a Popsicle)* Ummm!

SCHLOMO LEVITICUS: *(Backing away dizzily)* Hey—!

MADELINE X: What is it? What is it, Rabbi?

SCHLOMO LEVITICUS: Oh, my God. I feel strange.

MADELINE X: Do you feel okay?

SCHLOMO LEVITICUS: Not very. How do you feel after your injection?

MADELINE X: I feel fine.

SCHLOMO LEVITICUS: I think your injection is affecting me. *(He falls to the floor)*

MADELINE X: How could that be?

SCHLOMO LEVITICUS: Not everything is explainable.

MADELINE X: Oh, I'm sure there's an explanation.

SCHLOMO LEVITICUS: *(Still on the floor, struggling to rise)* Don't be foolish, Madeline X.

MADELINE X: Okay. However, if I'm a fool— *(She is repositioning the table so she can sit on it)*

SONYA VOVONOVICH: Leave the furniture alone!

MADELINE X: *(She jumps up and sits provocatively on the table)* I can't help it, can I? I wonder if this is really happening to me or I'm just hallucinating. I mean—he gives me an injection, then I feel fine, but he seems to be suffering— *(SCHLOMO is half up, and falls again to the floor with a heavy thud. MADELINE X turns and looks, then continues her train of thought)*—the results of my injection. But maybe that's only how it appears to me, as a result of my injection. What would I do in this situation? Especially since it may or may not be real.

SCHLOMO LEVITICUS: *(From the floor)* Very much like somebody having a dream.

MADELINE X: Not quite. Whether or not it's dreaming maybe depends on your reaction.

(The RINGMASTER enters with a world globe, which has a derby perched on top, and holds it against the illuminated movie screen)

SCHLOMO LEVITICUS: Oh, no—whatever I'm saying you flip-flop, so it's you talking.

MADELINE X: *(Taking the globe from the RINGMASTER, as LOLA MAE receives another from a CLOWN, as does SCHLOMO)* So whatever you say isn't important.

SCHLOMO LEVITICUS: That's not quite right.

MADELINE X: Hold it! Right there.

> (They run center lifting their globes—each of which is topped by a derby—into the air. Then they set them gently on the floor, and as the globes adjust themselves on the carpet, they all take three steps away and look back at them over their shoulders)

MADELINE X: It could be terribly important to start being stupid.

SCHLOMO LEVITICUS: Too easy.

SONYA VOVONOVICH: I don't know if Sonya Vovonovich finds this easy, but maybe it's because of my personality.

> (A little bell sounds once, and the CLOWNS run on and take away the globes.)

MADELINE X: Okay. Be just—a little more stupid.

SCHLOMO LEVITICUS: How about being totally stupid?

MADELINE X: No, just a little stupid. Stupid in a way nobody could possibly notice.

> (Another little bell, and the CLOWNS enter in silence in a conga line. Then music begins to rise. It quickly becomes quite loud, as the conga line circles the room and the others go to the walls and tear off paper, which they crumple and throw to the floor. Then the music lowers, and MADELINE X holds up her hands for attention)

MADELINE X: Now wait a minute, I know all about this craziness from before.

(*The music rises again, and all run to form two lines on either side of the stage. They flap their arms, run center and stomp, and react with a cry of pain as if each had received a stomp on their foot. They run back into their two lines and circle again waving their arms, and now as the music starts to fade,* SCHLOMO *comes out alone doing a funny dance step of his own invention. He suddenly realizes he is all alone and everyone is watching him. His face reddens. He runs to the table embarrassed, and reaches into a hole in the center of the table. All the others crowd around to see what he is going to extract. He lifts a white ice cream Popsicle into the air. The others retreat and he licks at it lasciviously*)

SCHLOMO LEVITICUS: Now Schlomo Leviticus feels like a human being again. How do you feel?

MADELINE X: No different.

SCHLOMO LEVITICUS: Would you like a Popsicle?

MADELINE X: Okay. (*She takes one from* SCHLOMO. *One of the* CLOWNS *has a mirror with handles that allows it to be whirled, casting flashes of light around the room. As it whirls and flashes,* MADELINE X *backs against the projection screen, dizzy from the flashing mirror*)

MADELINE X: How come you didn't offer me one of these earlier?

SCHLOMO LEVITICUS: Oh, it just didn't occur to me.

MADELINE X: But it occurred to you to give me an injection.

SCHLOMO LEVITICUS: Of course.

MADELINE X: How strange you are, Rabbi.

SCHLOMO LEVITICUS: You're sure you're being objective?

MADELINE X: *(Shielding her eyes)* No.

SCHLOMO LEVITICUS: After all, certain chemicals are, or could be, profoundly affecting the human brain.

(LOLA MAE and SONYA have each taken a small golden hammer, and they hold them up toward their heads)

LOLA MAE: Oh, shit, this is really gonna hurt. *(Both smash themselves and moan, then run and get Popsicles)*

MADELINE X: I know all about this craziness from before.

SCHLOMO LEVITICUS: Is everyone enjoying their Popsicles?

MADELINE X: I hardly started my licking my own.

SONYA VOVONOVICH: What flavor is this very peculiar Popsicle?

SCHLOMO LEVITICUS: It's my own invention.

SONYA VOVONOVICH: Shlomo Leviticus, what I said was—

SCHLOMO LEVITICUS: Shhh! *(He grins delightedly, as the music that has been playing in the background rises)* It's fish flavor. *(He whirls to the music, lifting his Popsicle)* It's fish flavor.

ALL: Ugh!

SCHLOMO LEVITICUS: See why I didn't offer you something I knew you wouldn't enjoy so much?

MADELINE X: Okay, why don't you try giving me another shot?

SCHLOMO LEVITICUS: Oh? Do I always do everything I'm told? *(He shrugs, takes out another hypodermic needle, but instead of giving MADELINE X an injection, he turns around and sticks himself in the behind. After an initial wince of pain, he puts away the needle and shrugs)* Schlomo Leviticus felt nothing. I must have developed an immunity.

LOLA MAE DUPRAE: *(She sits on the floor, legs spread like a little girl, and she holds out her Popsicle toward* SCHLOMO*)* How about a taste of this, Rabbi? *(The dotted string has again been stretched across the stage, and a small white panel is held behind* LOLA MAE, *framing her as she sprawls on the floor)*

SCHLOMO LEVITICUS: A fresh Popsicle, why not? I'm already habituated. *(He ducks under the string to join her in front of the panel. He takes her Popsicle and licks it, then offers to pass it back to her)*

LOLA MAE DUPRAE: Please, you finish it.

SCHLOMO LEVITICUS: We'll take turns.

LOLA MAE DUPRAE: I can't. Not after you've licked it.

SCHLOMO LEVITICUS: We've had a discussion, my dear. So whatever it is you're going to catch from me—you've catched it.

LOLA MAE DUPRAE: It's in bad taste, Rabbi. *(A* CLOWN *extends a stick, at the end of which is a white disk with painted eyes and a realistic three-dimensional nose protruding from its center. This is maneuvered in front of* LOLA MAE'S *face, and she holds the false nose with two fingers, as if it were her own)*

MADELINE X: Ah, that's why she's holding her nose. *(As she angles to get a better look, she walks into the dotted string, pulling it downstage with her body)*

LOLA MAE DUPRAE: Does this make me look pretty?

MADELINE X: Not at all.

LOLA MAE DUPRAE: Okay. Does it make me look disgusting?

MADELINE X: That could be a mental association.

(*The RINGMASTER holds another disk on a stick in front of the nose disk, hiding it. His has a checkerboard pattern*)

SCHLOMO LEVITICUS: (*Rising, going to a shelf to collect a wicker box*) It must be frustrating to find yourself continually in the neighborhood of associations instead of facts.

MADELINE X: I make up my own facts, thank you—even if they last only a fraction of a millisecond.

SONYA VOVONOVICH: This is more than a millisecond.

MADELINE X: That's because you're not paying attention.

SCHLOMO LEVITICUS: (*Holding out the box*) Here's for paying attention, ladies. Let's see what's inside the rabbi's box?

(*LOLA MAE comes, opens the box, and pulls out a stuffed rabbit. There is a pause*)

MADELINE X: Something's missing.

LOLA MAE DUPRAE: What?

MADELINE X: What's missing from this picture?

LOLA MAE DUPRAE: Hey, could you think of this as a picture? (*She ponders this, then puts the rabbit back in the box*)

MADELINE X: I think I know what was missing. (*SONYA offers a bouquet of red flowers. MADELINE X looks at her. Then turns away*) No. Wait a minute. (*She goes to the box, takes out the rabbit. It hangs down from her hand as she holds it by the*

ears, but she doesn't look at it. She stares into space)
Something's missing.

SCHLOMO LEVITICUS: You must be picking up on some revelatory quiver.

MADELINE X: Maybe I just glanced toward a mirror. *(A CLOWN passes by her, revolving a mirror which makes MADELINE X hide her eyes from its flashing)*

SONYA VOVONOVICH: At the exact moment all things were quivering?

LOLA MAE DUPRAE: Let's look again. *(She opens the box again, and takes out a velvet bag, which she holds against the projection screen as she fumbles inside it)*

MADELINE X: There's no mirror.

LOLA MAE DUPRAE: *(Looking in her bag)* Is God here?

MADELINE X: What a ridiculous question.

LOLA MAE DUPRAE: *(As she turns the bag inside out, and the six-foot-high God mask appears at the side for just a moment, before being covered by the ringmaster's red curtain and being whisked offstage)* Is God in this thing?

MADELINE X: I don't want to answer questions about that!

SONYA VOVONOVICH: Who asked?

LOLA MAE DUPRAE: Let's look again. *(She peers deep into her bag)* Is God here?

MADELINE X: Who?

SONYA VOVONOVICH: *(Whispering)* God god god!

(The three chair panels are carried quickly to position, and LOLA MAE, SONYA, and SCHLOMO try to sit and fall to the floor)

OTHERS: *(Whispering as they fall)* God god god!

LOLA MAE DUPRAE: *(Rising quickly and pointing to the bouquet of red flowers SONYA dropped earlier)* Look! The Rose Room!

(They are all hurled violently to the wall, as the lights change suddenly)

MADELINE X: What made those beautiful flowers tumble to the carpet?

SONYA VOVONOVICH: Sonya Vovonovich does not know.

MADELINE X: I repeat. What made the flowers tumble?

LOLA MAE DUPRAE: Isn't it beautiful in this room?

MADELINE X: See? You learned that from me.

LOLA MAE DUPRAE: Do you think I'm beautiful? *(In a far corner, three CLOWNS appear, each with a double-sided mirror with handles that they spin in front of them at chest level, and MADELINE X moves away from the wall)*

MADELINE X: What made the flowers tumble, what's causing my eyes to see, what's causing my tongue to move? Probably nothing.

LOLA MAE DUPRAE: Something must have made it happen.

SCHLOMO LEVITICUS: *(Pointing to the mirrors)* Schlomo Leviticus says optics—

SONYA VOVONOVICH: Of course. Of course.

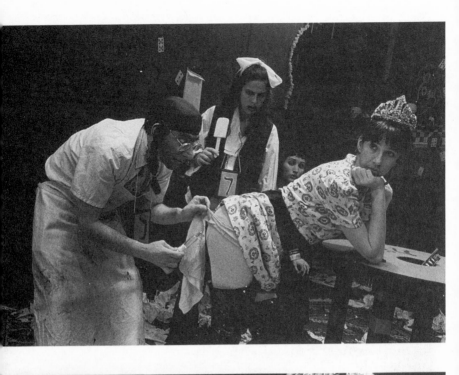

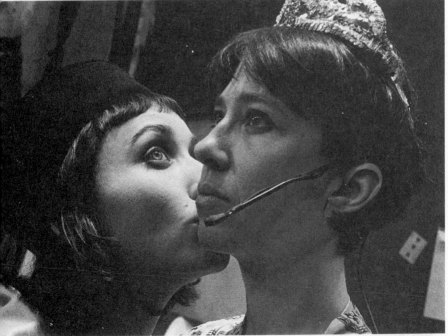

MADELINE X: (*Turns away momentarily blinded by the flash from the mirrors, which then exit*) Except the one thing I can't see is myself!

SCHLOMO LEVITICUS: Are you sure?

MADELINE X: I'm missing. Who's free to contradict that?

SONYA VOVONOVICH: Sonya Vovonovich would be happy.

MADELINE X: Somebody give me a kiss, please. (*SCHLOMO kisses her hand, and she pulls away*)

SCHLOMO LEVITICUS: Does this do anything for you, Madeline X?

MADELINE X: I don't think so.

SCHLOMO LEVITICUS: Look again, please.

MADELINE X: At what?

SCHLOMO LEVITICUS: That's not a relevant option.

MADELINE X: (*Taking a drink of water offered by LOLA MAE*) Okay—I just looked again. (*SONYA is holding out her arms toward MADELINE X*)

SCHLOMO LEVITICUS: —Saw?

MADELINE X: Nothing special. (*She takes another sip of water, and spits it out over SONYA*)

SONYA VOVONOVICH: Hey, now I am dirty!

MADELINE X: (*Crossing to in front of the white projection screen*) Okay. I was able to erase my thoughts for a fraction of a second.

SONYA VOVONOVICH: Thank you very much. Then what?

MADELINE X: Nothing. Thank you very much.

(A CLOWN carries out the white lozenge again, but this time holds it in front of MADELINE X's face. Then the RINGMASTER enters and holds a stick with a small white disk on the end in front of the lozenge. White on white. There is a pause)

MADELINE X: *(Hidden behind the disk and the lozenge)* I don't want a hole in the center of my life. *(Disk and lozenge are whisked off, and MADELINE X throws the stuffed rabbit into the center of the room)*

SONYA VOVONOVICH: Hey, I just saw it!

MADELINE X: What?

SONYA VOVONOVICH: That dead rabbit you've been carrying!

MADELINE X: But I'd already been holding it a long time.

SONYA VOVONOVICH: I just saw it!

MADELINE X: Okay. *(She picks it up again)* Me too. *(She drops it)* I just saw it. *(She starts stomping on it)*

SONYA VOVONOVICH: When I say "a dead rabbit," that takes considerable powers of discrimination—*(The stomping of the rabbit seems to make the three of them dizzy, and they fall to the floor around the rabbit)*

MADELINE X: Well, if you call those things we hold in common powers of discrimination.

SONYA VOVONOVICH: I do. Exactly right.

(*MADELINE X* rises quickly and throws the rabbit out of the room)

SONYA VOVONOVICH: (*Screaming in anguish*) You hurt the dead bunny!

(*There is a loud crash, and the lights flash blindingly bright for just a second, making everyone stagger. A* CLOWN *reextends the dotted string across the stage*)

MADELINE X: (*Holding her head from the crash*) That's not nice.

LOLA MAE DUPRAE: (*Recovering also*) Okay, okay, okay, okay! Let me play teacher for a moment and I'll ask you this: Did you ever try using a special focused beam of light to cast a shadow? Using your hands only—but manipulating them in such a way that the shadow cast is the shadow of a cute little rabbit? See? (*She makes a shadow rabbit, and* MADELINE X *comes to see and bumps into* LOLA MAE) Just stand back a little bit!

MADELINE X: Oh, that's so cute. Do it again. How do you do that?

LOLA MAE DUPRAE: You can do it too, Madeline X.

MADELINE X: Me?

SONYA VOVONOVICH: Try it.

(*MADELINE X looks at her hands, and plunges downstage, pulling the center of the string with her, as LOLA MAE and SONYA pull back against the walls as if afraid that MADELINE X is creating a warp in the space of the room. At the front of the stage, far away from the projection screen, which is at the back wall, MADELINE X holds up her hands, ready to make a rabbit*)

MADELINE X: I don't think this is going to work but I'm willing to try. *(She winds her fingers together)* This isn't working. There's nothing but light.

LOLA MAE DUPRAE: You haven't put your hands into it.

MADELINE X: Ah? You see? This is no recognizable rabbit. What's wrong?

SCHLOMO LEVITICUS: *(Entering at the side of the room)* Dear Madeline X, what's wrong? *(He taps her on the shoulder)* What's missing from this picture?

MADELINE X: Well, it's true—it could be thought of as a PICTURE.

SCHLOMO LEVITICUS: *(He stretches his arms and yawns)* Ah, that said of course, a multiplicity of other possibilities shut down for the night. *(He goes and curls up in a chair to the side, where he will soon fall asleep)*

SONYA VOVONOVICH: Interesting—what is missing from this picture?

MADELINE X: It's a hole. *(The electronic hum rises, and MADELINE X moves upstage to put her hands on the white projection screen. The noise stops)* It's a hole.

SONYA VOVONOVICH: Not a hole, but the opposite.

(Three CLOWNS enter with large books under their arms)

MADELINE X: That's what's missing.

SONYA VOVONOVICH: What is missing? *(The CLOWNS have opened their books, and revealed are three large pictures of an identical mountain)*

MADELINE X: Something really big.

LOLA MAE DUPRAE: It's a mountain.

MADELINE X: It's a hole in the opposite direction and that's what's interesting.

LOLA MAE DUPRAE: Really?

MADELINE X: Yes. Why do I have to repeat myself?

LOLA MAE DUPRAE: You don't have to repeat yourself, just put your money where your mouth is. Let's go mountain climbing. Isn't that what you were talking about?

(The CLOWNS have gone)

MADELINE X: How should I know?

LOLA MAE DUPRAE: I know—how about opening a new chapter of our mental experience?

MADELINE X: Where is this mountain we're going to climb?

LOLA MAE DUPRAE: I can make reference to it by showing you this tiny little representation. *(She takes a big book from a shelf and takes out a postcard tucked in its pages—one side of it shows a picture of the same mountain)*

MADELINE X: A real mountain? One that really exists? *(They are startled by a pair of mountain-climbing boots thrown in from offstage. SONYA picks them up and dangles them in front of MADELINE X)*

SONYA VOVONOVICH: Klippity Klopping up the cute little mountain. *(She knocks them together and lets them fall to the floor. The RINGMASTER has also entered carrying heavy boots. After SONYA'S boots fall, he lets his own fall to the floor with a thud. LOLA MAE picks up these boots and slowly crosses the room, as mystical music is heard in the distance)*

LOLA MAE DUPRAE: I can assure you . . .

MADELINE X: What?

LOLA MAE DUPRAE: Lola Mae Duprae says, Even though lots and lots of this particular mountain don't exist and therefore can be said not to exist, we can try climbing all the way to the top, even if it may be impossible to have the experience of doin' such a thing.

MADELINE X: Can I reinterpret that please? It's going to be sort of a mental adventure.

LOLA MAE DUPRAE: Oh, no, Lola Mae Duprae would never say anything that peculiar.

MADELINE X: Then can you explain how we go about climbing it?

LOLA MAE DUPRAE: Well . . . maybe once upon a time we did— but maybe we have to do it again without knowin' we ever did it before.

MADELINE X: This is not clear to me.

SONYA VOVONOVICH: *(The light in the room has become dim, and* SONYA *crouches in the shadows)* My dear, my most darling Madeline X—

(The mystical music rises as LOLA MAE *lifts her arms in the air to sing)*

LOLA MAE DUPRAE: Yodel-odel a-he hoo!

SONYA VOVONOVICH: *(Calling out over the music, as all the* CLOWNS *and the* RINGMASTER *reenter with books they place against the rear wall, and then open, displaying the mountain picture as if it were hanging on the red wall)* From her faraway mountain kingdom, Sonya Vovonovich says, Your hopes? They lie in the wrong direction.

MADELINE X: But I should be hopeful?

SONYA VOVONOVICH: Oh, no. I did not say that.

MADELINE X: (*Turning to study the mountain pictures*) A very interesting mountain after all.

SONYA VOVONOVICH: (*She has the little postcard, and holds it up*) This is your true opinion? For me, Sonya Vovonovich, here is the better little mountain.

(*The music rises again, and the CLOWNS and the RINGMAS-TER slowly turn and carry their pictures down to the front of the stage, displaying them to the audience. MADELINE X comes down with them, and peers at the pictures from between two CLOWNS*)

MADELINE X: Aside from their relative multiplicity, they look much the same.

SONYA VOVONOVICH: My little one is absolutely different.

MADELINE X: Why do you prefer that little one?

SONYA VOVONOVICH: Because my little one leads me to the other bigger ones.

MADELINE X: So in the end, you prefer that one. (*She indicates the bigger ones*)

SONYA VOVONOVICH: This is not what I am saying.

MADELINE X: (*Dizzy now, trying to clarify things in her mind*) But if that little one leads you to this one, and that fact is the reason of your preference—?

SONYA VOVONOVICH: You're not thinking about this clearly. (*LOLA MAE deposits a coil of heavy rope onto the carpet behind MADELINE X, who turns to see what it is*) Now you are trying too hard.

MADELINE X: What's that for?

LOLA MAE DUPRAE: Mountain-climbing equipment.

MADELINE X: I don't think climbable mountains abound here.

LOLA MAE DUPRAE: Guess what. Madeline X is right.

MADELINE X: Hey—should I put the rope back?

SONYA VOVONOVICH: I suppose for neatness. Okay. (*MADELINE X bends to get the rope, but freezes in that position*) What's wrong?

MADELINE X: Suddenly I feel dizzy.

SONYA VOVONOVICH: Sit down. (*MADELINE X collapses onto the floor*) Well, I didn't mean on the floor, Madeline X.

LOLA MAE DUPRAE: Sit on a chair, beautiful teacher.

MADELINE X: The teacher is too dizzy to get up.

SONYA VOVONOVICH: I didn't say get up, I said sit!

MADELINE X: Look. Anybody can do what you're doing—

LOLA MAE DUPRAE: What she doing, teacher?

MADELINE X: Causing a certain disorientation.

SONYA VOVONOVICH: I'm not causing any disorientation on purpose.

MADELINE X: Oh, yes.

LOLA MAE DUPRAE: Oh, no. (*MADELINE X struggles to get off the floor, but keeps falling back down*)

MADELINE X: Making the names of things questionable is an attempt at manipulation. And don't suggest I sit down because I already am. (*She finally gains her feet*)

LOLA MAE DUPRAE: I'm going to get you another drink of water.

MADELINE X: (*Sarcastically*) Well, thank you for your generous offer! (*She exits*)

LOLA MAE DUPRAE: I could refill the pitcher—

MADELINE X: (*Bounding back into the room*) Did you say PIC-TURE? (*A shocked pause. LOLA MAE looks about nervously*)

LOLA MAE DUPRAE: Which one?

MADELINE X: The little one.

LOLA MAE DUPRAE: (*Running to the center of the room, still carrying the pitcher she was about to refill*) Why the little one as opposed to the other bigger ones that were all over this place?

MADELINE X: Wait a minute! (*They wait*) That means you're as hungry for meaning as I think you are.

(*This accusation seems to upset LOLA MAE, who looks about for help, then pours herself a glass of water but in her nervousness spills it all over herself, and she shouts out to no one in particular*)

LOLA MAE DUPRAE: I am no such thing! (*She runs from the room*)

SONYA VOVONOVICH: Liar! That means I agree. (*She runs after LOLA MAE, and MADELINE X tries to follow, but slips and falls on the floor. There is a pause*)

MADELINE X: I guess that means I'm alone. Maybe now I can tell the truth about myself.

SCHLOMO LEVITICUS: Schlomo Leviticus is still here, my dear. (*He has been sleeping in his chair all this time*)

MADELINE X: (*Turning around, getting up*) Excuse me, I didn't know anything about that!

SCHLOMO LEVITICUS: I'm in plain sight, my darling, but I'm hidden.

MADELINE X: Hidden?

SCHLOMO LEVITICUS: Didn't you notice?

MADELINE X: Hidden? (*She covers her eyes and counts to ten*) I better make an inventory. (*A loud buzzer, and loud music, which then fades down as MADELINE X starts to take inventory, and all the others, CLOWNS included, come onstage and start checking the objects in the room*) This chair, that wall, that cabinet, this floor, carpet, bookcase, table, shelf— (*She stops and turns to the others, who stop moving*) Well, I am pleased to see everybody ready to learn something important. Question number one: How many of us does it take to change things in this universe completely? Twelve—? (*She turns one CLOWN to face her*) Including you? Seventy-five—? (*She turns another*) Including you? One thousand one hundred and twenty-one—? (*She turns a few more*) Including the rest of you? Answer. One person is enough to change things completely.

SONYA VOVONOVICH: This is new information.

MADELINE X: Of course. If I went crazy, all my problems would be solved. *(They all kneel to her, then quickly rise. But she gestures them to the floor, and they follow her instructions. Then she raises her arms, and they copy her, then she swings them down and they bow down on the floor to her. Satisfied, she continues her explanation)* Because I'd be in limbo. But the amazing thing is—your problems also. They'd be taken care of. Because—and this is going to be a big shock to your electrical systems, ladies—ZAP! *(As she imitates an electric shock, the music pops on again very loud, and the others run to the center of the stage, where MADELINE X stamps her foot once, and they all react as if she'd stepped down hard on each one's foot. They scream in pain and run off, except for LOLA MAE, who backs away, baffled)* Because I'm the only universe there is! Your universe doesn't exist. *(Pause)* What part of the universe doesn't exist, please? Whatever part isn't my own part. *(Pause)* Not convinced? To clinch my argument I will now act noninsane. *(A pause. LOLA MAE stares at her)*

LOLA MAE DUPRAE: It's kinda hard to tell. *(Another pause)* Well, I'm sorry, but this isn't the first time it was kinda hard to tell the difference between crazy and what seemed crazy and what wasn't crazy.

MADELINE X: Surprise!

(A loud crash, followed by music, makes LOLA MAE scream. She whirls to see a CLOWN in the doorway, holding the red-wrapped package)

LOLA MAE DUPRAE: It WAS a surprise! *(She takes the package and gives it to MADELINE X)*

MADELINE X: Yes, it was.

LOLA MAE DUPRAE: Okay. I can make an obvious gloss—well, two obvious glosses.

MADELINE X: Surprise!

LOLA MAE DUPRAE: First, you and me, Madeline X and Lola Mae Duprae, we are such reality-evading personalities that we prefer mystification to clarity, as an escape from a reality we're too weak or immature to handle. *(She brings her hand down in a hard slap onto the package, which falls from MADELINE X's hands. They both step back with a little scream as it hits the floor. The music stops)* But number two—somewhat more complimentary to the both of us—

MADELINE X: Is this what Madeline X is teaching?

LOLA MAE DUPRAE: All mystification—you know what I mean? *(There is a pause)*

MADELINE X: I know what you mean.

LOLA MAE DUPRAE: All mystification, before clarified, suggests a hidden something or other of great importance for which I, Lola Mae Duprae, have to confess— *(She takes MADELINE X's hand)* I am desperately hungry.

MADELINE X: This must be what I'm teaching, right?

(The music is heard quietly, as the CLOWNS again set out the painted chair panels. LOLA MAE crosses slowly to lean against the panels. As she does so, her personality seems to change. She seems to mature and her Southern accent becomes seductive rather than silly)

LOLA MAE DUPRAE: Not quite right, Madeline X. See, any premature clarification, because a clarification by definition is premature and reveals only itself, the premature, rather than the unfathomable something I've been able to intuit. *(She turns her back on MADELINE X)* You understand of course—?

MADELINE X: *(As if hypnotized)* I understand, of course.

LOLA MAE DUPRAE: That I'm speaking in your voice? *(There is a pause)*

MADELINE X: Of course I understand that. Free-associate.

(There is another loud crash and a flash of very bright light. MADELINE X winces and turns to hide her eyes, whispering, "That's not nice." But LOLA MAE seems unaffected and slowly puts on a pair of white gloves)

LOLA MAE DUPRAE: *(Her voice suddenly deep and languorous)* What drug are you really on, little lady?

MADELINE X: What drug are you on?

LOLA MAE DUPRAE: Oh, no. You tell me—what drug are you on?

MADELINE X: Would you believe me if I told you that what I want is to have a powerful drug experience without taking a drug?

LOLA MAE DUPRAE: All things are put together in a certain way.

MADELINE X: Right.

LOLA MAE DUPRAE: I just want them to be put together in a different way.

(The chair panels are taken away, and MADELINE X runs to one of the wall pads, tears off some paper, crumples it, and throws it to the floor)

MADELINE X: Okay. A follows B.

LOLA MAE DUPRAE: *(Tearing paper and throwing it to the floor)* Don't you mean B follows A?

MADELINE X: *(Running to a pad on the other side of the room, tearing more paper)* But B could be totally inside A. Think about it. Doesn't that mean B could be skipped—completely skipped? *(There is a pause)*

LOLA MAE DUPRAE: You look very satisfied with yourself, Madeline X.

MADELINE X: Maybe I'm on a very rare drug.

LOLA MAE DUPRAE: Lola Mae Duprae—remember her? She says, "What does it do? This very rare drug?" *(A pause)*

MADELINE X: Nothing. *(The RINGMASTER enters slowly, and places a white disk which is on the end of a stick, so it covers MADELINE X'S face.)*

LOLA MAE DUPRAE: If it doesn't do anything honey, it's not much of a drug.

MADELINE X: Wrong again.

LOLA MAE DUPRAE: How come?

MADELINE X: Because it's very powerful.

LOLA MAE DUPRAE: I'd say by definition— *(A CLOWN comes and places a similar disk in from of LOLA MAE'S face)*—if it doesn't do anything, it's not.

MADELINE X: That's why it's powerful.

LOLA MAE DUPRAE: Because it has no effect?

MADELINE X: It has a big effect.

LOLA MAE DUPRAE: What?

MADELINE X: It doesn't do anything. (*They both push away the disks, then* SONYA *appears, and all three run to separate corners of the room and take handkerchiefs from hiding places near each of them and hold the handkerchiefs up to their faces. They turn their backs to each other, breathe deeply, and fall to the floor, giggling*) See? It doesn't do anything.

LOLA MAE DUPRAE: Then I've achieved the same effect without drugs.

MADELINE X: (*Rising*) Wrong. (*She swivels her hips to unheard music*) That's where you are wrong, Lola Mae Duprae!

LOLA MAE DUPRAE: (*Giggling at* MADELINE X'S *dance*) That's not nice.

SONYA VOVONOVICH: (*Still on the floor*) Why is this happening to us?

MADELINE X: I can think of one reason. It would be the result of strong emotions.

SONYA VOVONOVICH: Why would anyone want strong emotions?

MADELINE X: I didn't say I want any such thing. I said it could happen.

(*There is a loud buzzer and* SCHLOMO *comes on with a suitcase. The electronic hum is discernible*)

SCHLOMO LEVITICUS: I have here a powerful drug, ladies. It's called "Drink me." (*He extracts a bottle with a label that reads "Drink me!"* MADELINE X *studies it for a few seconds*)

MADELINE X: Drink me . . .

SCHLOMO LEVITICUS: Ah, a very interesting interpretation.

MADELINE X: It wasn't an interpretation.

SONYA VOVONOVICH: *(Holding out a heavy book)* Can you read this, then—which might need a little interpretation?

MADELINE X: Hey, are you as hungry for meaning— *(She snaps her fingers and the hum vanishes)*—as I think you are?

SONYA VOVONOVICH: Read this and find out.

MADELINE X: No, thank you.

LOLA MAE DUPRAE: *(Far upstage in the corner of the room)* Okay, Madeline X—can you read the heartbreakin' thing that's carved in stone on the top of this doorway leadin' outa this room once and for all?

MADELINE X: I don't have to read that.

SONYA VOVONOVICH: It says, "Penetrate such a door and everything changes."

MADELINE X: *(Turning away from them, to herself)* Once upon a time I memorized those very words.

LOLA MAE DUPRAE: Read it anyway.

MADELINE X: *(Crossing up to the door)* What does it do when I read it?

SONYA VOVONOVICH: We don't know.

LOLA MAE DUPRAE: You tell us. We're scared.

(The electronic hum becomes very loud, as MADELINE X passes through the door. At the same moment, two CLOWNS run on with the white cloth; they hold it shoulder high in front of the door, between the rear wall and a side wall at a

45-degree angle, but *SONYA* and *LOLA MAE* immediately take over. *Each taking an end of the cloth from a CLOWN, they reverse sides, flip-flopping the cloth but keeping it taut at shoulder height as MADELINE X reenters and comes to stand behind the cloth, looking over its edge at the audience. The electronic tone stops suddenly, and there is dead silence)*

MADELINE X: Nothing.

SONYA VOVONOVICH: Right. But what's it like?

MADELINE X: Nothing.

LOLA MAE DUPRAE: You know—in that other universe?

MADELINE X: No communication is possible.

LOLA MAE DUPRAE: That's what I thought too.

SONYA VOVONOVICH: That's bullshit!

(MADELINE X walks quickly forward into the cloth, as LOLA MAE and SONYA close in behind her still holding their ends taut, so that MADELINE X appears encased in white from the neck down, with the two taut lengths of cloth like folded wings behind her. At the same time the CLOWNS set out the chair panels on a diagonal line that echoes the line of the white cloth that SONYA and LOLA MAE pull taut behind MADELINE X's shoulders. SCHLOMO creeps behind the chairs to watch what is happening)

MADELINE X: I mean, there's communication on certain subjects, but those are only the important subjects, which are therefore the important subjects.

SONYA VOVONOVICH: What a lot of bullshit!

MADELINE X: That's what I leave you with, ladies. Bullshit.

SONYA VOVONOVICH: Bullshit!

MADELINE X: Yes . . . But in some ways, this is really interesting.

SCHLOMO LEVITICUS: Please, my darling, continue to be interesting forever.

MADELINE X: *(She turns to him, and the cloth falls from her body)* Nobody knows how long it takes this drug to wear off.

SCHLOMO LEVITICUS: What drug?

MADELINE X: *(Going to the cabinet, she starts to toss items off the shelves)* The one I took.

SCHLOMO LEVITICUS: Where are the drugs? There are no drugs in this room.

MADELINE X: Oh, I didn't take DIFFERENT ones, Rabbi.

SCHLOMO LEVITICUS: All the same one?

MADELINE X: Evidently always the same ONE, Rabbi of my dreams.

(Mystic music has begun, and the CLOWNS and RINGMASTER enter and place open books against the wall, revealing in each book a large pictures of a rose)

SONYA VOVONOVICH: That is bullshit!

MADELINE X: Exactly what I leave you with, ladies. *(She exits)*

LOLA MAE DUPRAE: *(Calling after her)* The roses are for you, Madeline X!

MADELINE X: *(Reentering through another door)* Really? But there are no roses.

SONYA VOVONOVICH: Not even absent roses?

LOLA MAE DUPRAE But this room is NAMED the Rose Room—

MADELINE X: *(Ignoring the open books)* I would have thought that since there are no roses in the Rose Room, the fact of their absence would be especially potent.

SONYA VOVONOVICH: This room has been renamed— *(The CLOWNS and RINGMASTER, keeping the books up against the wall, turn a page to reveal pictures of the mountain)*—the room of invisible levitations.

MADELINE X: That doesn't interest me. I'd like to critique my own life, please.

SONYA VOVONOVICH: Go right ahead.

MADELINE X: My own life? I think it's brilliant.

SONYA VOVONOVICH: That's your subjective impression.

MADELINE X: Okay, let's try another perspective. It's a total failure. *(A pause, the CLOWNS leave quickly)*

SONYA VOVONOVICH: I'm sorry—I can't tell the difference. *(A CLOWN reenters with a bouquet of red flowers, which he hands to MADELINE X)*

MADELINE X: Ah—are those beautiful flowers for me? *(She lets the flowers fall to the carpet)* Well, excuse me if I'm a little dizzy, but don't suggest I sit down because I already tried.

SONYA VOVONOVICH: Please smell the flowers.

MADELINE X: *(Looking down at the flowers that lie at her feet)* That could be a terrible idea.

LOLA MAE DUPRAE: But why?

(The CLOWNS and RINGMASTER run back into the room and again place the open books with pictures of roses against the wall. Everyone but MADELINE X studies the pictures)

SONYA VOVONOVICH: *(Turning back to MADELINE X)* Beautiful?

MADELINE X: No, thank you. Let's just say— *(She crosses to the cabinet and leans back against it with her arms outstretched)* I've already been wounded. Badly.

LOLA MAE DUPRAE: I don't see any blood, Madeline X.

MADELINE X: It's pouring from all my pretend wounds in ways I predicted.

LOLA MAE DUPRAE: Oh, Madeline X, how did you get to be so Godlike?

MADELINE X: Godlike? *(She moves away from the cabinet and thinks, then nods her head slightly)* Well—

LOLA MAE DUPRAE: *(Very excited)* See? See the way you say "well" and nod your head?

MADELINE X: The way I say "well"? The way I nod my head?

LOLA MAE DUPRAE: The way you do that.

MADELINE X: Nod my head.

LOLA MAE DUPRAE: And say "well."

MADELINE X: Well— *(She nods it slightly)* It was involuntary. *(SONYA swoons to the floor)*

LOLA MAE DUPRAE: Involuntary? Are we in limbo?

MADELINE X: I have nothing to say.

SONYA VOVONOVICH: Hard to believe.

MADELINE X: Haven't I proved it? In retrospect? *(Mystic music is heard again)*

SONYA VOVONOVICH: I have nothing to say.

MADELINE X: Let me show you something. *(She takes a framed photograph down from a shelf)*

SCHLOMO LEVITICUS: I don't want to see that! *(He runs out)*

LOLA MAE DUPRAE: What's that?

MADELINE X: It's a snapshot I took of this room when nobody was watching. Now—where am I in this photograph that I took?

LOLA MAE DUPRAE: You're not in the photograph.

MADELINE X: Then I haven't been here, apparently, in spite of my vivid memories?

LOLA MAE DUPRAE: Of course you were here.

MADELINE X: I don't see myself in the photograph.

SONYA VOVONOVICH: Of course not. You took the photograph, so you were standing behind the camera, which also isn't visible. *(The CLOWNS and RINGMASTER have entered, each spinning a mirror in front of them)*

MADELINE X: Should I have pointed it toward a mirror?

SONYA VOVONOVICH: That didn't interest you.

MADELINE X: Why not?

SONYA VOVONOVICH: Obviously, it wasn't a mirror that attracted your attention, but the empty room. *(MADELINE X throws down the photo and runs from the room, as the spinning mirrors are directed toward the door through which she exited. Then the music suddenly stops, the mirrors freeze, and MADELINE X runs back into the room)*

MADELINE X: At the time, it's true, I thought there was magic in this room, but I wasn't enjoying myself. *(The mirrors begin to spin again, and MADELINE X runs to join hands in a circle with LOLA MAE and SONYA)*

LOLA MAE DUPRAE: Why not? *(They revolve the circle they have made)*

MADELINE X: Personal considerations were tormenting me. My emotional life was in upheaval.

SONYA VOVONOVICH: Is it now?

MADELINE X: Relatively. *(She breaks off the circle)*

LOLA MAE DUPRAE: Relative to what?

MADELINE X: I suspect that here, right now, I am surrounded by equal magic, but that doesn't redeem my current experience.

SONYA VOVONOVICH: Find a mirror.

MADELINE X: It would have to be a very powerful mirror, wouldn't it?

SONYA VOVONOVICH: What makes the power of a mirror?

MADELINE X: Its invisibleness.

LOLA MAE DUPRAE: Then maybe it's already here?

MADELINE X: Ah! *(She picks up the photograph, which had fallen to the floor)* I'm sure that's right.

SONYA VOVONOVICH: Okay, touch it.

MADELINE X: *(She studies the photo, then drops it again)* I can't.

LOLA MAE DUPRAE: Why not?

MADELINE X: I don't know why, but I can't.

LOLA MAE DUPRAE: That can't be right.

MADELINE X: Maybe it's optional! *(The CLOWNS run from the room)*

LOLA MAE DUPRAE: What I mean—you can touch it even if you can't touch what you're seeing.

MADELINE X: *(She starts dancing in place, swiveling her hips at LOLA MAE)* Your choice!

LOLA MAE DUPRAE: Don't bother. They took away the mirrors!

MADELINE X: *(Posing with her hands over her head)* How many mirror images do you need, darling? *(The CLOWNS have returned and are setting up photographic lights on stands, all aimed at MADELINE X)*

LOLA MAE DUPRAE: So what if it's a reflection? You can always touch the surface of things.

MADELINE X: Don't you get it, everything you've been taught is wrong ladies! *(She exits)*

SONYA VOVONOVICH: *(Calling after her)* Hey, I learned wrong things—?

MADELINE X: *(Reentering from another door—she goes and slams her hands against the still-illuminated projection screen and the music stops)* Madeline X says—That's wrong!

SONYA VOVONOVICH: Okay, then. All this time I learned right things?

MADELINE X: I'm sorry. If you add up your mistakes, there's no way to redeem them.

SONYA VOVONOVICH: Maybe with a kiss?

MADELINE X: *(Turning away disgustedly)* Certainly not with a kiss.

LOLA MAE DUPRAE: *(Tearing off paper and throwing it to the floor)* Kiss-kiss-kiss-kiss-kiss-kiss! This must be missed opportunity number one million one thousand one hundred and twenty-one.

MADELINE X: You mean the big bad door into this room should be opened permanently? *(The CLOWNS clap once, and music that had begun stops)* Or locked forever. Better still—is there a way to do both at once? *(All the others turn into the walls, turning their backs on MADELINE X)* Ah, this experience of turning away from each other, defeated by circumstances. But—not really defeated. Giving up on life? Yeah—in a way that could be productive.

SONYA VOVONOVICH: How could giving up on life, giving up on anything—how could that be productive?

(Music begins, and SCHLOMO reappears carrying three white Popsicles. MADELINE X, SONYA, and LOLA MAE each come and take one, and as SCHLOMO exits, they move slowly through the room, studying their Popsicles, as the CLOWNS set the chair panels around the room)

MADELINE X: (Thinking to herself) How could giving up on life be productive? To answer that very interesting question, try stretching out such a moment—

SONYA VOVONOVICH: This moment? (SCHLOMO has reappeared with a broom, and he is gently sweeping up at the rear of the stage)

MADELINE X: —any moment—till it lasts a whole lifetime here on gentle mother earth.

(SCHLOMO smiles and points offstage. Slowly, the RINGMAS-TER pushes onstage a three-dimensional tableau on a rolling platform. It features a thin red animal with a giraffe-like neck, topped with a white globe for a head, upon which the only feature is a grinning open mouth with bared teeth. On top of its head, a large white dunce cap. Skulls and naked baby dolls festoon its sides, along with streamers and strings of pearls and white flowers. As it's pushed slowly into position, gentle music fills the room, and everyone onstage stares at it in awe)

LOLA MAE DUPRAE: Oh, Madeline X, what's it like—really?

MADELINE X: Here on gentle mother earth?

LOLA MAE DUPRAE: Yes.

MADELINE X: (She turns away sadly) It's hard to touch base.

LOLA MAE DUPRAE: Come on, what's it like?

MADELINE X: Careful. Self-information doesn't surface so easy, ladies. Mostly, it's like something really well hidden.

LOLA MAE DUPRAE: But what's hidden?

MADELINE X: What's hidden? I could try to say what's hidden, but it's not like the thing that is hidden. (*She crosses to one of the painted chair panels, and prepares to sit*) it's more like . . . (*She sits on the painted chair, and falls to the floor*)

SONYA VOVONOVICH: (*After a pause, waiting for MADELINE X to rise*) Ah, more like the hiddenness itself?

MADELINE X: (*On her feet again, as if in a trance*) Careful. If I project any intensity, rest assured, I lie. (*SONYA comes and slowly plants a kiss on MADELINE X's cheek. MADELINE X waits a moment, then slowly walks away from her*) There is no real intensity inside me.

SONYA VOVONOVITCH: (*Whispers*) Liar!

(*MADELINE X has crossed to pick up a heavy red hammer that lies at the red animal's feet. She slowly comes down stage, caressing the hammer and holding it up inches from her head*)

MADELINE X: Oh, you can't begin to understand how perverse the rules of self-evolution really are— (*The others take a step toward her and she stops them*) No! Don't ask! (*She drops the hammer, and it hits the floor with a thud that makes everyone back away in fear*) Because instead of having a good effect on you— (*She bends down and picks it up again*)—it'll have a very bad effect on you. (*She crosses up to the animal*) And to say the least, ladies—(*She lifts the hammer, and all cower in fear*) You will be scared stiff. (*LOLA MAE and SONYA grab little gold hammers of their own and hold them up next to their heads. MADELINE X is whispering now)* Which is to say—you'll be scared shitless! *(She turns and hits the base of the red animal with three tremendous thuds—as terrible music rises, echoing those thuds. Everyone cowers in fear as the last blow sends MADELINE X ricocheting dizzily downstage, where she moans—)* Oh, this is really gonna hurt!

(LOLA MAE and SONYA hit their own heads and scream, as MADELINE X falls dizzily to the floor, and the lights snap out and the music is deafening. In the darkness there is a flash of light, then the lights return, and MADELINE X struggles to her feet and lurches over to the cabinet, falling against it with a thud. The music fades and they all turn their faces to the wall as MADELINE X recovers, and then steps forward and lifts a hand and speaks quietly)

MADELINE X: Okay. Hold it right there.

LOLA MAE DUPRAE: *(Turning from the wall to look at her)* What do you mean?

MADELINE X: What I said was—*(She takes one more step forward)* Click! *(She snaps her fingers)* Hold it right there.

(She turns her back to us, joining the others in turning her face to the wall. A gentle and happy music rises, and very slowly, the whole cast facing into the walls with their backs to the audience, the stage goes completely dark.)

THE END